PETRARCH
AND THE
RENASCENCE

J. H. Whitfield

HASKELL HOUSE

Publishers of Scholarly Books

NEW YORK
1966

PREFACE

THE consideration of the Italian Renascence is still largely dominated for us by nineteenth-century criticism. On the one hand, this laid emphasis on the moral superiority of its own time; on the other it tended to lose itself in examining the vast process by which the writings of antiquity were rediscovered. From that examination emerged the notion that the fifteenth century was too busy recovering, and imitating, the past to have a visage of its own. This lack of character was, in its turn, supposed to be responsible for unreality or paganism. Men lived in a past epoch instead of living in the present, and so they either lacked reality, or else theirs was a very wicked one. Such views are inconsistent, or inadequate. There was not only a process of recovery; there was also a use of antiquity recovered. And it is unreasonable to expect those who had sufficient enthusiasm to search out again the writings of the ancients to have had no attitude of their own towards them. Petrarch is the hinge of the door. His approach to antiquity is the reverse of Dante's, and it is Petrarch who, in giving a personal impulse to the fifteenth century, initiates a line which is visible there, and efficacious afterwards in the development of the European tradition. This study of the early Renascence has been written with the conviction that the tradition begun with Petrarch does not fade into the unrealities of form and imitation of which the Italian fifteenth century is usually accused. And I am equally convinced that the stream of humanism, as it develops from Petrarch down to Leon Battista Alberti, has not lost significance with the passage of time.

Finally, I wish to express here my thanks for the encouragement and help I have received, especially from Professor Foligno, Professor Ewert, Professor Boyd, and Mr. G. N. G. Smith; as well as my gratitude to the Curators of the Taylor Institution, Oxford, for generous help towards the publication of this book.

J. H. WHITFIELD

November 2, 1942

CONTENTS

PETRARCH AND THE RENASCENCE

I

WHAT OF THE RENASCENCE?

It is backed like a weasel.—POLONIUS.

A T the beginning of this century there was published a curious
commentary to nineteenth-century views on the Renascence,[1]
less important in its own achievement than in making explicit contradictions which had lain latent in the earlier interpretation. Monnier's
purpose, as announced upon his title-page, was to write an essay on
the literary history of the fifteenth century in Italy; yet he devoted his
first chapter to a study of the tyrannies in Italian states during that
period. So strong was the influence of nineteenth-century suspicion
of the Renascence, so firmly established the theory that its brilliance
and its corruption went hand in hand, that nobody has yet expressed
surprise at this inconsequence, or thought that a literary history of the
Renascence might more suitably have been begun by a consideration
of literary conditions. At first sight this may seem a local matter, not
deserving any particular notice. The work, though large in its scope,
was only superficially executed. Monnier's erudition was not always
sound, nor his judgment very solid; and he proceeded by a series of
descants which are often without any substantial basis. Moreover, the
nature of his first chapter—and it is easy to imagine without reference
to it the nasty episodes which the subject authorises, and the writer
looked for—attaches the book to a type of scholarship which has had
distinguished representatives, but which is not itself distinguished. I
mean the scholarship which deals with erudite subjects not for the sake
of erudition, but with a view to the extraction of scabrous details from
them; and it is not only Monnier's first chapter that displays this
sense of relish. On reflection, though, it will be seen that the matter
is of general importance. The unnoticed paradox, by which a literary
study of the *Quattrocento* begins with a political enquiry, is here at its

[1] P. Monnier, *Le Quattrocento* (1901), Essai sur l'histoire littéraire du XVe. siècle italien.

9

most acute and obvious stage, and we may reasonably be grateful for a reduction to absurdity. But the fact that the author's erudition is often second-hand suggests that the contradiction was hatched out before him, while a reduction to absurdity implies a previous existence of a fallacy in a state more difficult to detect. If we hold the open error in our hand we shall be better able to discover the lurking one.

No work affected the contemporary view of the Renascence quite so much as that of Burckhardt,[1] and none since has had quite the same international diffusion, or the same enduring popularity. It was written comparatively early in his life, and it is obvious that its scholarship has dated somewhat now, when we are almost a hundred years from the date of its first publication. It has as well its superficialities—what book dealing with so vast a field could hope to be without them?—but as by its merits it still holds a distinguished place, so in its time it underlay most of the conceptions of the Renascence put forward by later nineteenth-century criticism. Burckhardt undertook to cover the whole of Italian Renaissance civilisation and not literature only: it was natural, therefore, that his enquiry should lead him to discuss the political conditions of the period as well. His strength, and weakness, lay in finding one simple formula which explained all forms of human activity in this period as becoming conscious works of art: a phenomenon which he discerned in the political, as much as in the literary, field. The State, then, as a work of art obtained an equal place with literature in his book, and this time, perhaps, the fact that Burckhardt's study also began with the tyrannies, large and small, may occasion less surprise. At least, it is obvious that the coincidence is neither accidental, nor without its implications. Burckhardt's thesis is the recipe from which the later tradition copies, but it is not without its own antecedents. From Petrarch till the eighteenth century Europe echoes the gratitude expressed by Cicero at the beginning of the *Tusculan Questions* to those inventive minds to whom we owe the passage from the necessary to the more elegant arts.[2] On that gratitude was based the concrete achievement of the Italian Renaissance and the French *grand siècle*, and the eighteenth century in the main had little inclination to repudiate it. That is, until the voice of Rousseau rose against it. It is no accident that Rousseau reverses the language of Petrarch: for him virtue disappeared from Rome when Cicero appeared to

---

[1] Jacob Burckhardt, *Civilisation of the Renaissance in Italy* (German text first published 1860).

[2] *Opera*, IV. 106 (Bâle, 1534). 'Omnes magni, etiam superiores, qui fruges, qui vestitum, qui tecta, qui cultum vitae, qui praesidia contra feras invenerunt, a quibus, mansuefacti et exculti, a necessariis artificiis ad elegantiora defluximus.'

anatomise it;[1] for Petrarch Cicero was the spur to virtue. And at the same time Rousseau, in that childish but prophetic thesis thrust on him by academic success, maintained that the whole process was bad, leading from the primitive goodness of human nature, leading from an original equality straight to tyranny and inequality. Rousseau, of course, was not alone: Diderot, I think, denies literature as much in the implications of his theory as Rousseau condemns the arts and sciences. But without Rousseau the appearance of a Burckhardt would be less understandable. Not that Burckhardt, for all his curious simplification of a whole epoch, is single in his inspiration. In fact, the emphasis is rather on the refinement of the Renascence than on its corruption, the note of admiration sounded perhaps more frequently than that of condemnation. But despite his admiration for the brilliant era he was investigating, the thesis that the corruption of the fifteenth century flowered on the same tree as the Renascence, was part and parcel of the same movement, represents a variation on the fundamental theme of Rousseau. And after Burckhardt, as we have seen with Monnier, the accent shifts resolutely from brilliance to corruption.

For Burckhardt, then, tyranny was part of the Renascence—did not the tyrants combine with the refinements of cruelty an ostentatious admiration for the new learning, a desire to be surrounded with artists and men of letters? From this position the downward step to Monnier is easy: with the latter the refinement of cruelty, the luxury and the perfidy of dynasties, have become not only one factor in the general situation of Italy, but the very proem to the literature of the Renascence. It is the humanists who have been made responsible morally for the Visconti and the Borgia; it is the latter who suggest the moral value to be attached to this resurrection of pagan antiquity. To be fair to Monnier (I mean in the sense of limiting his responsibility) most of the conclusions had been drawn before him. De Sanctis in Italy, his follower John Addington Symonds in England, had drawn their pictures of a Renascence in which the political wickedness, the treachery as well as the talent and the culture of the despots were laid at the door of humanism. Neither of them gloated with the same relish over the inhumanity of the tyrants, but both were as convinced as Monnier that this inhumanity and this humanism were facets of one movement, the first an outward and visible sign of an inward and spiritual corruption.

[1] *Discours sur les Sciences et les Arts.* 'Jusqu'alors les Romains s'étaient contentés de pratiquer la vertu; tout fut perdu quand ils commencèrent à l'étudier.'

Now it is at first sight a little difficult to see how a renascent admiration for Cicero (to take an admitted idol of the humanists) could lead either to tyranny or to a cultured cruelty. The author of the *Tusculan Questions* and the *Offices* does not *seem* suited to the part. I do not think that this dilemma has ever been clearly stated; but that particular does not prevent it from having been resolved. Whereas Erasmus saw in Ciceronianism a tendency of his own time, and attacked this pejorative in its recent and its contemporary representatives, De Sanctis and Symonds extended it to the whole of humanism, writing it off as a rhetorical movement which polished the style, and perhaps also the intelligence, of its devotees, but left their consciences untouched. As the writers of maxims have assured us, it is our conscience which informs us of our duty; it is our intelligence which offers us the means of avoiding it. By developing the second and ignoring the first the Renascence reached its dual height: a race of writers who dealt in words (Ciceronian words), a race of rulers who used their culture to cloak their bestiality. Even worse than this, the writers of the Renascence also used their intelligence to laugh at the mob. For De Sanctis the main characteristic of Renascence literature, one which he saw from Boccaccio down to Ariosto, was a sceptical irony which finds its pleasure in the derision, moral or immoral or amoral, of stupidity. Buffalmacco was for him the symbol of the Renascence spirit, just as he was the symbol of the whole *Decameron*. In fact, it is not too much to say that De Sanctis included the *Decameron* in the Renascence because he saw this spirit as the main unity of the work.

Once this dilemma has been plainly stated it is clear that there are obstacles to its resolution in Desanctisian terms. For the intellectual to despise the vulgar is not unusual, and it was Petrarch, in one of his moments of praise for country life, who countered his friend's complaint about the cackling geese with the remark that it would be worse in town because of the most foolish din and clatter of the vulgar on the street-corners: 'Believe me, there is no beast at all more tedious than the vulgar.'[1] That contempt for those who had no concern with the matters of the mind was constant in Petrarch, and it was inherited largely by his successors. But what connection can be traced between it and the *Decameron*? The latter work was written before Boccaccio felt the influence of Petrarch; its formation may be said to have taken place before he knew him. And it is one thing to

[1] *Ep. Sen.*, VIII. 931. 'Ineptissimus in triviis vulgi fragor ac strepitus, nulla enim usquam bellua crede mihi, taediosior vulgo est.'

despise and shun, as Petrarch did, because one has worthier occupa-
tions: it is another to deride and take pleasure in the description of low
society. I do not think the unity of the *Decameron* is to be found in the
spirit of Buffalmacco (though that is a question with which I am not
here concerned), but that spirit existed, as the date of the *Decameron*
suggests to an unprejudiced enquirer, before the Renascence and
before humanism. It is popular, if not medieval; it may be found in
the *fabliaux*, and in the height of the Renascence it only appears
underground. De Sanctis's attribution of the spirit of the *beffa*[1] to
Ariosto was gratuitous, arising from a prejudice: where it does appear
is in the *Macaronics* of Folengo. Cingar, the prototype of Panurge,
uses all his cunning in making cruel sport of the rustic Zambellus
(*nomen et omen*), and the cruellest jest of all, the knife of St. Bartholo-
mew with which Zambellus cuts his wife's throat, hoping to effect a
homeopathic cure, derives from a popular story in verse of the late
fifteenth century. No evidence can be more unequivocal than this
continuity of the *beffa* in popular and semi-popular literature against
its ascription to the work of humanism. But if that evidence were
deemed insufficient by itself there is still its absence from the whole
of humanism to remain conclusive. It is not a characteristic of the
Renascence: its cynical irony belongs to the Middle Ages and to the
people.

The *beffa*, then, is popular, and its dismissal from the field of
humanism sharpens the paradox with which I began, since a main link
between the tyrants and the writers of the Renascence was that both
participated in this spirit of cunning triumphing amorally over stupidity. Now there is one curious particular which has not received an
adequate light. De Sanctis and Symonds did not only see in their
culture the explanation of their cruelty: they considered it also as an
aggravation. Of two contradictory assertions one must be false. If
the tyrants are made to say, with Ovid and with Petrarch,

E veggio'l meglio et al peggior m'appiglio,

it is unreasonable to make the better at the same time the cause of the
worse. The culture, in other words, must have a different origin
from the cruelty; and by now, I hope, it will begin to be plain
that had it not been for Rousseau ultimately, and immediately for
Burckhardt's thesis, the two would not have been confused. Just as
the *beffa* had a popular, and an antecedent, origin, so also had tyranny.

---

[1] The *beffa* may be illustrated in our own literature by *Gammer Gurton's Needle*, which is an
English *beffa*, and corroboration of the popular spirit.

This may seem a commonplace, too trite to be commented on; but in the criticism of the Renascence it is a commonplace which affects large issues. On the theory of a lapse of conscience (the theocentric conscience of the Middle Ages) accompanying the development of intelligence much has been built, and the moral downfall of Italy, the corruption of the papacy, the triumph of Charles VIII, the political servitude of Italy through several centuries have all been attributed to this fatal weakness. If political corruption was not the innovation of the Renascence, but was pre-existent, the main charges fall of themselves: the Visconti and the Borgia will have a tradition of their own, and will not have been wicked because of Cicero, but in spite of him. Symonds could write in a lyrical strain: 'Meanwhile amid apparent civility of manner, the violent crimes of a corrupt and servile race were frequent. Poisoning and secret assassination, acts of personal vengeance and the employment of hired cut-throats rendered life unsafe in that idyllic Italy.'[1] (No wonder that they film the Borgias; what more could the bourgeois want of history?) It could be only a strange fascination that saw this as the hall-mark of the Renascence. Turn back the pages of Italian literature, and who emerges from the *Inferno* of Dante Alighieri? The Malatesta for violent and treacherous assassination; Geri del Bello for blood feuds in families, acts of personal vengeance; Frate Alberigo and his dessert of hired cut-throats (his crime so common that Dante reserves the Tolomea for its punishment). These are random samples from the physical background to the *Divina Commedia*: surely it is obvious that their crimes must be attributed, not to the new learning, but rather to the old Adam?

The error of Burckhardt, then, was not that he covered too wide a field; it was, on the contrary, too narrow. He saw that the fifteenth-century rulers were both cultured and cruel; he could not have equated the two things if he had examined the history of the Middle Ages, for here he would have found the new culture lacking, but the cruelty present. The tyrannies sprang from the communes without any midwifery from literature, old or new; and as for an invaded Italy, had this been never known before? In the establishment of precedents we need not go back to the fall of the Roman Empire: a remark of Muratori on the torrent of English who poured in (along with Sir John Hawkwood) after the peace of Bretigny in 1360 may, for the one aspect of the question, be deemed sufficient: What else was lacking, after Italy had been trampled on by so many German and Hungarian troopers, than that there should come from far-off

[1] J. A. Symonds, *Italian Literature*, II. 456.

England new dogs to finish devouring her?'[1] It is a remark that is not very complimentary to our nation (as Gibbon observed, *more true than civil*), but what was left after it to say of Charles VIII? or with what justice can his repetition of the descent of Charles of Anjou be ascribed to the new learning of Italy? Nor had the popes awaited this movement of the Renascence before showing signs of degeneracy. Again, the facts are known, and may be stated briefly, since had it not been for Burckhardt's thesis confusion could hardly have arisen. Dante's remarks on Boniface VIII (to mention only one pontiff), Petrarch's letters *Sine Titulo*, Boccaccio's second story are fair evidence of a state of degradation in the Papal Curia before it could have felt the influence of humanism. It was Benedict XII who gave rise to the saying *Bibamus papaliter* long before Leo X talked of enjoying the papacy now he had got it. Of Clement VI Gibbon remarked: 'Under his reign, Avignon was the seat of pomp and pleasure: in his youth he had surpassed the licentiousness of a baron; and the palace, nay, the bed-chamber of the pope, was adorned, or polluted, by the visits of his female favourites.' It is Gibbon who wrote of John XXIII ('the most profligate of mankind'): 'He fled and was brought back a prisoner: the most scandalous charges were suppressed; the vicar of Christ was only accused of piracy, murder, rape, sodomy and incest.' What more was left to bring against Alexander VI? And if, alas, there are other charges to be preferred against this pontiff, does it not seem probable that they should be connected with the history of the papacy rather than with that of humanism?

If Burckhardt, then, and his successors had taken the sweep of Gibbon they would have realised that the violence and treachery which they found at the time of the Renascence will not serve to distinguish it from other epochs in the history of mankind, and that they have their origins in very different factors than the revival of antiquity. Nor perhaps could Burckhardt have proved that Boniface VIII or Frate Alberigo was any less conscious of what he was doing, the first in seeking to lay greedy hands on all Tuscany, the second when he murdered an unsuspecting relative at dinner, than the actors of the political scene at the end of the fifteenth century. Was Innocent III less secular in his ambitions than Julius II, or less aware of the scope of his actions? But since the theory was a dual one there is still one thing these critics had in common with Gibbon. They did not, it will have been seen, content themselves with saying that the new pagan learning underlay the wickedness of the despots; they maintained at

---

[1] Muratori, *Annali d'Italia*, XII. 197; and cf. Petrarch, *De Rebus Fam.*, XXII. xiv. 164-5.

the same time that it was a rhetorical movement dealing in words alone, and without the requisite attention to things. The two charges are in themselves, or would appear to be, mutually exclusive; but if the first is untrue, they still have the benefit of falling back with more insistence on the second. And in so doing they have powerful allies, even amongst those who have no axe to grind. A systematic scholar of the calibre of Sabbadini could write that all the historians of humanism repeat, and with justice, that the learning of those centuries (apart from some few results in criticism, in art and one or two other branches of knowledge) was an immense illusion, of which the Latinisers were partly authors and partly victims. All their complicated and vertiginous labours were on form, which was mistaken for reality: this was indeed the age of omnipotence for *form*.[1] If it is obvious that such an assessment cuts humanism adrift from Caesar Borgia (no-one has ventured to accuse him of mistaking form for reality), it is clear also that the allies here are not inconsiderable; and, as I have said, the position is strengthened by the concurrence of Gibbon, who, speaking the language—the very reasonable language—of the eighteenth century, had no respect for the medievals, and noted fully the necessity for their barbarous ignorance to receive the celestial dew of a classic revival. Yet 'the Italians were oppressed by the strength and number of their ancient auxiliaries: the century after the deaths of Petrarch and Boccace was filled by a crowd of Latin imitators, who decently repose on our shelves; but in that era of learning it will not be easy to discern a real discovery of science, a work of invention or eloquence, in the popular language of the country. . . . Such an intercourse must tend to refine the taste, and to elevate the genius, of the moderns: and yet, from the first experiment, it might appear that the study of the ancients had given fetters, rather than wings, to the human mind. However laudable, the spirit of imitation is of a servile cast.' Gibbon's commentary to this conclusion is very different from that of De Sanctis (for example): for Gibbon this seeding-time of humanism was not to be regretted since it, and it alone, led to the splendour of the vernacular Renascence. It would be foolish to express regret for a movement which prepared the 'incomparable Ariosto,' and all modern literature as well. But for De Sanctis Ariosto was a prolongation of the same movement of form without substance, and its echoes were to last in literature until Parini in the eighteenth century at least, in life, until his own time. If there is a gulf, however, separating the two conceptions it serves rather to

[1] Sabbadini, *Storia del Ciceronianismo*, preface.

emphasise the unanimity in the judgment on humanism: it becomes neutral ground, safely open to all combatants. One other voice may usefully speak here. The first volume of Saintsbury's *History of Criticism* ends with the *De Vulgari Eloquentia* and a brief chapter on the fourteenth and fifteenth centuries; the second begins with Politian. Saintsbury considered the advantage of being able to compare more than one literature as one of the foundations of a critical mind, yet what he says of Petrarch occupies a few lines only: 'He had indeed, as has been pretty universally recognised, nothing to do with the Middle Ages. Not only in his heart and desires, but in his nature, he is a man of the early—if of the earliest—Renaissance. Even in the vernacular he rings false as an exponent of anything medieval . . . Timotheus, not St. Cecily, has taught his strains. And in his "regular" writing he is severely, almost ludicrously, a classicaster.' One of the few general ideas which merge from Saintsbury's first volume is that he believed in the necessity for beautiful words in order to have beautiful literature. Hence his praise for the *De Vulgari Eloquentia*, though I do not suppose Saintsbury realised that he was committing himself to admire Dante's *canzoni* more than his *Commedia*. But it is astonishing to find this hiatus by which the whole of humanism from Petrarch up to Politian disappears from view, and not less astonishing because others have held that its weakness was the craving for beautiful words and the forgetfulness of realities. We might have expected Petrarch, with a wide knowledge of classical, patristic, Provençal and Italian literature (not to mention his small store of translations from the Greek) to have had more opportunities for critical development than Dante. We might have expected humanism with its love of form to have more claims on Saintsbury's attention than the remark that Petrarch was a classicaster (for I hope I have made it clear that the few negative sentences quoted are *all* Saintsbury says on humanism before Politian). The fact that to a critic whom we might have thought so favourably disposed the period is cold and dead affords extraordinary support to the concurrence of Gibbon, De Sanctis, Symonds and Sabbadini.

This stronghold of criticism has been so sure that few have ventured to assault it directly. Thus there have been some who have wished in recent years to claim poetic life for Petrarch's Latin epic. To the old assertion that the *Africa* was the 'poema dell'umanesimo' (and none the better for being so) the new apologists for Petrarch have replied that it is not what it is labelled. It is not, for example, a 'vana esercitazione estetica'—which it would be if it was a humanist's

production—but a medieval-Christian poem, complete with allegory. Petrarch had too much genius and originality to resign himself
to a cold, lifeless, and, at the best, rhetorical repetition of classical
motifs, or to reduce his poem to the humble rank of a cento.[1] This,
it will be observed, is the vanishing-trick, at least as far as Petrarch is
concerned. The judgment on humanism remains unchallenged and
unaltered: it was cold and servile. The rescue of Petrarch—the father
of humanism for the earlier critics, is effected by the repudiation of
his offspring. I am not at present concerned with testing the validity
of the assertion that Petrarch was a man of talent and a Christian and
therefore a medieval, not a humanist. But it is obvious at least that the
redemption would not have been made in these terms had not the
rhetorical nature of humanism seemed ascertained beyond dispute.
Is the respect for the fortress justified, or has it been exaggerated? The
question is suggested by these opposing views of Petrarch (he is bad,
therefore he is a humanist; he is good, therefore he is not a humanist).
What if the first critics were wrong in his badness, right in his humanism? what if the second were right in his medievalism, wrong in
his goodness? It is plain that these questions can be answered only
when the charge of words, words, words has been examined.

I should be disingenuous if I did not mention here that I had heard
of the Roman Academy, and of the scandalous conduct attributed ,
several of the humanists. Pomponius Laetus may have thought
he lived in ancient Rome, but it is only when we have no clue to the
main development of any movement that we can make the mistake
of judging it by its aberrations. Similarly, as the *Anti-Ciceronianus* has
been extended to provide a rod for all the humanists, so the failings
of some have marred the reputation of many, and with little distinction of outlines. It is no uncommon thing to find editors expressing
surprise at an insistence on goodness, or a manifestation of it, in a
particular author, Petrarch, the humanist educators, Alberti, Castiglione, while remaining convinced that the general trend of culture is
towards corruption. And, once again, wickedness has been attributed
to learning, not to the defects of human nature. But although no-one
insisted more sharply than Petrarch on the danger of being clever
without being good the more general question is the most urgent one.
Why were they all concerned with words? Why were they not also
men of action, or at least men who applied the wisdom of antiquity
to the solution of modern problems? The second half of the
question we must not prejudge; the first has been answered by

[1] Tonelli, *F. Petrarca*, 101.

implication already. If I were dealing with the late, and not with the earliest, Renascence, I might ask: Why did not Caesar Borgia ask the advice of Machiavelli? The answer to that question is simple, and, I think, conclusive: Machiavelli was a humble employee of the Florentine Republic. His superiors listened to his reports, but they did not solicit his counsel; and how should Caesar Borgia anticipate our judgment on the superiority of Machiavelli? We could not make that judgment if we despised words in favour of actions, or if we were bound by the distinction of persons. It is, however, precisely this distinction and this contempt that we must bear in mind most clearly in considering the work of humanism. John XXIII was not to be expected to reform the Church; the *condottieri* in their rise to despotism, had little leisure to consider the benefit of the governed. The men of action were in power, and they continued without much reflection the traditions deriving from the Middle Ages. It could not have been otherwise. Those who, like Petrarch, devoted themselves to study stood outside the course of events. Dante exercised as little practical influence as any humanist. And yet the ultimate influence of humanism was more effective than the power of the Visconti or the Borgias; and it was its work to change, in the short space of a hundred years, the mind of Italy and the course of European civilisation. Perhaps that judgment is anticipatory; but it should be clear that the hope for improvement in the medieval scene lay with those who believed in Cicero, not with the men of action. And if we may have to record an abuse of Ciceronianism in the later Renascence—the abuse pilloried by Erasmus—we must still admit that the choice of Cicero in the beginning was a healthy element. Petrarch once remarked on the superiority of the written over the spoken word: an argument committed to writing will be more useful than a spoken one. Words flee, but books remain; the first reach few, the second many; the ones reach only those who are present, but the others reach the absent and posterity as well.[1] Not only do actions partake of the same disability as spoken words, but they were also vitiated in the fifteenth century (I speak of course of the public actors, Popes, *condottieri*, rulers and aspirants) by barbarous traditions. The future lay with Petrarch.

While I am concerned with general, and not with particular, questions the point which I have shelved above demands attention. Gibbon and Voltaire knew the difference between the Middle Ages and the eighteenth century; they never doubted that the polish and

[1] *Ep. Sen.*, IX. i. 93.

the humanity of the latter were the work of the Renascence. And both might equally have derided the notion that there was a peculiar wickedness in the Renascence, deriving from its pagan connection. But Gibbon and Voltaire no longer hold the field, and we have seen the claim advanced that Petrarch must be medieval on the grounds that he is Christian, and because he is claimed to be more than a mere servile imitator. We have seen that the assertion was in the nature of an *échappatoire*; but since there have been many, and not only neo-scholastics, ready to believe in the superiority of the Age of Faith over the age of culture it was an escape that might hope to avoid pursuit. Again, I am convinced that the confusion derives in no small part from Burckhardt, and I may be forgiven if I state common-places which have not always been applied in the last hundred years to the sequence of the Middle Ages and the Renascence.[1] When a house is sacked we do not expect it to be ready for normal occupation without some lapse of time and some expenditure of energy. When a civilisation is destroyed the interval and the effort must be greater, since the means of rescue have disappeared as well. As Siciliano has observed, we know what the barbarians destroyed better than we know what they brought as their contribution; and to a large extent it was they who remained in possession of the house. Now it is true that the Church, in its own interest, clung to the remains of Latin learning (not to the Greek, for that was the language of heresy); but so long as the work of Comparetti[2] stands unrefuted it is obvious within what narrow limits this is true. Until the rise of the vernacular literatures, and after them of humanism, the means of expression remained largely a monopoly of the cleric; and it is self-evident that it will be, in form at least, a Christian expression. 'Qui Christum scit, satis est si cetera nescit.' The ascetic side of the Middle Ages is in no danger of being forgotten, because it was the most articulate one. But it does not follow that it represents a picture of the period: on the contrary, it represents the reaction against the picture of the period, and from the violence of the one half we can form an estimate of the violence in the other. Nor were there con-tradictions lacking in the Church itself. Scholasticism can seem a unity to us only because we have forgotten it: in itself it was a war of words from which the orthodoxy of St. Thomas Aquinas did not emerge until the Council of Trent; his supremacy was reserved for

---

[1] I am indebted to Siciliano's brilliant little book against the French claims to have inaugurated the Renascence, *Medio Evo e Rinascimento* (1936).

[2] Comparetti, *Virgilio nel Medio Evo* (1872).

the Council of the Vatican. The Middle Ages was the time of rampant heresies and of attempted reform. It was the age of absolute papal and imperial power, but also of such struggles as that over investitures. The successor of Caesar was often excommunicate, the successor of Peter not inviolate in his own person. Under the theory lay its denial in practice; by the side of the literature lay the life of the Middle Ages.

Again, I may be accused of dealing in commonplaces. If they are such my task is lightened, but I can only repeat that they have not always been used as such since the eighteenth century. Voltaire wrote of the strange folly of the Crusades: 'Les Croisés mêloient les débauches les plus scandaleuses et la fureur la plus barbare, avec des sentimens tendres de dévotion; ils égorgerent tout dans Jérusalem, sans distinction de sexe, ni d'âge; mais quand ils arriverent au saint Sépulcre, ces monstres ornés de Croix blanches, encore toutes dégouttantes du sang des femmes qu'ils venoient de massacrer après les avoir violées, fondirent tendrement en larmes, baiserent la terre et se frapperent la poitrine, tant la nature humaine est capable de réunir les extrêmes.'[1] Gibbon and Montesquieu speak the same language in their account of the Crusades;[2] but the nineteenth century did not choose to insist on the stains which blotted the white robe of churches, and other and curious contradictions have resulted from the neglect. A follower of Carducci, the staid Bartoli, had to claim the irreligion of Rutebeuf or the disrespect of the *Carmina Burana* for the Renascence, because, of course, the spirit of the Middle Ages was pure asceticism.[3] De Sanctis, in the same way, claimed the *Decameron* for the Renascence, and uttered a cry of relief that the ascetic, the abstract Middle Ages were over, and we were back to positive reality, down to good earth once again. He saw the *Decameron* not as an expression of, nor as an evolution from, the Middle Ages, but as a catastrophic revolution which destroyed it: in it 'trovi il Medio Evo non solo negato, ma canzonato.'[4] But as at the same time De Sanctis himself revolted against the cynicism and the immorality which he found in the *Decameron* he left an easy game of skittles to be played by the Catholic apologist for the Middle Ages. Olgiati, for instance, remarks drily after setting forth these contradictory positions of De Sanctis: 'Da Dio passiamo all'uomo; dalla trascendenza all'immanenza; dal dover essere al-

---

[1] Voltaire, *Essai sur la Poésie Epique*, VII.
[2] cf. *Decline and Fall*, LVIII, and *Grandeur et Décadence*, XXIII.
[3] A. Bartoli, *Storia della Letteratura Italiana*, I, *passim*.
[4] Olgiati, *L'Anima dell'Umanesimo e del Rinascimento*, 115. One of the main merits of this book is its clarity in summarising the various critical approaches to the Renascence.

l'essere; da Tommaso d'Aquino a Giovanni Boccaccio.'[1] As at the beginning of the period, so at its end De Sanctis fell into the same inconsequence, and left a similar game to be played with his judgments on Machiavelli. With him he saw the Middle Ages crumbling in all its bases, religious, moral, political, intellectual. But that was not the end of the world: it was its renewal. Confronting theocracy there arose the autonomy and the independence of the State.[2] And again by the side of his relief at the escape from abstractions lay his repudiation of the immorality he found in Machiavelli's political ideas, so that Olgiati had only to remark on the significance of the history of the Renascence, on the ruin of the country which had been rebellious to God, lacking in moral sense, and oblivious of the Transcendental. The demolition is most neat; but it is De Sanctis who remains the victim. If the strength of Olgiati's apology for scholasticism lies quite often in the exposition he gives of critical theories about the Renascence, its weakness consists in his having chosen the critics as his opponents, and not the facts. On the one side he equates the position of St. Thomas with the medieval scene; on the other he establishes the superiority of this latter over the Renascence by accepting the lowest estimate which has been set on it. To buy the Renascence cheap and sell the Middle Ages dear must always be the duty of the neo-scholastic. I do not want to enter yet into a defence of Machiavelli; but even without that, it is clear that Olgiati's position is damaged by the historical position as suggested above. If Italy was ruined in many ways before the Transcendental had been abandoned for the positive, where, then, is the efficacy of the former, the deleterious action of the latter? And if the theory of Aquinas was the reality of his own time what need was there for Dante to castigate Popes of Thomas's own century? or what account are we to take of the physical background to the *Commedia*? Was that already the wicked ferment of the Renascence? And at the other end, how can we account for the flourishing state of Italy in the years which run from the peace of Lodi down to the time when the character and policy of men like Lodovico il Moro (neither scholar nor humanist) brought the intrusion of Charles VIII to overthrow the equilibrium of Italian politics? There is at the beginning of Guicciardini's history of Italy a celebrated picture of Italy on the brink of the invasion: brought wholly to the greatest peace and tranquillity, cultivated no less in the most mountainous and sterile

---

[1] Olgiati, *L'Anima dell'Umanesimo e del Rinascimento*, 115. [2] ibid., 266-71.

places than in the plains and fertile regions; subject to no alien rule, not only most abundant in inhabitants, merchandise and wealth, but made illustrious by the magnificence of many princes, by the splendour of many noble and beautiful cities, by the seat and majesty of Religion.[1] It would perhaps be discourteous, but it could not be impertinent, to ask the neo-scholastic to account for this accurate picture of an Italy not yet plunged into the miseries that began with Charles VIII. Here, I think, the facts speak for themselves; with regard to Boccaccio there is a little more to be said. Olgiati accepted willingly the label and the estimate of De Sanctis for the *Decameron*; but the label, as we have seen, was ill-applied. Boccaccio's genius allowed him to develop admirably the short story at the moment of its emergence from subordination in the guise of the *exemplum* (and the *exemplum* is much more the progenitor of the *novella* than the oriental apologue). It allowed him—had his admiration for the hundred cantos of the *Commedia* nothing to do with it?—to frame his work more surely than had been possible before him. It did not allow him to alter the character of the society which he depicted (apart from his infusion into Tuscan life of the aristocratic elements learnt in Naples—which is another matter), or to anticipate the work of Petrarch and of humanism. For the first time, then, in the history of the *novella* a comedy of character is possible; and it is a medieval character and a medieval society. The book is neither a catastrophe, nor a revolution: it is, on the contrary, a fulfilment. It is the inarticulate side of the Middle Ages come to definite expression, and it has more claim to represent the reality of the medieval scene than the theocracy of Olgiati and Aquinas.

I have said *inarticulate*, but it is clear from the history of medieval literature that the word is an exaggeration. The *fabliau* and the farce paint an even grosser picture. But apart from the abundance of light that can be thrown on the medieval by the primitive nature of the first vernacular literature there is other, and perhaps even more important, evidence at our command. In defining the limits of medieval culture Comparetti remarked on its inability to raise minds much above the popular and vulgar level: the most worldly monk, the most enamoured of classical literature, is always infinitely nearer the people than the last of the Latinists of the Renascence can ever be.[2] It is this which authorises us to take into account not so much the great system of Aquinas—which is impressive because it

---

[1] Guicciardini, *Storia d'Italia*, 4 (1803). [2] Comparetti, 228 (ed. 1896).

is an abstraction from the medieval reality—as the humbler writers who betray unconsciously the limits of their time. The passage of the word *legend* from a recommendation to read what was edifying to a suggestion of absurdity in the events narrated is effected by the ecclesiastical writers of the Middle Ages. It is no insignificant revolution. The practical worth of medieval Christianity is to be tested in the minor writers as much as in the greater ones: Jacques de Vitry, Passavanti or the *Gesta Romanorum*, to name samples from three different countries in a similar key, speak, perhaps, even more authoritatively than Thomas Aquinas as voices of the medieval world. Let us listen, almost at random, to just one of the stories with which the Bishop Jacques de Vitry refreshed his sermons. And is it not a little significant that the sermons having vanished out of sight only these *exempla* still remain? 'I heard of a certain demoniac who told publicly the sins of those who came to him. So when a certain noble and powerful lord suspected a certain knight of his of adultery with his wife (and in truth it was so), he said to him: 'Let's go to that demoniac and question him.' But the knight, full of fear for himself, went to confession. When, then, they were before the demoniac the lord said: 'What sort of woman is my wife?' And the demon: 'An adulteress, stained by foul lust.' 'Who sins with her?' But he began to think, and when he could find no-one to name, he said: 'A little while ago I knew, but now I don't.' And looking through all his papers he found the knight's sin blotted out. This plainly shows the worth of true confession.'[1] EX QUO PATET QUANTUM VALEAT VERA CONFESSIO—it is the voice of Boniface VIII asserting to Guido da Montefeltro his powers of absolution; and the efficacy of that *true confession* is echoed in the miracles accomplished by the Virgin Mary in Jacques de Vitry's pages, as in those of other collections. When we evaluate the merit of monasticism in preserving what we have of classical literature we must do so in the light of Boccaccio's visit to the library of Monte Cassino; before we accept the bland assertion of the neo-scholastics that the *Summa* of Aquinas *is* the Middle Ages we must gloss it in the light of history and of this topsy-turvy literature. Ex

[1] J. de Vitry, *Exempla*, CCLXI. 109 (ed. Crane). 'Sicut de quodam demoniaco audivi qui peccata venientium ad se publice dicebat. Unde, cum quidam nobilis et potens miles quemdam militem suum suspectum de adulterio cum uxore sua, et in rei veritate sic erat, dixit ei: 'Eamus ad demoniacum illum ut interrogemus eum.' Ille vero valde sibi metuens ivit ad confessionem. Cum autemcoram demoniaco stétissent, dixit dominus: 'Qualis est uxor mea?' Cui demon : 'Adultera est et fetore libidinis inquinata.' Et ait: 'Quis est qui peccat cum ea?' At ille cepit cogitare et cum non posset reperire, ait: 'Paulo ante sciebam, sed modo nescio.' Et inspiciens omnes cartas suas invenit quod deletum erat militis peccatum. Ex quo patet quantum valeat vera confessio.'

quo patebit quantum valeat vera christianitas—I mean, the Christianity of the Middle Ages.

'Ignorance is a great poverty of the mind, than which there is no greater, except vice.'[1] That the Middle Ages knew both these forms of poverty is apparent, and though I have only suggested an approach to the question, the doors of the medieval world are open and a further view is easy to obtain. Perhaps nothing can convince so readily of the insufficiency of the Middle Ages as the attempts that have been made to take the Renascence out of Italian keeping and push it back to the twelfth century, or even to Carolingian days. It is quite natural that the date 1453 should have fallen (like Constantinople itself) as the birth-year of the Renascence, but its fall has left scholars pushing back until they found whole series of separate renascences, or no need for one at all. I do not imagine that such views are entirely honest, but at any rate they carry with them their own retribution. 'Que dire,' says Bremond, 'du *Roman de la Rose* et des *Carmina Burana*?' And did not the rage they had for thinking themselves descended from the Trojans (compare the *Roman de Troie*) prove the continuity from the ancient world?[2] And it was Haskins who remarked, when he had told the tale of Frederick II shutting one man in a wine-cask to prove the soul died with the body and disembowelling two others to show the respective effects of sleep and exercise on the digestion: 'All in all, quite enough to demolish the legend that Roger Bacon was the first experimenter of the Middle Ages.'[3] There would be little point in my tilting at the *Roman de la Rose* or at the *Carmina Burana*; I may, however, refer their supporters to Siciliano's account of them.[4] What is more important is to observe the hedges which Haskins put round his twelfth-century renascence: 'There was always a sea of darkness beyond the known world.'[5] The classics were taken largely at second-hand, 'through the Fathers, the Latin grammars and glossaries, and the various collections of extracts.'[6] They were accepted uncritically and without any discrimination. The real successes were the epitomisers, those who worked (as we know from a reduced edition of Donat) 'pro fratrum mediocritate.'[7] In its culture, then, a servile age, one which poorly imitated a few words from the classical inheritance, and missed the substance.

---

[1] Petr., *De Ignorantia*, 51 (Capelli). 'Magna animi paupertas ignorantia est, et qua nulla maior praeter vitium.'

[2] *Histoire littéraire du sentiment religieux en France*, 4.

[3] *The Renaissance of the Twelfth Century*, 335.　　[6] ibid., 115.

[4] *Medio Evo e Rinascimento*, 103.　　[7] ibid., 226; Comparetti, 162.

[5] Haskins, 336.

There is a remark in Haskins which would be worthy of Gibbon, had its author intended it to be a general, and not a particular, judgment; if it had been a satire, and not a piece of naivety: 'If the physicians of Salerno did not dissect the human body, they at least studied the anatomy of the pig.'[1] It is a dubious *proxime accessit*: what more, or indeed, what less, could the uncharitable say about the Middle Ages?

It is possible now to examine humanism in a less odious light. The wickedness with which its conscience has been burthened was a legacy from the past, existing on very different levels from the one on which humanism could develop. Voltaire's answer in 1755 to the thesis of Jean-Jacques is valid for the work of humanism also: 'Les grands crimes n'ont guère été commis que par de célèbres ignorants. . . . Les lettres nourrissent l'âme, la rectifient, la consolent. . . .' The flattering epithet of Christian sorts ill with the nature of the Middle Ages; it was the revival of antiquity which promised and allowed a decrease in the bestial elements in man. When the confusion caused by Rousseau and Burckhardt is removed we are back on ground the eighteenth century knew; but we have still to bear in mind Gibbon's charge of fetters and imitation. And it is against this background that I propose to begin the study of Petrarch. As a preliminary at least it is comforting to remember that Erasmus called Petrarch the founder of the Renascence in Italy, praised his lively mind, his erudition, his eloquence, but blamed him for insufficient skill in the Latin tongue, complaining that all his style suffers from the harshness of his century. Not the least surprising thing about this judgment (for those who conjure up a Renascence all of form and void of substance) is that Sabbadini quotes it on page 10 of the same work the preface of which I have quoted above in a very different sense.[2] But we must remember also that, since those who have seen good in Petrarch recently have been anxious to exclude him thereby from the Renascence, the continuity affirmed by Erasmus is not to be neglected.

---

[1] Haskins, 332.   [2] cf. *supra*, 16.

II

PETRARCH: FORM OR SUBSTANCE?

SAINTSBURY asserted, then, without otherwise examining the situation, that Petrarch was ludicrously a classicaster. Erasmus maintained his style was not sufficiently polished for him to be a classic. The two judgments might be reconciled, but as such a reconciliation would depend more on an exposition of Saintsbury and Erasmus than on Petrarch it is more profitable to consider Petrarch's own intentions in this matter of style. One, at least, of the passages in which he refers to these intentions is well-known: 'I confess it is my intention to adorn my life with the words and counsel of others, not my style, unless I mention the author, or effect some signal change, as by the alchemy of bees one honey is made from many and various flowers; besides, I should much prefer my style to be my own (even though unpolished and uncouth), like a cloak made to the measure of my own nature, preferable to someone else's, richer with ambitious ornament, but coming from a greater nature, and unfitting in its ampleness for the stature of a humble one. Any robe suits an actor, but not any style a writer: each must form and keep his own.'[1] On the one side, it is better to be oneself than to appear in a disguise; on the other (as Petrarch put it in the other similar passage), the bee is preferable to the silkworm.[2] To an age which thinks in terms of self-expression and originality this may seem a confession of inferiority, and silk may seem more precious than honey. Petrarch thought differently; for him the process of learning was the acquisition, and the application to oneself, of a pre-existent wisdom. Doubtless he was not inventing the Latin language, and he had read his authors till they were second nature: so that there will be echoes, and how many![3] But the style of Petrarch is not based on stylistic imitation, and he absorbs elements of writers who are removed from Cicero: St. Augus-

---

[1] *De Reb. Fam.*, XXII. ii. 124. 'Vitam mihi alienis dictis ac monitis ornare fateor est animus, non stilum; nisi vel prolato auctore, vel mutatione insigni, ut mutatione apium e multis et variis floribus mel unum fit: alioquin multo malim meus mihi stilus sit, incultus licet atque horridus, sic in morem togae habilis ad mensuram ingenii mei factus, quam alienus, cultior ambitioso ornatu, sed a maiore ingenio profectus, atque undique defluens animi humilis non conveniens staturae. Omnis vestis histrionem decet, sed non omnis scribentem stilus: suus cuique formandus servandusque est.'

[2] ibid., I. vii. 58. [3] cf. esp. *Fam.*, XXII. ii. 123.

27

tine and Seneca are partly responsible for the later disapproval of his
latinity. But the essential point is that before the more famous assertion
of Machiavelli Petrarch asserted the unity of mankind and the relevance of the lessons of antiquity to present conduct; and after him
Europe spoke his language until the eighteenth century. The passage
that I have quoted is echoed so strikingly in Montaigne's essay *De
l'institution des enfants* that it might be possible to claim Petrarch as an
inspiration there, rather than attribute it direct to classical sources. Or
if we take Villey's suggestion of Castiglione and numerous other
authors of the sixteenth century as a source for Montaigne we may
still find ourselves led back eventually to Petrarch.[1] Nor is Petrarch's
conclusion at this point foreign to the temper, or unechoed in the
expression, of Montaigne: 'I would sooner have no leader than be
compelled to follow my leader everywhere.'[2] Truth and wisdom
are no monopoly and no new creation. They are to be gathered
wherever they are to be found, but they must be assimilated. Petrarch,
Montaigne and Pascal (need I add Pope?) speak the same words: 'You
say that Seneca said that. Who would deny it? I say it too, and so
will many after me, and so perhaps did many before him; and whoever says it, provided only that he does not lie, will have said a fine
and splendid thing.'[3] 'La vérité et la raison sont communes à un
chacun, et ne sont non plus à qui les a dites premierement, qu'à qui les
dict apres. Ce n'est non plus selon Platon que selon moy, puis que
luy et moy l'entendons et voyons de mesme.'[4] 'Ce n'est pas dans
Montaigne, mais dans moi, que je trouve tout ce que j'y vois.'[5]

Modo ne mentiatur — but the suspicion that Petrarch was really
concerned with the adornment of his style, not of his life, has been
so widespread that we cannot absolve him on a single showing. His
statement that in his letters to friends he wrote without attempting
eloquence (for what is a friend but another self, and who thinks of
style when communing with himself?) may be accounted disingenuous; though it will be much more readily reckoned so by those who
have not read Petrarch's correspondence than by those who have.
And if he did think of saying well what he had to say he had a very
sufficient reason. In the presentiment of Machiavelli to which I have

---

[1] *Essais*, I. xxvi (ed. Villey), and for sources, III. 466. Montaigne only quotes explicitly the
Canzoniere, and as his editor has looked for direct classical sources to the essays the Latin works
of Petrarch do not appear in the list. But there are affinities in method and outlook.

[2] *Fam.*, XXII. ii. 125. 'Sum qui satius rear duce caruisse, quam cogi per omnia ducem sequi.'

[3] ibid., V. xviii. 299. 'Seneca, inquis, hoc dixit. Quis negat? Et ego dico, et multi dicent
post me, et ante eum multi forte dixerunt; et quisquis id dixerit, modo ne mentiatur, egregium
magnificumque verbum dixerit.'

[4] Montaigne, I. xxvi. 195.   [5] Pascal, 345 (ed. Brunschvigg).

alluded Petrarch said: 'Believe me, Caesar, the world is the same it was, the sun the same, the elements the same: virtue alone is diminished.'[1] In his partial rejection of Aristotle in the *De Ignorantia* he attributes the apparent harshness of Aristotle's style to the incompetence of his translators, and notes especially the *Ethics*, which are to be mastered 'not that we may know, but that we may become good. What use would it be to know what virtue is, if when known it were not loved?'[2] The spur to this love lies, not in the unpleasing style of Aristotle, but in the eloquence of Cicero. If Petrarch, then, is disingenuous in disclaiming eloquence, his concern with it is not a matter of imitation, or a departure from a concern with reality. On the contrary, eloquence is an important part in the persuasion to virtue; and his lament of the rareness of virtue implies the need also for its eloquent advocacy. Nor did Petrarch make the idealist's mistake of dreaming of a universal higher education, or place the means above the end. To force the mind beyond its capabilities is useless; it must be helped by study and meditation, but it cannot be compelled to heights beyond its reach. 'Otherwise, apart from the fact that the effort is vain, it will often happen that we neglect the possible in seeking the impossible.'[3] There is an infinity of different degrees of capability, and the world would be ill served if all were poets or philosophers: it is goodness which is the common goal. 'And so the lack of eloquence or knowledge is more tolerable than that of virtue, for those qualities belong to a few, but this to everybody. . . . For as truth is the goal of the understanding, so goodness is the goal of the will. Not all can be Ciceros, Platos, Virgils or Homers; but all, except the unwilling, can be good. A ploughman, fisherman or shepherd, if only he be good, has his value. And finally if one or other must be lacking, I prefer (to turn Themistocles' remark from riches to knowledge) a man without letters to letters without a man.'[4] That is explicit, and there is nothing in Petrarch's life to contradict it.

---

[1] *Fam.*, XVIII. i. 463. 'Crede enim mihi, Caesar, mundus idem est qui fuit, idem sol, eadem elementa: virtus sola decrevit.'

[2] *De Ignorantia*, 68. 'non ut sciamus, sed ut boni fiamus. Quid profuerit autem nosse quid est virtus, si cognita non ametur?'

[3] *Fam.*, I. vii. 60. 'Alioquin praeterquam quod conatus erit irritus, saepe accidet ut dum impossibilia cupimus, possibilia negligamus.'

[4] ibid., XIX. xvii. 562-3. 'Unde fit ut tolerabilior sit defectus eloquentiae aut scientiae, quam virtutis, quod illae scilicet sint paucorum, haec est omnium. . . . Ut enim veritas intellectus, sic bonitas voluntatis obiectum est. . . . Non possunt sane omnes Cicerones esse vel Platones, non Virgilii vel Homeri; boni esse autem possunt omnes, nisi qui nolunt. Et arator quoque piscatorque et pastor, modo vir bonus sit, suum pretium habebit. Denique si alterutro sit carendum, ut Themistoclis dictum de divitiis ad literas traham, malo virum sine literis, quam literas sine viro.'

The more quoted terms of Petrarch's letter to Boccaccio on the superiority of a learned piety over a *devota rusticitas* must be examined in the light of this attitude; and it will be seen that, if the exercise of goodness is sufficient, that does not preclude from setting a higher value on the study, and consequently the inculcation, of virtue. 'What then? I exhort and I beseech, let us with all our vigilance, with all our strength, drive out ignorance, the darkness of the mind. Let us strive to learn something on earth which may become our path to heaven.'[1] Intelligence has become more a part of goodness than obedience to a rule.

Such are the terms of the question as it presented itself to Petrarch, and there is an instructive commentary to them in a place where we might least have expected to find it. Indeed, amongst the charges brought against him none has been more sharply urged than that of political insufficiency. Some have accused him of inconsistency, others of speaking in idealistic terms to deaf ears, or rather, to ears which were flattered by his eloquence, but unresponsive to his matter. Perhaps the sharpest words were spoken by an admirer, one of those who praise him in general terms as the father of a great movement, and then belittle his achievement in its detail. Here is Voigt's remark on Petrarch's memoir on the government of Rome (I quote him, as I shall do again on occasion, in the French translation): 'Rien ne sert mieux que ces écrits à montrer la présomption de Pétrarque et en même temps son incapacité à distinguer le monde réel de celui de ses études. . . . Pétrarque a souvent été loué comme un grand patriote, et, en effet, personne ne s'est rencontré pendant bien des siècles après lui, qui ait déploré avec tant de passion les maux de sa patrie et qui ait cherché autant que lui à la ramener à son ancienne et glorieuse unité. Mais de sacrifices personnels, il n'en fit jamais ni à l'Italie, ni à Rome.'[2] Coming from one who was a professed admirer the accusation is as harsh as it is explicit. But if we ask ourselves what were these sacrifices Petrarch should have made we shall find it almost as difficult to determine them as to imagine the active part he might have played in the events of his century. Should he have become a *condottiere*, aspired to a bishopric, become a papal secretary? The

---

[1] *Fam.*, I. vii. 59. 'Quid ergo? Hortor atque obsecro, ut omni vigilantia et summis viribus animi tenebras, ignorantiam depellamus, enitamurque in terris aliquid addiscere, quo via nobis ad coelum fiat.'

[2] Voigt, *Pétrarque, Boccace et les Débuts de l'Humanisme*, 62-3. It is odd that so many scholars have devoted their labours to the study of Petrarch and humanism while considering both to be of doubtful worth. Can one devote one's life to the study of a mirage, and have retained oneself a feeling for realities?

latter two, at least, were ambitions which he sacrificed. He would
not have been greater, he would not have been great, if he had yielded
to them. And another sacrifice he made: it was to speak the truth
as he saw it with the knowledge that it would be unwelcome. If he
had not been independent of the actors of his century he could not
have done so with the same force. I do not know what part his letter
to Urban V had in the temporary return of the papacy to Rome;
but no-one can read it and deny the sincerity of Petrarch when he
speaks of himself as confident that truth, though somewhat bitter,
would be dearer to Urban than honeyed blandishments.[1] Incidentally,
nowhere better than in this letter is Petrarch's contempt for the mere
rhetorician expressed. In the same category belong his letters to
Charles IV; and it is in the series to the Doge of Venice that a striking
testimony of Petrarch's integrity, as of his acumen, is to be found.
That Venice and Genoa, two flourishing cities, the two eyes of Italy,
should make war seemed to Petrarch, as it may to us, unfortunate.
He urged on Andrea Dandolo these ideal reasons, and the practical
consideration that war is a contagion which cannot be kept within its
boundaries. It seemed to be with Genoa only, and that already was
a calamity, now it is with all Liguria. What is the cause for strife?
'Peace is expedient to you both, or rather it is necessary to all, except
to those who live by rapine, trading much blood for little revenue. . . .
These lead a wretched and calamitous life for infamous wages.
Rightly do they fear peace, and in peace, starvation: they love war,
and like wolves or vultures, find delight in slaughter of men and in
corpses. Are you to act like these wild beasts? . . . I beseech you not
to let the flourishing Republic committed to your care, and all this
rich and lovely part of Italy which lies between Alps and Apennines,
become the prey of hungry foreign wolves, from whom wise Nature,
as I constantly repeat,[2] has separated us by the ridges of the Alps themselves.'[3] It is by cultivating peace between the towns of Italy that the
troopers from north of the Alps can be cheated of their victim. Thus

---

[1] *Epist. Rer. Sen.*, VII, i. 914. 'Fisus tibi amariusculam veritatem, quam melliculas blanditias
chariorem.'

[2] cf. *Rime*, I. cxxviii. 33-5.

> Ben provide natura al nostro stato,
> Quando de l'Alpi schermo
> Pose fra noi e la tedesca rabbia.

[3] *Fam.*, XVIII. xvi. 509-10. 'Pax utilis est ambobus, imo cunctis necessaria, nisi illis qui rapto
vivunt et exiguum censum multo mercantur sanguine. . . . Hi sunt qui infami stipendio calami-
tosam et miseram vitam trahunt. Iure igitur pacem et in pace famem metuunt: bellum amant,
et lupi velut ac vultures, strage hominum et cadaveribus delectantur. Hisne tu belluis morem
geris? . . . Noli, quaeso, noli committere ut florentissimam tuae creditam custodiae Rem-

ran Petrarch's appeal, and in the light of history few will contend that
it was without either eloquence or a firm base in truth and reason.
What response did it evoke? It was brought to Andrea Dandolo a
few days before his death, and he expressed to those who stood
around his bed his sense of shame that he could not answer it as
eloquently as it was written. And Petrarch commented on this
answer: 'As if he thought it most shameful that he could not match
my style (the one thing he could most easily achieve, as above all a
man of letters and a skilful speaker). But that which was most
difficult, I think, he did not mind: I mean, to rebut and to confute my
ideas. Skilled in speech and practised with words he could not fear
a wordy contest: but what is there for you to do with the facts themselves, or answer to patent truth? Nothing but silence, or assent.
Compose words, you may be equal or superior; in things you must
remain inferior. Bare truth can often conquer ornate eloquence.'[1]
It is a curious reversal of the allotted rôles, this Doge who thinks in
terms of rhetoric, this Petrarch who talks in terms of truth. We may
be readier now, after bitter experience, to listen to the language of
Petrarch than was the world of his own time. I do not mean only
because we have seen the function of the Alps (which he and Napoleon
so clearly recognised) restored, and then atrophied. *Docet experientia*,
but only through the words of those who can discern her lessons; the
majority of mankind do not learn directly by experience, even when
they learn at all.[2] And if we can understand the language of Petrarch
better than Andrea Dandolo, it is thanks partly to Petrarch for having
spoken it. There is in Barozzi's excellent study of Lorenzo Valla a
relevant conclusion: it is that when literature places its finger insis-
tently on a social evil, even though those who are attacked be powerful
and make fierce resistance, yet sooner or later it produces the desired
effect, if its work is continual and incessant.[3] That may seem to us

publicam, atque omnem hanc, quae inter Apenninum et Alpes interiacet, opulentissimam atque
pulcherrimam Italiae partem externorum ac famelicorum praedam facias luporum, a
quibus bene nos, quod in ore semper habeo, ipsarum iugis Alpium solers natura secreverat.'
    [1] *Fam.*, XIX. ix. 538. 'Quasi summo pudori duceret non aequasse stilum, quod unum
facillimum illi erat, litterato in primis disertoque homini. Id enim, puto, quod erat difficil-
limum non curabat, retundere scilicet et confutare sententias. Verbis equidem atque dicendi
exercitio ornatus, verborum certamina non timebat; sed quid rebus ipsis facias atque apertis-
simae veritati quid respondeas, nisi ut taceas aut confirmes? Verba enim compares, aut par aut
superior esse potes, rebus inferior sis oportet. Saepe phaleratam eloquentiam nuda veritas
vincit.'
    [2] cf. Machiavelli, *Principe*, XXII. 'E, perché sono di tre generazione cervelli, l'uno intende
da sé, l'altro discerne quello che altri intende, el terzo non intende né sé né altri.'
    [3] Barozzi, *Studi sul Valla*, 180.

now a piece of nineteenth-century optimism; but at least we may be prepared to admit that progress towards a peaceful society is more likely to come from the men of reflection than from the men of action, a somewhat over-valued category. In many ways that work could be begun with Petrarch, both because of the ability of the man himself, and because of the state of Italy as well. Dante, it will be remembered, looked backward. His praise was for the *popolo vecchio* in Florence, and its equivalent elsewhere. We may see in the rise of the Arts in Florence, and the end of the imperial power, steps forward to the picture of Italy in the fifteenth century as I have given it in the words of Guicciardini. But Dante saw decay and misdirection, and looked back to modesty, sober manners, liberal and knightly virtues in the past. His insistence on this theme in Canto xvi of all three canticles, *Inferno*, *Purgatorio* and *Paradiso*, proves how central is this idea for him. Just as in Ulysses he damned the sin of curiosity which sent men searching through the world for knowledge, so in Florence he abhorred commerce, the foundation of her greatness:

> La gente nuova e i subiti guadagni
> orgoglio e dismisura han generata,
> Fiorenza, in te, sí che tu già ten piagni![1]

Petrarch does not make the same mistake, and his emphasis on the flourishing state of Italy (*'florentissimam . . . Rempublicam; opulentissimam atque pulcherrimam Italiae partem'*) represents a different orientation from the invectives of Dante. The house was being put in order, reflection on its uses had become possible as use itself became legitimate. The thought of the Middle Ages had been abstract because the house of civilisation was in ruins: it could more easily be denied in favour of the other world than it could be examined, organised or enriched. The Christianity of the Middle Ages was other-worldly by force of circumstance: the *De Contemptu Mundi* was a line of least resistance.

Barozzi was bold enough to place Machiavelli in the line of descent from Valla; he did not appear to have observed the close dependency of Valla on Petrarch. The position of Valla (which had swung a full half-circle, but on the same centre) I shall consider later, but since I have linked the names of Petrarch and Machiavelli I must justify myself. At first sight it might seem an odious conjunction, profitable to neither of the parties; though, here as before, I shall not attempt a set defence of Machiavelli. Since the distrust and the contempt

---

[1] *Inferno*, XVI. 73-5.

aroused by his name is founded on ignorance, or what is worse, on partial knowledge, it will already serve towards showing his essential goodness and honesty to emphasise his contacts with Petrarch. And since Machiavelli has not usually been considered (any more than Caesar Borgia) to have occupied himself with form to the exclusion of substance, the connection between them will serve also to clear Petrarch from the charge of being a dreamer only. The elements of a comparison are known, of course, to be there: Machiavelli quoted Petrarch in his eloquent peroration to the *Prince*; Petrarch anticipated Machiavelli's objection to the use of mercenary troops. But there is more than elementary contact. Petrarch had a theoretic reason for claiming that monarchy was the ideal, providing the monarch was just. It is an argument which will recur in Castiglione rather than in Machiavelli, and I need not reproduce it; but Petrarch added a reflection of a different sort: 'Of course, in the present state of our affairs, and in this unappeased discord of men's minds, I have no doubt at all that monarchy is the best means to recruit and repair the strength of Italy, dissipated by the long fury of civil strife . . . and I confess the hand of a king essential for our ills.'[1] It is, in substance, and in language also, the view of Machiavelli. In him its statement appears in the *Discorsi*, both many times and in many guises, but it underlies the *Principe* even if it does not find overt expression there, since it is the very reason for the latter treatise being written. 'La ragione è questa, che dove è tanta la materia corrotta, che le leggi non bastino a frenarla, vi bisogna ordinare insieme con quelle maggior forza, la quale è una mano regia, che con la potenza assoluta ed eccessiva ponga freno alla eccessiva ambizione e corruttela dei popoli.'[2] And Montesquieu adds the commentary to both of them: 'Pour qu'on ne puisse abuser du pouvoir, il faut que, par la disposition des choses, le pouvoir arrête le pouvoir.'[3] Where the abuse of power is greatest, there obviously the power to check it must be greatest also. It is within these limits that the *Principe* obtains; without corruption to redress absolute power is excessive, and Machiavelli's idealism demanded that the hand which curbed corruption should also frame the laws, because 'un principe sciolto dalle leggi sarà ingrato, vario e imprudente più che un popolo.'[4] That also is a presumption which

---

[1] *Fam.*, III. vii. 150-1. 'Certe, ut nostrarum rerum praesens status est, in hac animorum tam implacata discordia, nulla prorsus apud nos dubitatio relinquitur, monarchiam esse optimam relegendis reparandisque viribus Italis, quas longus bellorum civilium sparsit furor . . . fateorque regiam manum nostris morbis necessariam.'

[2] Machiavelli, *Discorsi*, I. lv; and cf. the end of I. xviii.

[3] *Esprit des Lois*, XI. iv.　　　　[4] *Discorsi*, I. lviii.

underlies the *Prince*, and is echoed constantly in the recurring passages where Machiavelli recommends the favour of the people as the surest safeguard to the ruler. Petrarch had offered the same counsel to the prince: 'Let him create in his heart a love for those he rules; for both love is won by loving, and also there is no surer rule than over willing subjects.'[1] Machiavelli urged the prince to encourage commerce and aid prosperity, to leave his subjects secure in the possession of their goods; and in the same passage which I have just quoted Petrarch required of him that he should prefer abundance for his subjects to that of his treasury, that he should realise the lord of a rich kingdom cannot himself be poor.[2] Now it is well known that Machiavelli's *mano regia* did not come (if it came at all, perhaps as an accident and a bye-blow in 1796) in his own lifetime. We do not for that dismiss him as a dreamer, or as an empty rhetorician. Nor should we stand on any better ground in thus dismissing Petrarch. If he had spoken a language immediately and wholly intelligible to Andrea Dandolo, and to other worser actors of his century, it would have been a limitation in him, and not a virtue. Reduce Machiavelli to the level of the younger Medici, of Giuliano and Lorenzo, and what becomes of his stature? Again, I may appeal to Montesquieu with the sure knowledge that Petrarch could not have spoken differently: 'Les vertus . . . ne sont pas tant ce qui nous appelle vers nos concitoyens, que ce qui nous en distingue.'[3] That is not unreality: it is the statement of the means of progress.

I am not sure, though, that we cannot take the agreement between Petrarch and Machiavelli further still. Those who have held the shallowness and inconsistency of Petrarch's political views to be proved by the fact that he appealed *successively* to Robert of Sicily, Cola, Emperor and Pope, have not always mentioned that he had the same programme to propose to each. That is already an important qualification to the charge of inconsistency. Still more, in writing to Charles IV he urged the example of Cola di Rienzo. Cola had proclaimed himself the assertor of Roman liberty (*obscuri hominis clara confessio*). They are not things which we have read, says Petrarch, but which we have seen: justice and peace, their companions, fair faith and tranquil security seemed to presage the age of gold. Cola

---

[1] *Fam.*, XII. ii. 165. 'Inducat in animum amare quos regit: nam et amando amor quaeritur, et nullum certius regnum est, quam praeesse volentibus.' cf. Machiavelli's quotation from Livy in *Disc.*, II. xxiii: 'Certe id firmissimum imperium est, quo obedientes gaudent.'

[2] *Fam.*, ibid. 'Malit subiectos abundare quam fiscum, et intelligat divitis regni dominum inopem esse non posse.'

[3] *Esprit des Lois*, IV. ii.

C

failed, but if a Tribune (the humblest office) could achieve so much, what shall the name of Caesar do? Petrarch adds the warning against delay (that delay which made him so often renew his appeal), because delay is fatal: the empire falls, and liberty is lost.[1] Cola and Charles IV, with varying chances of success deriving from their rank, have the same function to fulfil; and the keynote is *liberty*. Its application to the attempt of Cola di Rienzo is obvious enough: it is, however, an odd word to propose to Caesar, though it is one we cannot ever accept safely without a gloss. This Petrarch supplies a little later in his letter. Justice is prostituted in the brothel of avarice, Caesar shall place her on her throne again. 'It is for this that you are born; you are destined to this task of abolishing deformities in the State and giving back its pristine appearance to the world.'[2] It is only justice which distinguishes the king from the tyrant; justice and magnanimity, which is the *sine qua non* of a kingly mind. Humanity, if it is present, is not a virtue in man, but his nature; if it is lacking the result is monstrosity rather than vice. Thus liberty is to be defined in terms of law, and kingship in terms of both; the world is to be restored to a state of order which it knew in the days of Roman peace, and which it lost through corruption. The *regia manus* of Petrarch and the *mano regia* of Machiavelli have the same office, and both think in terms of restoration of order to a world of chaos, by the same means and for the same purpose. It is probably impossible to determine how much of Petrarch Machiavelli had read, or to decide if we may in this speak legitimately of influence; but the fact that they speak the same language is something by way of testimony to the strength, and the validity, of the humanism generated by Petrarch. The man of action is not necessarily the realist: he may be the one to destroy realities which are appreciated by the reflective mind. An observation of Petrarch on conquerors and victories is relevant to this point. 'There is no full victory while an enemy with arms survives; although, if you destroy this one, others will rise against you, and one may say that certain victories are as the seeds of war, for hatreds cut down with the sword spring up again, and warriors are born again to come to battle.'[3] Does not such an observation prove the unreality of the conqueror's dream?

[1] *Fam.*, XVIII. i. 464. 'A noble claim in an obscure man' and 'Ruit Imperium, perit libertas.

[2] ibid., 468. 'Ad hoc enim natus, huic officio destinatus es ut Reipublicae deformitates aboleas et pristinam faciem mundo reddas.'

[3] *De Remediis*, I. ciii. 87. 'Non est plena victoria, ubi armatus hostis superest, quanquam et si hunc oppresseris, alii renascentur, quasdam nempe victorias, ceu sementem dicas esse bellorum, sic odia ferro trunca repullulant, densanturque, et redivivi in aciem redeunt bellatores.'

There arises at this point a formidable name, one that may seem to forbid the banns I have proclaimed, or rather to assert itself as the inspiration of both parties to them. Dante lamented the chaos of Italy, and urged an Imperial return:

> Ahi gente che dovreste esser devota
> e lasciar seder Cesare in la sella,
> se bene intendi ciò che Dio ti nota.[1]

In some ways Petrarch is, of course, the obvious heir to Dante, or, at least, to Dante's time. He inherits the twin ideals of Papacy and Empire, but the detail which I have quoted is significant of the change which has taken place: Cola could replace Caesar in Petrarch's thought; as Dante's tercet shows, the question was prejudged for him, and Caesar alone could sit in the saddle of Empire. It has been said (and most admirably said) that with Dante the rational faculty is taken as a premiss, while with Petrarch it is a conquest. With Dante the restoration of the Roman Empire was a return to the divine order of things, and therefore a sovereign and indisputable remedy: it is part of a theological problem, and as such it has a theological solution. There is no question of ways and means, and no possibility for another to usurp the place of Caesar, precisely because it is the name and not the virtues of an emperor which is envisaged. It is this that makes the political theory of Dante the last dream of the Middle Ages, and an abstraction without a consequence. Despite his astonishing perception of the actors on his stage he left the solution to a *deus ex machina*. It is the logical corollary to the backward glance, the praise of the *popolo vecchio* of Florence, and the distrust for the new life which was preparing the prosperity of the fifteenth century. But for Petrarch a decline in virtue is to be countered by a return to virtue, nor is there any machine which can deliver us. That is why it is Cola's business as much as it is Caesar's, and why, if Cola has more virtue, it is more his than Caesar's business.

We have returned, it may seem casually, to Petrarch's business also: the inculcation of virtue. The consideration of his political ideas is not, however, a digression, since it has allowed me to state a part of what I take to be the essential advance of Petrarch, and since the distinction between Dante and Petrarch is fundamental. But others also had noted before Petrarch the dangers of ignorance, and without

---

[1] *Purg.*, VI. 91-3.

carrying our search back to Thomas Aquinas we can find the assertion in Guittone d'Arezzo:

> Nescienza, e piú scienzia carnale
> E secular, di mal tutto è cagione;
> Che conoscendol chiar, nullo ama male;
> Né mette, in che non ama, operazione.[1]

Not so much ignorance then as knowledge of this world: that is the medieval Christian recoiling from the task of organising the world in terms of virtue. The innovation of Petrarch is that the *scienzia carnale e secular* is not excluded, but acquires in this connection a peculiar and a predominating importance. When he discusses the question of reading the books of the Gentiles he refers to St. Augustine's debt to Cicero and Plato: the saint had candidly confessed his familiarity with both, as well as his finding in Plato a great part of our faith, while in the *Hortensius* of Cicero he had found a turning-point by which he was converted to the study of truth alone. Augustine was worthy to have received the praise of Cicero; there was no need for him to blush in acknowledging the leadership of Cicero. Why should he blush? 'No leader is to be despised who points the way to salvation.'[2] Petrarch's rejection of the primacy of Aristotle rests largely on this conception of Plato as closer to the Christian position. His affirmation of the merit of Cicero rests strongly on his conviction that there is nothing in Cicero to contradict, and very much to support, the Christian thesis. Cicero, for example, had written a work *De Natura Deorum*, and its title might be taken as evidence against him, since it involves plurality instead of unity. But even in this work Cicero blames those who cannot see a motor and a governor behind the visible universe; and elsewhere he accepts the unity of that motor from the Greeks. His real sense is this, and the deviations from it represent a momentary deference to tradition and temporal authority. When he speaks with his true voice, then you might think it was an apostle speaking, and not a pagan philosopher.[3] If Cicero, then, in affirming repeatedly that the world is established by divine providence, and governed also by the same, speaks the language of St. Paul, what explanation can we give? There is, for Petrarch, one only: if Cicero speaks not so much with a philosophical as with a theological locution, the truth he utters flows from God. 'Since God is living truth; since, as St. Augustine says, any true thing

---

[1] Guittone d'Arezzo, CXXI (ed. Valeriani).
[2] *Fam.*, II. ix. 122. 'Nemo dux spernendus est, qui viam salutis ostendit.'
[3] *De Ign.*, 45. 'Interdum non paganum philosophum, sed apostolum loqui putes.'

is true by derivation from the truth, without doubt whatever anyone says that is true derives from God.'[1] The conclusion of Petrarch at this point in the argument is very well known: What then, are we to account Cicero a catholic? 'I wish I could. O would that it were possible!'[2] But Cicero's eyes were closed in death a few years before the birth of Christ, and Petrarch can only bewail his misfortune. Petrarch is not a theologian, and he does not speculate at any point upon the chances of salvation and damnation for Cicero. I do not think that in his affection for Cicero he ever had recourse to the loophole offered by St. Augustine which found controversial employment in Voltaire;[3] though doubtless Petrarch would have subscribed unconditionally to it. In fact, what is it but another version of the claim for divine inspiration for Cicero, and whoever else in antiquity spoke moral truths? But Petrarch has so little of the preoccupations of the Middle Ages that he seems oblivious of the whole problem of damnation: it is regret for Cicero's not having known the whole truth, rather than fear for his fate, which underlies his sentiment. Nor have I idly cited Voltaire, though there are obvious and important distinctions to be seen between the two: 'C'est bien dit, quoique cela n'importe guère. Quels que soient l'origine et le destin de l'âme, l'essentiel est qu'elle soit juste; mais j'aime toujours à traiter cette matière, qui plaisait tant à Cicéron.'[4] Voltaire attacked by skirmish the absurdities of Christianity, in order to concentrate attention on a pure and natural religion, with a main concern for moral questions and the conduct of life in this world. The emphasis of Petrarch is not different, though the polemical note is lacking, since Petrarch does not deny Christianity itself. On the one side he saw the major revelation of Christianity, which he accepted without feeling the necessity to attempt its systematic organization into a speculative theology; on the other he saw the minor revelation (*omne verum a veritate verum*) of antiquity. The one is a simple and central truth, and Petrarch accepts St. Ambrose cheerfully on the futility of metaphysical speculation;[5] it is the second which allows, or indeed requires, the investigation of the human mind; and the moral problems of

---

[1] *Fam.*, XXI. x. 86. 'Cum enim Deus veritas viva sit; cum, ut ait pater Augustinus, omne verum a veritate verum sit, haud dubie quidquid ab ullo verum dicitur a Deo est.'

[2] *De Ign.*, 52. 'Vellem posse. Et o utinam liceret.'

[3] Voltaire, *1ère Anecdote sur Bélisaire.* 'Depuis le commencement du genre humain, tous ceux qui ont cru en un seul Dieu, et qui ont entendu sa voix selon leur pouvoir, qui ont vécu avec piété et justice selon ses préceptes, en quelque endroit et en quelque temps qu'ils aient vécu, ils ont été sans doute sauvés par lui.' Voltaire cites also St. Jerome, St. John Chrysostom and St. Paul, *Ep. to Romans*, II. 10-14.

[4] *L'A, B, C*, 2e. Entretien sur l'Ame.   [5] *De Rem.*, I. xlvi. 45.

conduct surround us at every turn. In the conduct of one's life Cicero can give the greatest help: it is the goal beyond this life of which Cicero is ignorant. 'For even if our goal is not in virtue (where the philosophers have placed it), yet the path is straight through virtuous acts towards our goal; through virtues, I say, not so much understood, as loved.'[1] It was Cicero that Petrarch was quoting above, Cicero even who thought of this life as the way to heaven.[2]

When this new direction given to enquiry by Petrarch is borne in mind it will be seen how odd are many of the ready-made judgments upon humanism. In one of his descants Monnier remarked, *a propos* of Nicholas V and Pius II: 'L'humanisme qui est né en dehors de l'Eglise, qui, à tout prendre, est né contre l'Eglise, est accaparé par l'Eglise.'[3] That is not so much a taking everything into account, as an ignoring all the essentials. And the danger of beginning one's study of humanism in the fifteenth century, and with the tyrants, will by now be more apparent. Petrarch is not concerned with imitating antiquity, but with improving man; and as for being outside, or against, the Church, we shall see the clearness of his stand.

Now that we can see that the case against Petrarch as one concerned with form alone is hard to establish, it is instructive to observe that what has been asserted as the cardinal defect in Petrarch and in humanism has also been asserted as a virtue in the Middle Ages; and this often by the same person. M. Gilson was at some pains to prove that there were medievals who were fascinated by the form and style of the ancients, and whose love for classical literature was based on a conception of its beauty.[4] The difference between the two terms, medieval humanism and renascence, should be, then, one of degree: the development of studies allowed a more adequate, and a more general, conception of pure latinity. But the search for style, and the models of style, were not new simply because they were improved phenomena. Gilson's conclusion is: 'La différence entre la Renaissance at le moyen âge n'est pas une différence par excès, mais par défaut. La Renaissance, telle qu'on nous la décrit, n'est pas le moyen âge plus l'homme, mais le moyen âge moins Dieu, et la tragédie, c'est qu'en perdant Dieu la Renaissance allait perdre l'homme lui-même, mais ce serait une autre et longue histoire à raconter.'[5] In so far as this judgment attributes to the action of the Renascence con-

---

[1] *De Ign.*, 68. 'Etsi enim non est in virtute finis noster, ubi eum philosophi posuere, est tamen per virtutes iter rectum eo ubi finis est noster; per virtutes, inquam, non tantum cognitas, sed dilectas.

[2] cf. *supra*, 30, n. 1.   *Fam.*, XVII. iii. 424.   [3] *Le Quattrocento*, 90.

[4] Gilson, *Humanisme médiéval et Renaissance* (in *Les Idées et les Lettres*).   [5] ibid., 192.

ditions which represent a continuation from the Middle Ages we have already seen its injustice; in so far as it follows Olgiati's bland assumption that the Middle Ages and the system of St. Thomas Aquinas are one and the same thing we are in a position to call it mistaken. In all this we are on familiar ground; but the real interest, and the real weakness, of M. Gilson's own contribution to the argument is hidden in the 'telle qu'on nous la décrit.' In itself it is, of course, no novelty: Olgiati also accepts ready-made views of the Renascence. In Gilson's application of this convenient telescope the Renascence has no concern with anything but form, copied from antiquity; and that obviously can only be a defect. But M. Gilson claims the same research for form as having been conducted by the medievals; and this anticipation of the Renascence is obviously a virtue. To be more logical, though: M. Gilson maintained that the medievals were, in desire at least, rhetoricians. I am very willing to concede the point, the more so because Dante himself exclaimed to Virgil:

> Tu se'lo mio maestro e il mio autore;
> tu se'solo colui da cui io tolsi
> lo bello stilo che m'ha fatto onore.[1]

I am not sure to what exact extent Dante's style can be called Virgilian, but the passage to Petrarch's affirmation of Cicero as an ideal is significant: it represents the end of the period in which antiquity is a mere ornament. Petrarch nowhere imposes Cicero as the master of his style, and nowhere recommends him as the arbiter of style in others. He praises, it is true, Cicero's eloquence; he had read him until he was part of his own mind. But he recommends him as *magister vitae*, because he examines, and persuades to, virtue. Virgil (and Ovid) supply Dante with apparatus, rather than with ideas; his *magistri vitae* are to be sought rather among the theologians, in Aquinas and in St. Bonaventure, and it is the next life, more than this one, which is important. But in Petrarch the attention is shifted from the goal to the path towards it, not by the negation of the first, but by the insistence on the necessity of progressing towards it. The sense in which the elaborate theology of the Middle Ages is abstract is this scanning of the heavens when the path to them was untracked, or else consisted in the renunciation of a path. As Bishop Blougram observed to Mr. Gigadibs:

> How should you feel, I ask, in such an age,
> How act? As other people felt and did;

[1] *Inf.* I. 85-7.

> With soul more blank than this decanter's knob,
> Believe—and yet lie, kill, rob, fornicate
> Full in belief's face like the beast you'd be!

What else is Browning's gibe against the noodles who praise the Middle Ages but the echo of Gibbon and Voltaire on the contradictions of the Crusades? But if it is possible to link Petrarch, the acknowledged father of humanism, with Machiavelli, proclaimed generally as a realist, it is through this changed vision of antiquity. To those who may still object to the danger of the link, asserting that Machiavelli, and the Renascence with him, has forgotten the medieval God, I will reply that in the works of Machiavelli the name of God is never taken in vain. In the Italian works of the medieval Boccaccio the name of God is always taken in vain.

It is clear that by establishing this difference we are absolved from weighing too nicely M. Gilson's claims for the Latinity of his clients. It is true that the encomium of Bishop Stubbs on twelfth-century Latin (for him it was 'fairly good and grammatical Latin; adjective agrees with substantive and verb with its nominative; ut governs the subjunctive. . . .'[1]) hardly seems more persuasive than Bremond's insistence on the merits of the *Carmina Burana*—where Bartoli, in his absolute belief in the asceticism of the Middle Ages, thought he saw the Renascence shining whenever a couple of students were gathered in a tavern to sing of wine and women. But as long as its apologists remain on the ground that the Middle Ages must have been a renascence because it was imitative of antiquity *qua* form they may safely be referred to Comparetti for the delineation of the limits within which their praise is justified. In so far as they imply strictures on the Renascence itself, these are non-suited by the position of Petrarch, and by the direction which he gave to humanism. With this development I shall be concerned later on, but meanwhile, to make the matter clear, by the side of Petrarch's affirmation of the relevance of Cicero there stands his denial of the learning of the Middle Ages. Since these are halves of the same question consideration of the one must follow that of the other. Voigt already has noticed the rarity in Petrarch's writings of the religious paraphernalia of the Middle Ages: 'Il est vraiment singulier que Pétrarque, dans ses écrits, parle si rarement des saints et des hérésies, des miracles et des reliques, des visions et des révélations. . . . Pour tout ce que l'Eglise a fait, depuis l'époque des premiers Pères, pour tout ce mélange qui est en elle de paganisme et de superstition, pour sa hiérarchie enfin, il n'a que de

---

[1] Haskins, 129.

l'indifférence.'[1] The word *indifference* is, perhaps, too weak. Petrarch spoke so boldly against the display of luxury in church adornment that Fracassetti hesitated to affirm the genuineness of the letter, though it is supported by his general sentiments.[2] Offhand I can only recall one reference to the cult of relics in the whole body of his letters: it is in the long reproach to Philippe de Vitry for considering Cardinal Guido's journey to Italy as an exile, instead of an opportunity for seeing and learning.[3] Since it concerns the relics of Rome it may be attributed to Petrarch's veneration for what he considered the holiest soil in Christendom; but as it is a single, so also it is a discordant note. Even the famous *canzone* to the Virgin is unechoed in his letters, and Petrarch's appeal here is invariably to Christ, never to the Madonna and the saints. In fact, it is unprepared for in the *Rime* themselves, and not only comes after the genuine close to Petrarch's theme, but even may seem to contrast with this. The three sonnets which immediately precede the *Canzone alla Vergine*, and in especial the last of these, are the real ending to the *Rime*; and the contradiction between the sonnet CCCLXV and the *Canzone* is an encouragement to those who have ventured to see coldness and artificiality in this celebrated composition. For the rest, the superstitions of the medieval mind find no echo, but only an opposition. Where M. Bremond sees a continuity, Petrarch saw a break and a renewal. It was his boast to Boccaccio that he had restored a study long neglected, that he had urged the minds of many in Italy (and perhaps some outside Italy as well) *to these our studies, neglected for so many centuries.*[4] By the side of that affirmation of a conscious renewal stands Petrarch's constant scorn for the learning of the Middle Ages. The four young men whose devotion to the *ipse dixit* of Aristotle (the Averroistic Aristotle) drew down on them the treatise *De sui ipsius et multorum aliorum ignorantia* are not represented as fit judges in the matter of ignorance. It is not, says Petrarch, a thing of which you can judge, as you can best of other things, by having a lot of it.[5] But one of them, at least, possessed some sort of learning. 'So he knows many things about beasts, birds and fishes: how many hairs the lion has on its head, how many feathers a hawk has in its tail, with how many tentacles the octopus binds a shipwrecked man, how elephants copulate backwards and gestate for two years . . . how the sea-urchin checks the movement of a ship, though taken from the waves it can do nothing; how

---

[1] Voigt, 85.   [2] cf. Fracassetti's note to *Fam.*, VI. i, 309.   [3] *Fam.*, IX. xiii. 49.

[4] *Sen.*, XVI. ii. 1067. 'Ad haec nostra studia multis neglecta saeculis multorum me ingenia per Italiam excitasse, et fortasse longius Italia.'

[5] *De Ign.*, 31. 'Nemo peius de ignorantia iudicat quam ignorans.'

hunters deceive tigers with a mirror, etc. . . . Which things are for the most part false . . . but finally, even were they true, they have no relevance at all to the blessed life. For what, pray, will it profit to have known the nature of beasts, birds, fishes and snakes, but to be ignorant or to despise the nature of man—why we are born, whence we come and whither we go?'[1] Since the young man is anonymous it is pointless to enquire whether such an indictment against him personally is valid; the triumphant fact is that the learning of the bestiaries and the lapidaries, the fables of Pliny as the fictions of the alchemists, is cancelled from Petrarch's mind. It is not an asset, but an encumbrance. He does not deign to sift it, to determine in it the large element of the fabulous and the little grain of truth. He is content with declaring its irrelevance. It was for him more praise-worthy to be overcome by truth than to overcome by falsehood; whatever cause was truer was also for him more honest.[2] But the truth he sought was relevant to one central issue: the nature of man was to be studied. By the side of this the knowledge of the Middle Ages was ignorance. His affirmation of centuries of neglect is sup-ported by his individual judgment on almost all the branches of medieval learning. Philosophy was for him (as it was to be for the eighteenth century) the love of wisdom, a word reflecting the modesty of the man who first rejected the proud name of *Sophos*: 'O name once venerable, now prostituted to vanity and insipience.'[3] His attitude to the chop-logic of the Schools is summed up in his anecdote of Diogenes: 'You are not what I am. I am a man. Therefore, you are not a man.' Diogenes replied: 'The last bit is false: and if you want to get it right, begin with me.'[4] To dismiss almost with one anecdote so much of the mental background of the Middle Ages

---

[1] *De Ign.*, 24. 'Multa ille igitur de beluis deque avibus et piscibus, quot leo pilos in vertice, quot plumas accipiter in cauda, quot polipus spiris naufragum liget, ut aversi coeunt elephantes biennioque uterum tument . . . ut echinus quovis actam impetu proram frenat, cum fluctibus erutus nil possit; ut venator speculo tigrem ludit etc. . . . Quae quidem vel magna ex parte falsa sunt . . . quae denique, quamvis vera essent, nichil penitus ad beatam vitam. Nam quid, oro, naturas beluarum et volucrum et piscium et serpentum nosse profuerit, et naturam hominum, ad quod nati sumus, unde et quo pergimus, vel nescire vel spernere?'

[2] cf. again Voltaire's objection to the pious fraud (in *Entretiens Chinois*). *Le Jésuite*: 'N'est-il pas permis de tromper les hommes pour leur bien?' *Le Mandarin*: 'Je crois qu'il n'est permis de tromper en aucun cas, et qu'il n'en peut résulter que beaucoup de mal.'

[3] *Sen.*, XIV. 1043. For the eighteenth century, cf. Voltaire, *Le Comte de Boulainvilliers*: 'Qu'entendez-vous donc par philosophie?—J'entends l'amour éclairé de la sagesse, soutenu par l'amour de l'Etre éternel. . . .'

[4] *Fam.*, I. vi. 55. Again, cf. Voltaire, *Les Anciens et les Modernes*: 'Nous sifflons les scolastiques barbares qui ont régné longtemps parmi nous; mais nous respectons Cicéron et tous les anciens qui nous ont appris à penser.

suggests a strong degree of dissociation from it. And so much were the battles of the scholastics outside the range of Petrarch's interests that the only reference—I think; certainly the only praise—he gives to Thomas Aquinas is in his attack upon the Gaul who defended medicine and condemned poetry. For Petrarch the University of Paris was not a French achievement, but rather a rustic basket full of noble fruits picked from other trees; and had not Italy contributed Peter Lombard, Aquinas, many another to the teachers of Paris? That is part of a polemic; for the rest, Petrarch is content to leave the nominalists and the realists and all the rest alone, contenting himself with the Bible and the Fathers of the Church. From St. Augustine he derives, indeed, the conviction that the obscurity of the Scriptures is useful, since it allows different minds to seize different truths, one man understanding one thing, others another. But it is sufficiently obvious from Petrarch's writings that this latitude, this liberty of judgment, operates outside the central truths of the Christian religion, and that he saw no pretext here for indulgence in the speculation and the bitter quarrels of the scholastics. He was content with the examination of conduct, and here he refused to limit the freedom of man's choice by dependence on the pseudo-science of astrology. 'Why do you wish to make yourselves slaves of the unfeeling stars when you are born free?'[1] And there is a pleasant little dialogue in the *De Remediis* on the promises of alchemists. *Hope* pins her faith in their greatness, and *Reason* answers: 'Tell your alchemist to perform on his own behalf the things he promises to others, and banish first his own poverty; there is a begging sort of men who, while they confess themselves poor, want to enrich others, as if the poverty of other people was more distressing to them than their own.'[2] People called him a necromancer, because he admired and read Virgil, but his attitude to magic, divination and astrology is one of constant exclusion. Consulted on the value of dreams he replied that twice in his life he had dreamed correctly of an absent friend, but that he was no more prepared to put his faith in dreams because of that than Cicero himself, who did not think the chance truth of one dream reason enough to be involved in the obscurity of many.[3]

His attitude to law is already clear from the discussion of his

[1] *Sen.*, I. v. 827. 'Quid vos liberos natos, insensibilium syderum servos vultis facere?'

[2] *De Rem.*, I. cxi. 94. 'Dic ut ea sibi praestet, quae promittit aliis, primumque suam pellat inopiam: est enim fere mendicum genus hominum, cumque se pauperes fateantur, ditare alios volunt, quasi aliena illis, quam propria molestior sit paupertas.'

[3] *Fam.*, V. vii. 278; and cf. *De Rem.*, I. cxii. Contrast Dante's acceptance, with the theologians, of dreams and magic; the latter real enough, but born of a pact with the devil.

political position, and what is to be added is well known: he considered the time that he had spent by his father's orders in the legal studies of his time as wasted. The vast body of glosses which obscured the principles of justice offered an intricacy, the threading of which was nothing else (to use the splendid words of Boccaccio) than to waste irrecoverable time to no purpose.[1] The attack of Valla, and of Voltaire, will not have a different burden.[2] Petrarch had not had to study medicine, but his attitude to its current practice is the counterpart of his attitude to the law. In his old age a doctor sent him advice on the better conduct of his life: he was not to drink water, but only wine, as more warming to a frigid age. He was not to eat fruit or vegetables, and above all he was not to weaken himself by fasts. Who could possibly be well fasting? But against this collection of vulgar prejudices Petrarch could oppose the whole practice of his life. From his youth he had found the practice of fasting when he was unwell to be salutary, and he did not propose to abandon so much more useful a remedy than those offered by the doctors. 'As often as I cease to be well, I shall not only be able to fast, but I shall be compelled to.'[3] As for the virtues of wine and water, he had seen a gout-ridden friend so crippled that it seemed he would never walk again; and ten years after had found him as sprightly in his gait as if he had never known the gout. Wine had bound him; water had loosed him again.[4] Petrarch's frugality (he ate little meat, and took one main meal a day) was not without some reference to antiquity: Vespasian found massage helpful, and fasted regularly one day a month; Aurelian when he was ill never called a doctor, but fasted instead— and Petrarch drew a comic picture of the princes of his time in their strait dependence on doctors as a contrast to these two.[5] But when he rejected these proposals of a doctor with regard to the conservation of his old age he could do so with a reference to the practice of his whole life; and there was nothing servile or chimerical in his respect for the example of antiquity. Rather, the absurdities were uttered by the doctors, against whom the *vis comica* of Petrarch and Molière (to go no further) found ready play. But in spite of Petrarch's letter to Clement on the surest way to death, in spite of the invectives

[1] *De Genealogia Deorum*, XV. x. 'Non recupe: abile tempus in vacuum terere.'

[2] For Valla, v. *infra*, 122. Voltaire, *André Destouches à Siam*. 'Nous n'avons point de lois, mais nous avons cinq ou six mille volumes sur les lois.'

[3] *Sen.*, XII. ii. 1006. 'Quotiens enim sanus esse desiero, ieiunare non tantum potero, sed compellar.'

[4] ibid., XII. i.

[5] ibid., V. iv. 884. 'Nostri vero nunc Principes nec ructare, nec spuere quidem audent, absque Medicorum permissu, neque ideo tamen aut melius quam illi vivunt aut diutius.'

against doctors generally, he did not deny medicine, any more than he denied law: 'I have no doubt that Medicine both exists and is of great importance.'[1] But it was to be a medicine in conformity with Nature, not one established by the *ipse dixit* of Hippocrates. 'I have obeyed Nature, and would always do so, unless the power of one greater opposed, not Hippocrates, that is, but God.'[2] This, like his remarks on Aristotle to the young men of the *De Ignorantia*, suggests no blind dependence on antiquity.

In all this it will have been observed how constant is the note of exclusion. The mind of Petrarch was so positive, and so intent on the examination of conduct and the persuasion to virtue, that he never set himself the deliberate task of refuting in detail the learning of the Middle Ages. The invectives form a minimum part of his work: the *De Ignorantia*, for example, was written casually, a year after the accusation which underlies it,[3] when he was descending the river Po by boat and without any other pressing occupation. The weight of Petrarch's work lies in the firm re-establishment of a study which had been neglected for centuries (and which is, of course, not so much antiquity, as moral philosophy with the guidance of antiquity); the work of detailed refutation was left for the patient scholarship of the fifteenth century. I have insisted on correspondences with the thought of Voltaire, because it is the differences between the two that are most striking. Petrarch has not, of course, any basis for the irreverent persiflage of Voltaire, though if he had been so constituted, there was much to ridicule in the Middle Ages. He constantly, however, averts his gaze. Once more, though, it is clear that he does not depend in any servile manner on the antiquity to which he looks for guidance. 'I am not ignorant of what Aristotle and Epicure say on this point: but the authority of the philosophers does not prevent freedom of judgment.'[4] That is a passage which will be found echoed in varying terms, often better known than this (as in the famous assertion that he was neither Platonist, Aristotelian nor Ciceronian, but Christian[5]) through the whole body of his letters; and to those who read Petrarch rather than his detractors there is little reason to doubt his sincerity or his accuracy. Instead, then, of a

---

[1] *Sen.*, XII. ii. 1002. 'Ego vero et esse Medicinam, et magnum aliquid esse, non dubito.'

[2] ibid., XII. ii. 1004. 'Parui ego naturae, et parerem semper, nisi maioris obstaret imperium, non Hippocratis scilicet, sed Dei.'

[3] That he was a good man, but unlettered.

[4] *Fam.*, III. vi. 148-9. 'Non sum nescius quid de hac re Aristoteles, quid Epicurus sentiat: sed philosophantium auctoritas non impedit iudicii libertatem.'

[5] *De Ign.*, 77. 'Non Ciceronianus certe nec Platonicus, sed Christianus sum.'

humanism born outside the Church, and even against the Church, we have a humanism which is born, and consciously engendered, within the bosom of the Church. How could the Church temporal, even in the moment of its abasement and degeneracy,[1] reject St. Augustine and Petrarch, or deny the contribution of Cicero? The freedom of judgment which Petrarch claimed could be established only because of the unimpeachable orthodoxy of his personal position. The fervour of the Renascence in its search for ancient learning (and it must be borne in mind that the corpus of ancient writers was almost complete in 1430, a bare fifty years after Petrarch's death) could continue unhindered, even encouraged, by the Church just because of the authority of Petrarch. Two and a half centuries were to elapse before the Church threatened Galileo, or burnt Giordano Bruno; this when the human mind had made a different use of its freedom not anticipated by Petrarch. It had not only, as Petrarch himself had done, abandoned the fabric of the superstitious and credulous Middle Ages; it had also attacked the central revelations of Christianity itself, and the reaction of the Church was in the Council of Trent, and in such acts as the suspicion of a Galileo—who asserted natural truths before they were recognised as such, and the execution of a Bruno—who was, in fact, a heretic. According to the range of one's sympathies or one's convictions one may applaud or condemn the use, or the abuse, of spiritual authority; but at least I hope to make it clear that the reason for its remaining in abeyance at the opening of the Renascence lies in the nature of Petrarch's thought.

Petrarch replied to the doctor who forbade him to eat fruit that it would be very wicked and step-mother-like of Nature to hide poison in honey. And the authority of Cicero, as well as his own experience, was with him; while the fifteenth century, as we shall see, was to draw large conclusions from this simple base. For Petrarch, indeed, the statement in Cicero that to fight against Nature was nothing else than to make war like the giants against the gods was unforgettable.[2] It was to be read, of course, with the reservation which I have already quoted, but within that limit it still held important implications. He had maintained, with regard to his assertion of the existence of a science of medicine, that even if there were no men left alive this and other arts would still exist in abstract in the mind of God; but it does not suffice for them to exist thus to be of help to man—they must be known to man as well.[3] What he held in this

---

[1] It is the century of the Babylonian captivity. The Cardinals, says Petrarch, preferred the wine at Avignon.

[2] *Sen.*, XII. ii. 1006.   [3] ibid., 1002. 'Notae hominibus sint oportet.'

particular case he repeated for the general. He maintained that Cicero's whole conclusion is that 'everything we see with our eyes, or understand with our mind, has been made divinely for the good of man, and is governed by divine counsel and providence.'[1] With such a conclusion he is, naturally, in complete agreement. What is included in the *everything*? There is the manifold commodity man draws from the brute creation in food, labour, traction; there is the remedy of diseases, hunting and fowling, building, navigation, with all the innumerable arts either found in Nature or invented by man's mind.[2] Cicero, it will be remembered, remarked with a sense of gratitude on the greatness, the superiority, of all those who had found out fruits, clothing, shelter, the protection against wild beasts, the refinements of life by which man is polished and made milder, so that he can move on from the necessary arts to the more elegant ones, *a necessariis artificiis ad elegantiora*.[3] The conclusion and the gratitude seem natural enough; their expression might seem superfluous if we did not remember also Jacopone da Todi stripping man of every external desire, despising all things:

> Spogliar si vole l'omo d'ognecovelle,

breeding hatred of all creation from the theory of divine love:

> L'amor vero, liale,—odia sé per natura,
> vedendosi mesura—terminata.[4]

The fierce spiritual nihilism of Jacopone may seem, and doubtless is, an extreme position; but the thoroughness with which he carried out his programme serves only to reveal the repulsive nature of the programme itself. And Jacopone was not the author of the very general sentiment:

> Certe qui suavius—hic vixerunt, gravius
> sentient infernum,
> ubi stridor dentium, ululatus flentium
> erit in aeternum; [5]

while St. Ambrose, when he met the landlord of an inn who had no troubles, but only prosperity and family bliss to recount, was imme-

---

[1] *De Ign.*, 51. 'Omnia quaecumque cernimus oculis vel percipimus intellectu, pro salute hominum facta esse et divina providentia ac consilio gubernari.' For Cicero, cf. esp. *De Officiis*, II (*Opera*, IV. 319).

[2] ibid., 'Et artibus innumeris, omnibus vel ingenio vel natura inventis.'   [3] cf. *supra*, 10.

[4] Jacopone da Todi, *Laude*, XCII. 64; XCIX. 15 (ed. Laterza).

[5] Sapegno, *Frate Jacopone*, 92. 'Of course, those who have lived more comfortably here will feel hell more sharply, where there will be for ever gnashing of teeth and the howling of those who weep.'

diately certain that God was not with him. And indeed, St. Ambrose had hardly called his servants, saddled his mules and ridden a hundred yards before he saw the inn, the landlord, his family and his domestic animals swallowed up into the bowels of the earth.[1] *Ex quo patet . . .* as Bishop de Vitry would remark. If that was true of the comforts, it should be doubly true of the elegances, of life: and in fact where the Middle Ages gropes towards these it does so by a cheat. It is no accident that the art of medieval Europe is Christian, rather than mundane. There was no other possible excuse for the satisfaction of so natural an instinct. But the strength of that instinct can, I think, suitably be judged by such episodes in early Christianity as the battle with, and the victory over, the Iconoclasts, as well as by medieval religious art in general. It is again no accident that the Reformation and the Counter-Reformation, in that they bridged to some extent the gap between theory and practice, were sterile (and have remained so) in art. But by the sixteenth century the aesthetic instinct had other means of expression, and this logical sterility could pass unobserved; the Middle Ages could only become articulate aesthetically in the service of the Church, and the gargoyles and the misericords and some of the capitals offer the same commentary which the *Gesta Romanorum* give in literature.[2] That is a digression, or rather, it is a variation on a theme already developed; but the theme is an essential to the business of assessing Petrarch's position. Dante inveighed against the followers of St. Francis, who had abandoned his lady Poverty bequeathed to them:

> ai frati suoi, sí com'a giuste rede,
> raccomandò la donna sua piú cara,
> e comandò che l'amassero a fede. . . .

> .   .   .   .

> Ma il suo peculio di nuova vivanda
> è fatto ghiotto. . . . [3]

But Petrarch ignores St. Francis[4] as thoroughly as he does Aquinas or

---

[1] Passavanti, *Lo Specchio della Vera Penitentia*, 60 (ed. 1856).

[2] With what pleasure would Voltaire have pounced on the idea of Gregorovius and Symonds that Gothic Art was more Christian than neo-classic, or was, in fact, *simpliciter* Christian. cf. Greg., *St. di Roma*, VIII. 158: 'Chi si fa per la prima volta davanti al San Pietro, è tratto a confessare che la figura gotica esprime l'idea archetipa di una chiesa, e forse quella della religione cristiana, con forme piú decise etc.' And Symonds, *Revival of Learning*, 342: 'What the cold churches of Palladio are to Christian architecture. . . .' cf. Voltaire, *Catéchisme de l'honnête homme, Dialogue du douteur et de l'Adorateur, Dîner du Comte de Boulainvilliers*, II.

[3] *Paradiso*, XI. 112-4, 124.

[4] cf. however, *Sen.*, VIII. iii. 835 for his opinion on St. Francis's stigmata as due to auto-suggestion through intensity of thought. And Segré, *Studî Petrarcheschi* (1903).

St. Dominic. And with the *omnia quaecumque* he stated also, in a letter dissuading a friend from taking monastic vows, his agreement with Cicero on the value of *society*: 'For nothing, he says, can be more acceptable on earth to God the prince who rules all this world than the unions of men with laws of association, which we call cities.'[1] The footnote to this passage in Petrarch on the legitimacy of the innumerable arts offered by Nature or invented by the wit of man is the production of the fifteenth century; and so far as theory is concerned Valla will offer the commentary to Petrarch's affirmation of Nature as a goddess to be followed in the words of Cato, which Petrarch quotes from Cicero):[2] if the gifts of Nature, strength and beauty, are placed in man, is he to think so badly of her as to suspect a deception and not an honour? The identity of that question with Petrarch's own on poison in honey serves as a sauce to the difference between them: Valla's question, as we shall see, is part of the treatise *On Pleasure and the True Good.*

[1] *Fam.*, III. xii. 166. 'Nihil enim est, inquit, principi illi Deo, qui omnem hunc mundum regit, quod quidem fiat in terris acceptius, quam concilia coetusque hominum iure sociali, quae civitates appellantur.'

[2] *Sen.*, XII. ii. 1004.

III

PETRARCH'S CONFLICT: ANCIENT AND
MODERN AGAINST MEDIEVAL

IT was Pascal who observed that the Old Testament must have one
overriding sense, or have no sense at all; and though its application
in that case depends on a presumed unity of inspiration it is a valuable
maxim in dealing with a single author. In accordance with it I have
tried to determine the central position of Petrarch, substance not form,
that because of which he was of value to the generations (and how
many generations?) succeeding him. By virtue of that position there
fall, I think, both the assertion that Petrarch was medieval because
he remained Christian, and that he was a mere imitator because he
sought wisdom in the writings of antiquity, instead of seeking only
an aid to style. The contradictions in De Nolhac's judgment on
Petrarch (to quote one of the most patient investigators into the
physical phenomena of Petrarch's library and writings) are easily
apparent: 'Son oeuvre est calquée sur celle de l'antiquité qu'il a
exhumée. Elle manque d'originalité dans la forme et souvent dans le
fond; elle prépare une littérature d'imitation, qui entravera presque
autant qu'elle servira le développement des littératures nationales;
mais cette imitation, malgré tout, est un grand pas en avant et une
nouveauté d'une portée extrême. Elle contribue à former des généra-
tions rares et vigoureuses, qui vont mettre, de gré ou de force, les arts
et les lettres au service d'un idéal oublié.'[1] These acrobatics, by which
his weakness becomes their strength, and his retreat their advance,
are rendered unnecessary if Petrarch has lost the servility of the
medieval compiler without developing a new servility of his
own towards antiquity. But although the truer form of the paradox
might be that Petrarch is not medieval *because* he is Christian, rather
than that he must be medieval, being Christian, it does not follow
that there is in him no residue of the Middle Ages. Such a deposit is
visible in one of his Latin works—the one perhaps which has received
more than its fair share of attention owing to its connection with the
Rime. The *Secretum* has been called the conscience of the *Rime*, a
definition whose accuracy it is not my intention to examine; but in
any stricture on, or any praise of, Petrarch as a medieval the work

[1] *Pétrarque et l'Humanisme*, 16.

52

demands consideration. The first dialogue analyses, at what may seem to some exasperating length, Petrarch's inability to get the best out of the contemplation of death in spite of elaborate precautions. 'So may God's pardon be granted me, I do plunge myself daily in these thoughts; especially at night, when the mind freed from daily cares withdraws into itself. Then I compose this body in the manner of the dying, and intently imagine for myself the very hour of death, and whatever in it the mind finds horrible. So much so that I seem placed in the struggle of dying, seeing sometimes hell, and all the ills you tell of. By this vision I am so grievously disturbed that I rise up terrified and trembling, and often to the horror of the bystanders I burst out in these words: "Alas, what is my state? what suffering? To what wretched end does fortune destine me?" '[1] This refinement of self-torture has no connection with Cicero's assertion that the whole of life is a commentary to death. It seems, in Petrarch's own words, to have *nichil penitus ad beatam vitam*.[2] But it cannot easily be divorced from the spirit of Jacopone and his lights. The blessed Jacopone da Todi mortified his own gulosity by hanging up the *coratella* he had coveted in his cell. When the desire to eat was on him he countered it by smelling at the lights; and this practice he continued until the morsel itself was so advanced in its own beatitude as to poison with its stench his cell, the dormitory, and all the building.[3] Kill the appetite for the things of this world by the smell of their dissolution: that is the medieval-Christian in Petrarch as in Jacopone, and it rests with our individual convictions whether we are prepared to equate the terms. 'Le plus simplement se commetre à nature, c'est s'y commettre le plus sagement.'[4] But although Montaigne appeals to Cicero, as Petrarch did elsewhere, and is perhaps ultimately dependent on the direction given to humanism by Petrarch, there had been time for him to avoid the contradiction into which Petrarch fell. It has been fashionable in recent years to mark off Petrarch's life in times of crises and of a *dissidio*. The true contrast is between the

---

[1] *Secretum*, I., 380. 'Sed si mihi Deus veniae largus sit, ut ego per dies singulos in has cogitationes immergar, praecipueque noctibus, cum diurnis curis relaxatus animus se in ipsum recolligit, cum corpus hoc in morem morientium compono, ipsam quoque mortis horam, et quicquid circa eam mens horrendum reperit, intentissime mihi confingo; usque adeo, ut in agone moriendi positus mihi videar, interdum tartara, et quae narras omnia mala conspicere, eaque tam graviter visione conturber, ut exterritus, tremensque consurgam, et saepe usque horrorem astantium, haec in verba prorumpam: Heu quid ago? Quid patior? Cui me exitio fortuna reservat miseriae?

[2] *De Ign.*, 24 (cf. *supra*, 44).

[3] cf. the legend of Jacopone da Todi, in *Zeitschrift für Romanische Philologie*, II. 1878, 26.

[4] *Essais*, III. xiii.

legitimisation of nature and of the elegances of life, of human and social activity (the sphere of practice for virtue), and the contempt for this world which Petrarch inherited from the Fathers of the Church and the medieval tradition. The *Secretum* has another title also, not much used now, but serving to link it with the *De Vita Solitaria* and the *De Ocio Religiosorum*: it is a treatise *De Contemptu Mundi*. These works were the product of the time in his life when he could write that he had read formerly what pleased, and now must read what profited; when he could think of abandoning Cicero wholly for St. Paul.[1] This desertion did not take place, and Petrarch never sank to the level of the Thebaid, or of Jacopone; but it is not possible to assess him without taking both sides into account, the negative, that is, as well as the positive.

The *De Ocio Religiosorum* and the *Vita Solitaria* are both definitely devotional in tone; and they are, perhaps in consequence, amongst Petrarch's dullest writing. The first is given over, as indeed its title indicates, to a praise of the retirement of the monks. *They* are free from the cares, and the knavery, of this world; and by way of contrast Petrarch paints an unflattering picture of the tumultuous and unprofitable manner in which various classes of citizens spend their days. Trickery here, dishonesty there, never repose, never innocence. The superiority of the contemplative over the active ideal is an old theme (and it assumes almost the air of a caricature here); but it is obvious that there is no reconciliation possible with the praise of cities and of civil society as most acceptable to God. The *De Ocio* is relieved by an occasional independence of thought. It is here that, in opposition to his favourite Augustine, he denies any intention to prophesy on Virgil's part in the IVth Eclogue. Pursuing a line of thought familiar with him, he asserts that if Virgil could have known the Christian faith he would have applied his words to it; but that, in the absence of such knowledge, he applied them to the highest that he knew. The opinion was no less daring for being hidden in a haystack. But the *Vita Solitaria* has even less to recommend it. It soon resolves itself into a catalogue of the gentlemen, of the Thebaid or of more placid tastes, who had retired into solitude. Would that St. Simeon Stylites obtruded himself to lend colour to this pallid throng! but none of them, at least in Petrarch's recital, has any relief, or any particular interest. Nor are there scattered in it many of the passages which redeem to some extent its companion treatise. The reason for the artificiality of these two works lies, I think, in Petrarch's

[1] *Fam.*, XXII. x. 148. 'Legi quae delectabant, lego quae prosint.'

good intentions, coupled with his own inaptitude for a monastic solitude and obedience. He catalogues and repeats because he has nothing really genuine to say; nor does his own love of solitude alter the issue. He filled that solitude with a much more human activity than he could chronicle or prescribe with regard to the Carthusians, or catalogue in the long list of hermits. 'All my life has been spent on letters'—the study of antiquity, and of man as a moral being.[1]

Closer to the mood of the *Secretum*, more irritating in its method and in its insistent theme than either of these last treatises, is the long work *De Remediis Utriusque Fortunae*. It is here that Petrarch corroborates that first dialogue of the *Secretum*: Stay in bed and reflect on death![2] It is here that he joins hands most nearly with Jacopone: If your house is small, think of your tomb![3] Petrarch puts as a consolation what Jacopone put as a remedy to pride:

> Quando t'alegri, omo de altura,
> va', pone mente a la sepultura.[4]

But the contradiction between the two passages is merely formal: the spirit is identical, and the form might have been so as well had Petrarch's recommendation happened to be in the first, and not in the second, book. The remedy to good fortune is to prove the inanity of earthly goods; the remedy to bad fortune is to consider it   . as an exercise for death. Thus the whole work demands a constant negative: no man happy before death, and no man happy except in death. Add to this theme a dialogue form in which Reason pontificates, and Hope, Joy, Sorrow, Fear repeat their lines plaintively, providing, not an interlocutor, but a sort of bell-press to start Reason off again. The result should be the most tedious in Petrarch's catalogue, and its situation on the threshold of the folio editions may well have turned many a reader away from Petrarch's works! But it is Medieval-Christian-renunciatory in its conception, not entirely in its execution. It sweeps this world away in favour of the next; it gives a free play to Petrarch's misogyny, his hatred of servants, a dozen other pessimisms and exclusions. But even where Petrarch seems to speak with the voice of Jacopone most clearly he adds reflections which Jacopone could never afford. The latter's motto had been: to despise the world, to despise oneself, and to despise the fact of being despised.[5] It is advice which Reason repeats in the dialogue on Contempt: Despise the world, despise nobody, despise oneself and be despised

---

[1] *De Ign.*, 35. 'Omne meum tempus in literis actum est.'   [2] *De Rem.*, II. xcv. 187.
[3] ibid., II. lxiii. 156. 'Visne tibi domus omnis amplissima videatur, sepulchrum cogita.'
[4] *Laude*, XXV. 51.   [5] 'Spernere mundum, spernere seipsum, spernere se sperni.'

oneself, this finally is what is needed.[1] But when Grief repeats the cry:
I am despised by others, Reason adds: Remember, whether you
despise others, or have despised them: this is the way of men, to
despise and be despised. You reward each other with a mutual hate,
a mutual contempt, and you wish to be venerable to others while
venerating nobody.[2] That has nothing to do with the theme of the
book as enounced; it has nothing to do with the ascetic counsels just
quoted. It is an observation on human conduct which implies a
recommendation for its improvement, and therefore also implies a
recognition of conduct in this world: something quite different from
the *spernere mundum* with which we began. This constant tendency to
observe, reflect and generalise initiates the modern European tradition,
and sharply distinguishes Petrarch from Dante. Dante starts from the
general pattern to which man ought to conform, and in the light of
this observes individual sins and virtues. It is a method in which the
reflection does not occur: so that Petrarch is of the same family as,
for example, La Rochefoucauld, but not Dante. The richness of
this reflection even in so fundamentally arid a work as the *De Remediis*
is surprising; but it is a phenomenon with which I shall be more
concerned later on, and what is immediately more important is the
contradiction by which Petrarch upholds what his book purports to
call in question. From the very beginning the possibility of this is
clear: life, if rightly lived, should be the most happy and the most
cheerful of things.[3] That is a different statement from the better-
sighs-than-singing mood,[4] from the rejection of building or painting.[5] It links with the passage in the second book (and it is in
the second book that the richest chapters are to be found) on the
benefits of life. The argument against sadness begins with man's
likeness to the image of God; it proceeds through the qualities of the
mind, the arts invented by the mind and those which serve the body,
both in necessities and for enjoyment, down to the gifts of nature and
the pleasure in the handiwork of nature, which is subject to man.
Such store of roots, so many juices of plants, such a fair assortment of
so many flowers, of scents, colours, tastes and sounds, with harmony
springing from opposites. Add the animals that people the ele-

[1] *De Rem.*, II. xxxvi. 138. 'Spernere mundum, spernere nullum, spernere sese, se sperni, hoc
tibi ultimo opus est.'
[2] ibid., 'Recordare, an tu alios aut spernas, aut spreveris: hic est mos humanus, spernere et
sperni, mutuo vos vicissim odio, mutuoque praemitis contemptu, et vultis aliis esse venerabiles,
neminem venerantes.'
[3] *De Rem.*, Preface. 'Quae si rite ageretur, foelicissima prorsus ac iucundissima rerum erat.'
[4] ibid., I. xxiii. 21.   [5] ibid., I. xxxiv and xl. For sculpture as vanity, cf. xli.

ments; add the view of hills, sunny valleys, shady woods, snow-clad mountains and warm sea-shores; add ripening corn and jewelled vineyards; add the convenience of the town and the leisure of the countryside[1]—and you have a picture of human life to be appreciated by Virgil or Horace, whom Petrarch quotes, but not the medieval *spernere mundum* with which the work should be concerned. Not that Petrarch has ceased to be Christian in ceasing to be medieval: all in nature is for the rule of man if he eschews sin. The main statement, admirable in its warmth and colour, is an illustration of Petrarch's acceptance of a general conclusion from Cicero, as we have seen it above. It is no accident that the predominantly medieval tone of the *De Remediis* is contradicted by passages such as these: from their juxtaposition with so much that is tedious they represent all the more obviously the vital contribution of Petrarch.

Harshly, then, as the negations of nature and society which are to be found scattered throughout the *De Remediis* contrast with the affirmation of these in Petrarch, they do not cancel it; and the fact that the spiritual crisis was surmounted without the abandonment of Cicero and Antiquity diminishes their importance. But there was another negation in Petrarch which cannot be cancelled. It is well known that his love for Laura lay in the Provençal tradition, and had nothing to do with the institution of matrimony. For this institution, and for women in general, his letters reveal the contempt and distrust which I have noted as characteristic of the *De Remediis*. 'Let those have wives who take delight in endless company with women, nightly embraces and wranglings, the wailing of babies and sleepless nights; those who think in that way to build up the nobility of their name and perpetuate their family (though nothing is more uncertain than this). We, if it may be, will propagate our name not by marriage but by our talent, not by children but by books, not by the aid of a woman but of virtue. He trusts little in himself and God who seeks the help of a wife for the favour of posterity and for glory; for a wife will give you sons, and grandsons, with a fertile succession, but she

---

[1] ibid., II. xciii. 184. 'Non parva enim vobis gaudii causa est, imago illa similitudo Dei creatoris, humana intus in anima, ingenium, memoria, providentia, eloquuium, tot inventa, tot artes huic animo famulantes, huic corpori, quibus necessitates vestrae omnes divino beneficio comprehensae sunt, tantae quoque opportunitates, necessitates, et tam variae rerum species, non necessitati tantum vestrae, sed oblectationi servientium miris, et ineffabilibus modis, tanta vis radicum, tot herbarum succi, tot florum tam iucunda varietas, tot odorum, et colorum, et saporum, et sonorum, ex contrariis orta concordia.' ibid., 'Adde collium prospectus, apricationes vallium, umbrosos saltus, algentesque alpes, et tepentia littora . . . commoditates urbium, et ruris ocia.'

will give you also cares and labours.'[1] A lasting name, then, must be one's own production: what would Plato, Aristotle, Homer and Virgil be if they had relied on their wives for their fame? To such a question Petrarch unites a list (a medieval list) of those who have suffered from the molestation of their wives. He does not bring it to date, for fear of truth being offensive, not for lack of conviction or evidence: you have only to go out, he asserted in a moment of enthusiasm, to be assailed everywhere by the laments and clamour of the married. The general judgment may seem pleasant enough, and not so far removed from the sage reflection of Chanticleer. In fact, many of the misogynistic remarks of the *De Remediis* have an unconscious humour: 'I hope my wife is coming.' 'If you hope for that, I don't know what you fear. But so it is, some expect their wife, and some the fever.'[2] 'I have lost my wife. So you say *I have lost*, almost as one will say *I have lost the fever or the itch*, where sometimes loss is a sort of gain. . . .'[3] But the personal note in Petrarch is more bitter. In spite of the persistence of the investigators into Petrarch's biography, in spite of the polemic which has ranged round the plurality or the singularity of his love, the birth of his children Giovanni and Francesca has remained obscure. What seems certain, at least, is that their mother (if she was one person) was of humble status, and that it did not occur to him to connect his parenthood with the poetic tradition of Love. Rather, it is possible to think of Laura as having been envisaged, at least at times, as an ideal above 'l'usanza ria,' and as an escape from it—not the last of the oscillations of the *Rime*. Indeed, if the famous debate in the IIIrd Dialogue of the *Secretum* has any sense at all, or any sincerity, it must surely be that Petrarch could think of this poetic tradition, and of Laura in consequence, as a means of escape from the senses. Otherwise Laura herself incurs the contempt which Petrarch had for women. 'Resort to women, without which I had at times thought I could not live, I now fear worse than death; and though I am often disturbed by the sharpest of temptation, yet when there comes into my mind what woman is, all temptation

---

[1] *Sen.*, XIV. iv. 1035. 'Uxores habeant, qui muliebri sine fine consortio et nocturnis amplexibus atque conviciis vagituque infantium, et insomni negotio delectantur, eoque modo, maxime claritatem nominis, et perpetuitatem familiae moliuntur, quo nihil incertius. Nos si dabitur, nostrum nomen non coniugio, sed ingenio, non filiis, sed libris, non foeminae, sed virtutis auxilio propagamus. Parum sibi, parum Deo fidit, qui ad gratiam posteritatis, ac gloriam opem poscit uxoris, uxor enim et filios, et nepotes foecunditate successuum, et curas tibi pariet et labores.'

[2] *De Rem.*, I. cxiv. 97.   [3] ibid., II. xviii. 125.

immediately departs.'[1] There is in Jacques de Vitry the story of a hermit who was troubled by temptation even though he knew that the object of his desire was dead. At last he went to her tomb and cut off a morsel of her flesh, so that when he was tempted by carnal desire he could put the decomposing flesh to his nose and reproach himself with the baseness of the object. 'And when he'd done this once or twice his lusts died away and ceased.'[2] These are not two, but one remedy: the second being only the physical version to fortify the mental image. It is a *remedy* in the special sense of the *De Remediis*, and of Jacopone. But the statement in Petrarch is, I think, obviously genuine, though it may seem to us to bear too much the bitter and inhuman stamp of St. Jerome; if it is here in its extreme form it is because the statement dates from that central part of the century when Petrarch had overcome the *delicta iuventutis meae*, but while horror for them was still sharp. There is no other passage with quite so strong a repugnance in his letters; but only once or twice—to those who asked his counsel—does he give any approval to matrimony for others. Once only does he embark on any praise of the female sex, and as this is in a letter congratulating the Empress of Charles IV on the birth of a daughter it is not in itself very conclusive. His more general sense is that of Chanticleer, his fixed conviction with regard to a wife 'that to be without her is sure tranquillity.'[3]

It would scarcely be necessary to quote Montaigne again, or Valla in the *De Voluptate*, to prove that a different conclusion might logically be drawn from Petrarch's view of the unreasonableness of expecting to find poison in honey. To follow nature *tanquam Deam* might be taken to preclude the bitter contempt (*dum in animum redit quid est femina*) for women generally. The appeal to Plato and Aristotle, Homer and Virgil offers little foothold, since it is obvious enough that their being wived or not has no inevitable connection with their philosophical or poetic merit. One does not *necessarily* cease to strive for the perpetuation of one's name by reputation on the grounds that it is already in process of perpetuation in one's children. This illogicality is not hard to grasp, and the implied contradiction between Petrarch's praise of nature and his dispraise of matrimony is equally near the surface. But it must be remembered that the problem

---

[1] *Fam.*, X. v. 100. 'Consortium feminae, sine quo interdum aestimaveram non posse vivere, morte nunc gravius pertimesco, et quamquam saepe tentationibus turber acerrimis, tamen dum in animum redit quid est femina, omnis tentatio confestim avolat.'

[2] *Exempla*, CCXLV. 102. 'Et cum aliquotiens hoc fecisset mortue sunt et cessaverunt ejus concupiscentie.'

[3] *Sen.*, XIV. iv. 1034. 'Qua caruisse tranquillitas certa est.'

does not exist in a vacuum, nor is it confined to the mind of Petrarch
alone. In his exclusion of medieval learning, in his intuition of the
value, and his grasp of the substance, of the learning of antiquity
Petrarch could stand alone. His task, and his merit, was enormous;
but it was nevertheless a task within the compass of a single mind.
His attitude to women implied a relationship, and that relation could
only be with woman in her contemporary status. That is why we
have on the one hand the courtly ideal of Laura, which is not advanced
as a solution to the problems of life (it is disappointing that there is a
lacuna in the letters of Petrarch from 1326-1333,[1] so that Laura
receives scant mention in the correspondence as it remains); on the
other we have the rejection which concerns the tradition dating from
the Fathers of the Church and involving a very medieval misogyny.
The positive element, on which Valla seized and later generations
built, is there in Petrarch; but there was no room physically as yet
for a conception of society such as we shall find in the *Cortegiano*.
This latter work echoes antiquity as much as any other book in the
Renascence, yet the society which it depicts is as different from that
of antiquity as the architecture of Michelangelo is from that of
ancient Rome. Nowhere is it more different than in the status of
women; and Petrarch, who opens the path which leads to Castiglione,
would have found himself ill at ease at the court of Urbino. In spite
of the *Rime* Petrarch's attitude to woman remains negative.

I have said that this is a negation which cannot be cancelled in
Petrarch, and that I think is strictly true. But apart from the explanation there is also an affirmation which does not lie very far away, and
which may be counted as an attenuation: Petrarch's conception of
friendship. It has been said by those who have insisted most on
Petrarch's vanity and his desire for glory that this never allowed a true
equality: it was a sovereignty rather than a correspondence between
friends. In support of this, for example, Francesco Nelli has been
adduced, counting himself lucky to have been born in a century illu-
minated by Petrarch. But the danger of judging by scraps and anecdotes instead of attending to the general sense of an author can be
nowhere very much more apparent than in this question of Petrarch's
character. That there were people who considered themselves fortunate in being Petrarch's contemporaries is doubtless true: it was a
very perspicacious gratitude to one who meant so much to the
intellectual, and the moral, fortunes of Europe. But that he attempted
in return to play consistently the *Roi-Soleil* is disproved by the whole

[1] cf. Fracassetti, *Prefazione alle Lettere Familiari*, 45 (1863).

tone, and the whole sense, of his letters. Petrarch writes mainly with
modesty, often with humility, rarely with scorn for an individual.
The unfortunate person who thought Cicero a poet and counted
Valerius Maximus the greatest of the moralists receives a fairly sharp
rebuke, but Petrarch took the trouble to answer him patiently; and
where he is writing to his friends he writes with no sense of superiority
assumed. The charge has been brought against him that in his letters
he is concerned with himself alone, and that others are for him an
audience only. It is a strange charge, and I can only repeat that it
will not easily be accepted by any one who has read the letters of
Petrarch in their entirety. Rather is there a constant and an intimate
concern with the welfare of others, and an affection which enters into
his friends' affairs with an unfailing interest. It is, in short, as strange
a charge as that other which maintains that his letters are mere
artificial pieces in imitation of Cicero's, now short as one of Cicero's
Familiar Letters, now puffed out by rhetoric to the length of a treatise
and stuffed pedantically with quotation from the Latins. Such a view
consists equally of levity and ingratitude. Petrarch quoted liberally
of what he had read, and for those who are inclined to see in this a
new defect of the humanist age it may be well to refer to earlier
practice. The charge of burdensome quotation has been preferred
against the *Convivio*, and has been rebutted by the Dantists with the
admission first that good taste now would not tolerate so much, but
with the contention that anterior and contemporary medieval compilations were nothing but a repertory of sentences strung on the
thinnest thread of thought: in the *Convivio* Dante wrote whole
chapters by himself![1] As we have seen before, if Petrarch was
merely imitating antiquity *qua* form he was continuing the Middle
Ages. But from the erudition of Dante, wrestling, as it does, with the
subtle and aprioristic theories of the medieval mind, to the prose of
Petrarch in the letters there is an interval. We read Dante's treatises
out of homage to the author of the *Divina Commedia*, and it is for the
most part a fatiguing effort of respect. Petrarch's preoccupations are
entirely different from those of Dante, and what he absorbs from the
ancients suffers no distortion to strange arguments. He quotes the moralists as moralists, and as part of the observation of human conduct.
The result is to make them once again assimilable. We must be grateful
to Petrarch for quoting: how else could he have communicated his
own enthusiasm or his own understanding to those who lacked the
apparatus of classical learning? Such a procedure was not pedantry

[1] Zingarelli, *Dante*, 404.

but the life-blood of a new movement. It is true also (and it has been urged against him) that Petrarch valued the letters he wrote sufficiently to keep minutes, and even duplicates of them. It is an argument which would be more cogent of a later writer, when the fashion of presenting the world with a collection of one's letters was well established. But it does not follow that they could not still be concerned with real things, and must perforce have less value for us precisely because they obviously had more for Petrarch himself! I have myself quoted liberally from Petrarch's letters, and I think the quality of what I have quoted is fairly indicative of the nature of Petrarch's writing in them, its concision and its care for things rather than words. 'The discipline of the tongue alone is easy, we must philosophise in things as well if we wish to be saved in reality.'[1] It is a remark to which Petrarch very often returns. And I may add my feeling that there is scarcely more than a handful of letters which are vitiated by being written for writing's sake—a thing which is by no means the same as writing for the sake of writing something important. Amongst the dross in the *Letters* I would stigmatise the VIIIth Letter of the VIIIth Book in the *Familiares*: it has a very medieval pedantry. But it stands, so far as I am aware, alone in the collections as we have them.

I have discussed this charge here because it makes a difference to our conception of friendship in Petrarch: the less value we attach to the letters, the less also to the writer. But what *Laelius* and *Socrates* recognised as friendship stands, I think, above suspicion. ' I desire the same good for you as for myself: the blessed life, for which many long, to which few attain.'[2] There is nothing more amiable than virtue, nothing more attractive; and it is the duty of friendship to share what seems most precious. Virtue, then, is the foundation of friendship, and mutual love preserves it. But that does not prevent Petrarch from concluding that the sum of the whole matter is to seek friendship alone in friendship, *in amicitia sola amicitia quaerenda*. To these sentiments his letters are the commentary: in them the praise of friendship is a constantly recurring theme, just as the practice of friendship lies at their base. His laments are many as he outlives his generation, his consolation is often given to absent friends in that true friendship knows no absence. It was not a generosity in friendship that was

[1] *Sen.*, I. ii. 815. 'Levis est enim solius linguae disciplina, philosophandum nobis et rebus est, si re ipsa salvi esse cupimus.'

[2] *Fam.*, IV. ii. 203. 'Illud bonum tibi cupio quod mihi; beatam vitam, ad quam multi suspirant, pauci perveniunt.'

limited to a few only (to *Laelius* and *Socrates* with a few chosen Florentines). Petrarch gave freely of himself to his century, and we may judge of his generosity by the fact that the letters he retained represent a fraction only of those he wrote. The number of his correspondents, and his readiness in answering those who were unknown to him, gives point to his claim to have brought many *ad haec nostra studia*. If the letters to unknown correspondents were put into a separate corpus it would be found that Petrarch is as much concerned with the persuasion to virtue and to study as with the traditional sunning of his vanity; the separate consideration of those to friends will show the same equality as in his proposals for a communal life. And the general sense bears out his affirmation that there was nothing dearer in human life to him than friendship. This constant insistence on the value of friendship, and of its meaning, has nothing in it to surprise us if we remember Petrarch's dependence on Cicero and his contact with antiquity: as he observes, it was Horace who called Virgil *half of his soul*. It is only if we bear in mind the Middle Ages that surprise is possible at the completeness with which Petrarch could recover the conception, and the practice of friendship. The Middle Ages is rich in pairs of names which we remember— Héloise and Abelard, Tristram and Isoldt, Floire and Blanchefleur and the rest (not forgetting Paolo and Francesca); but on the whole they concern the first relationship, love between man and woman. I call it first, because it is fundamental, and its absence would surprise much more than its presence. But unless I am mistaken the second relationship—the conception, and the achievement of friendship—is deficient in the Middle Ages. The reason for this is implicit in every commonplace which I have so far applied to that period: without the restoration of moral philosophy the Ciceronian, and the Petrarchan, conception of friendship is impossible. The first step from a medieval to a civilised society lies in this re-establishment of the link between man and man by means of ideas and reflection. *Parce que c'était luy, parce que c'était moy* is not so casual as it seems. But with the reappearance of this link we have at once the sign of a society which is settling down of itself after the dark ages, and the hope for future progress. Petrarch could claim so many friends because of the first process; and he could wield such enormous influence because of the second fact. By the side of this relationship the *Divina Commedia* seems almost a work written in a vacuum. The friendship of Dante for Guido Cavalcanti or for Cino da Pistoia may be prophetic, but the vagueness of the outlines, and the lack of connection with the *Com-*

media, is significant. In spite of Petrarch's coronation on the Capitol
(and the part which this played in his life bears little relation to the
insistence on it by the biographers) it is Dante rather than Petrarch
who is dependent on the 'gran disio dell'eccellenza.' The tranquillity
of Petrarch's life at Vaucluse or at Arquà was not given to Dante: it
would have suited neither the time nor the man. This does not
diminish the poetic stature of Dante (and there will be many
to whom it will seem rather to enhance it); but it does something to
account for the ease with which he was supplanted as an influence. To
practise virtue in the Middle Ages one retired from the world to the
monastery (a theological, and not a moral, solution); and the *Divina
Commedia* is much more concerned with the relationship between
man and God—that is, with prescribing rules for the conduct of man
—than it is with reflection on the relationship between man and man.
Dante was abandoned as a medieval, and this I take to be an underlying cause to the specific charges of harshness of form: it is easy to
pass over imperfections of form where the sense is congenial, and the
accusation of their existence may often obscure effectively a real
dissatisfaction. To ask oneself what logical continuation was possible
to the *Divina Commedia* (in spite, or because, of the multiplying of
manuscripts, glosses and expositions) is to realise the extent to which
it is a stop rather than a pointer; and where else was there any basis
for the creation of a conception of society other than in Petrarch's
return to Cicero, and in his affirmation of virtue as the first half of the
business?

I have returned inevitably from the negative to the affirmative, so
strong is the balance in Petrarch in favour of the second. But there is
still another point which claims discussion in this context: Petrarch's
conception of poetry (of Latin poetry, that is). It will not have been
forgotten that Saintsbury's judgment of Petrarch in his regular writing
as ludicrously a classicaster presumably concerns the *Africa* more than
it does the letters; nor that modern apologists have claimed the *Africa*
instead as a Medieval-Christian poem. The latter assertion we need
not, perhaps, take very seriously. It arises from prejudice, and not
from discussion: Petrarch's Latin works are living, therefore they cannot be dead, therefore they are medieval and not humanistic. Nevertheless, it is true that his conception of poetry is medieval. When
King Robert examined him, prior to his coronation on the Capitol,
he confessed that he had never known there were so many things in
Virgil before. Petrarch put forward his interpretations of Virgil with
some diffidence, but only because the labour of decoding a poet who

had written more than a thousand years ago seemed hazardous to him; that did not prevent him being sure that the *Aeneid* contained hidden moral truths. In the IXth Book of the *Africa* he states the theory: the poet has not the licence that men imagine. He must build firmly on truth, but resting on this foundation he may hide himself under a fair cloud, and leave the reader a long and pleasant task in the discovery: the deeper buried, and the longer looked for, the sweeter is the finding of the hidden truth. Such is the method.[1] The material for poetry is history, the cult of virtue, whatever teaches the way to live, all study of nature. But especially they must be cloaked, the eyes cheated by a thin veil of ornament, through which instruction at times breaks out, but mainly shuns the view. The ornament is the invention of the poet: if he invents the whole he is no poet, but a liar.[2] If logically applied this game of hide-and-seek reduces poetry to the level of the crossword puzzle, but nobody reads a crossword puzzle when it is solved: the cracking of the nut is all its interest, and it has little food value. Doubtless, this idea of camouflaging what Petrarch thought of as the substance of antiquity and calling it poetry will be condemned as misguided, and in any case as erroneous in its judgment on the ancients themselves. It formed part in the beginning of the cheat by which the writers of the pagan world were preserved at all: what excuse had the early Christians for clinging to heathen poetry if they could not represent it as allegory, and erect this excuse into a rule for writing? But in Petrarch this mode of *writing* (as apart from *thinking*) affected mainly the *Eclogues,* which he concocted in the then accepted manner so obscurely that, if we had not his own key for

---

[1] *Africa*, IX. 90.

> Non illa licentia vatum est
> Quam multis placuisse palam est . . .
> Scripturum iecisse prius firmissima veri
> Fundamenta decet, quibus inde innixus, amoena
> Et varia sub nube potest abscondere sese,
> Lectori longum cumulans placitumque laborem,
> Quaesitu asperior quo sit sententia, verum
> Dulcior inventu.

[2] ibid., 97.

> Quicquid labor historiarum est,
> Quicquid virtutum cultus documentaque vitae,
> Naturae studium quicquid, licuisse poetis
> Crede; sub ignoto tamen ut celentur amictu,
> Nuda alibi et tenui frustrentur lumina velo,
> Interdumque palam veniant fugiantque vicissim.
> Qui fingit quodcumque refert, non ille poetae
> Nomine censendus, nec vatis honore, sed uno
> Nomine mendacis.

their unlocking, they might have remained hermetic for ever. As it is, nobody, I think, has ever claimed much poetic life for them. I do not think that the defects which have been attributed, rightly or wrongly, to the *Africa* are due to its possession of a secret code; but since from the first nineteenth-century scholar to examine the work down to the modern apologists for the poem opinion has swung to the full opposite, it is well to determine both what Petrarch intended, and what he achieved. Zumbini's original negative judgment I will give as a pendant to the opposite one of the apologists: 'Il poema, che pure segna il periodo in cui ferveva nel Petrarca l'amore per il mondo romano, e piú egli si sforzò di farlo rivivere, in cui la venerazione per l'antichità classica fu tanta da soggiogare in lui il sentimento cristiano, si ridusse in realtà ad un grande tentativo fallito, ad una splendida versificazione della storia romana ricalcata pedissequamente su Tito Livio.'[1] It is to be noted first that this does not square with Petrarch's intentions as to poetry. History may be its matter, but the corollary of *documentaque vitae* forbade the abandonment of Christian feelings, as also of what Petrarch took to be Cicero's contribution to Christian conduct. His intentions, in any case, are not exhaustively stated in the passage from the *Africa* just quoted, though that statement itself is repeated in various places in Petrarch's works. He was ready to meet objections against the paganism of the ancient poets—a fault which they shared with the philosophers of antiquity. That was not a failing of poetry, but of individuals, not of art, but of the times; it need not prevent, in other times, with a different mind and with larger grace, a poet from being both pious and eloquent.[2] The formula of poetry is one and the same, that is to say, but *we* are not limited (if I may speak paradoxically) to the polytheism of antiquity. Rather, it is possible for a new and Christian poetry to arise which has the advantage over the pagan, in that it is built on truth. If some one, inspired by pious feelings, relies on the Muses to adorn truth and to write the life of Christ in noble verse, or any sacred subject, or even a profane one (so long as it is not a forbidden one), what could be better?[3] By this the way is prepared both for the *De Partu Virginis* and for the

---

[1] Zumbini, *Studii sul Petrarca*, in Gerosa, *L'Umanesimo Agostiniano del Petrarca*, 11.

[2] Petr., *Contra Medicum Quendam*, III. 1221. 'Non id certe Poeticum, sed humanum fuerit, temporumque crimen vel ingenii, non artis, ut dictum est, neque quod alio tempore, atque alio ingenio, et ampliori gratia Poetam esse, pium disertumque prohibeat.'

[3] ibid., 1218. 'Si quis ergo talis, pio instigatus affectu, ad ipsius veritatis ornatum, musarum praesidio niteretur, et vel sacrum aliquid, vel profanum etiam, modo non vetitum, celebraret, quod nostrorum quidam fecerunt, quamvis praeter legem carminis, nullo poetico artificio usi sint, quis putas id melius posset implere?'

Christias, those forgotten poems which made the nineteenth-century critics cry out on pagan profanation (though if their authors had wished to be pagan it would have been easy to choose some other subject; and is not *Paradise Lost* also provided for in the formula of Petrarch?) But apart from this anticipation, the *vel profanum etiam* refers transparently to Petrarch's intentions with regard to the *Africa*. Not only is there no need for him to abandon his Christian position because his subject is profane, but even the need is the opposite one, to assert it. And from this clear statement we can deduce the legitimacy of the search for subjectivism in the *Africa*. Nor was the subject itself so profane in Petrarch's eyes as it may be in ours. As he says, with some emotion, in the *De Viris Illustribus* the prize at stake was not one city or a kingdom (as is usual in warfare)—*sed merces victoriae orbis erat*. For Petrarch as well as for Dante Rome had a Christian destiny.

Such, then, was the intention; what of the achievement? When we strip the apologist's formula of its mistaken form there is left the claim that it is a living and not a dead poem, a success and not a failure. I do not feel disposed to make so high a claim for it. On the one hand, it is not a mere servile copy from antique models; on the other, its original elements are not sufficient to give poetic life to the whole. In the *Rime* Petrarch inherits from a living tradition: whatever one's judgment on the Provençals, the Sicilians and the *dolce stil novo* one cannot deny their existence. In the *Africa* he was not developing in a tradition: he was attempting to resurrect one. Now in the resurrection of the flesh we may hope to recover our bodies without the infirmities of old age or disease through which we shall have left them; but in the resurrection of literary traditions there is an unconscious, and an unfortunate, tendency for them to pick up where they had left off. Petrarch may have compared himself in his own mind with Virgil; but in actual fact he must more probably be measured with Statius. That is to say, that we may expect parts of the *Africa* to impress us, but that we can hardly expect the whole to do so. The general coldness of effect is not due to Petrarch's lack of enthusiasm for his task; it is to be ascribed to the effort of starting the machine, a machine that had not been working since late Roman times, and then only feebly. The labour of producing a long series of hexameters is more likely to be successful when their handling has been rendered easier by the handling of one's predecessors (in spite of Croce's odd idea that there is no such thing as a tradition in literary technique[1]).

[1] cf., for example, Croce, *Giosuè Carducci*, 135 (ed. Laterza, 1937): 'Come se ci fosse un progresso dell'arte dello sciolto, per sé considerato!'

E

In default of this the labour of producing hexameters may well be mistaken for the production of poetry. This, I think, is the defect of the *Africa*; but we may expect it to be most eloquent where the contribution is most definitely from Petrarch himself, rather than from Livy or Florus (for even here Petrarch did not copy servilely: he attempted, as he stated in the preface to the *De Viris Illustribus*, and in so far as his limited apparatus would allow, to sift his historical authorities and to hold to what seemed truest). Within these limits there is probably an exception to be made. At the beginning of the poem Petrarch proceeds from the invocation of the Muses to the name of Christ, and there is a certain awkwardness in the procedure. In Book VII similarly Jove himself appears in response to the prayers of the women who personify Rome and Carthage. Round him are choirs of angels singing peace (*atque agmina nuntia pacis*), as though it were the night of the Nativity, to which indeed, by a daring prophecy, he alludes. Again, the position is an unexpected one, and not entirely successful; but the awkwardness is due to the novelty of the departure, and the proper judgment is, I think, to discount this awkwardness on account of the difficulty of the transaction, and to read the passages in relation to the notion of poetry which I have quoted. In fact, this intrusion of Christian sentiments into places which do not seem easily to admit them is a proof that elsewhere Petrarch will not forget his own ideas in his zeal for copying Livy. His enthusiasm for antiquity is never a retrogression from his Christian faith. *Omnis veritas a Deo*, and Petrarch, who knows one God, cannot hobnob with others. In the *De Viris Illustribus* he may mention that Hannibal offered sacrifices to his gods: it would have been enough to pray to One, he adds with something of a snort. He does not forget that history is example when he is treating it in verse any more than he did in prose. In Scipio's dream his father assures him that this life is comparable to death and that the soul is immortal. Scipio enquires, most logically, what is the point of delaying here; but his father answers with sound sentiments that God and nature have fixed the soul within the body till it is called away (*edicto donec revocetur aperto*). It is wrong to hasten that call, and in the meantime the trials of this life must be modestly borne, and this code kept in mind:

Tu sacra fidemque
Iustitiamque cole; [et] pietas sit pectoris hospes
Sancta tui morumque comes, quae debita virtus

Magna patri, patriae maior, sed maxima summo
Ac perfecta Deo; quibus exornata profecto
Vita via in caelum est. . . .[1]

I need scarcely refer back to show that Petrarch owes nothing here to
Livy, much instead to his conception of the Christian nature of
Cicero's ideas; and by the strength of a passage such as this striving
after purely classical effect often seems childish. I have in mind
particularly one simile when Scipio's father first appears, and his son's
lament disturbs the chorus of the radiant stars, as when a fish has fled
the saltness of the sea and tasted the sweetness of fresh water: but the
sea returns in sudden strength, and bitterness disturbs the pleasure.
It is a laboured, and an inaccurate, simile.[2] Nor does the rest of the
poetic *apparatus* (with a reliance on serpents as the chief stock-in-trade
of similes) show any unexpected virtue. It is the straightforward
expression of Petrarch's mind which is important, and the passage
quoted shows clearly enough that it is the Petrarch of the letters who
will be revealed.

No-one, I imagine, will accuse the *Trionfi* of being un-Christian
in their inspiration. The progress through the triumph of death,
fame, time, to that of divinity may be dull, but it cannot be claimed
to be unedifying. And it is most closely paralleled by the sentiments
of Scipio's father on the three deaths which await his son. The
physical death can be vanquished by reputation: Petrarch will come,
like another Ennius, to celebrate Scipio at the end of centuries. But
books themselves will die, and only one thing is left to compensate
for this successive mortality. The lips of the elder Scipio fashion
themselves to a Christian doctrine of eternity, and preach the pursuit
of Virtue not Glory (the second being only the shadow of the first):

Gloria si fuerit studiorum meta tuorum,
Pervenies equidem, sed non mansurus, ad illam.
Praemia sin autem caelo tua nate, reponis,
Quo semper potiaris habes sine fine beatus
Et sine mensura.[3]

The identity with the letters is here complete, but all that I have

[1] *Africa*, I. 482. 'Honour sacred things, justice and faith. Let holy piety be the guest of your
bosom, and the companion of your manners. It is a virtue owed greatly to a father, more to
one's country, but most of all to God. If life is adorned with these it is the way to heaven.'
[2] ibid., I. 210 ss.
[3] ibid., II. 478. 'If glory is the goal of your endeavour, reach it you will indeed, but only
for a while. But if you lay up your rewards in heaven, my son, you have what you may possess
in blessedness without end and without measure.'

quoted so far lies outside the *action* of the poem: the invocation of Christ, the apparition of Jove, the sentiments of Scipio's father expressed in a vision can only be taken as an earnest for the main body of the work. It is an earnest which will not be refuted, and the positive opinions of Petrarch, as I have quoted them from the prose works, will find almost all of them their corroborative in the *Africa*. It has been pointed out that even in the most epic moments of the poem, in the very attainment of victory (the victory, be it remembered, of Rome itself, predestined to Christian primacy), there emerges, not any exultation in battle and conquest, but a sense of the uselessness of these two things, and of the effort and suffering which even victorious war demands. In the minds of the warriors themselves there is something of an un-Roman nostalgia for peace.[1] The Petrarch of the closing lines of *Italia mia* is not unrecognisable in the author of the *Africa*:

> Heu furor! et quanto satius vixisse quietus
> Finibus in patriis populus potuisset uterque!
> Non sinit ambitio caecique superbia cordis
> Et sitis, aeterna quae spe succendit habendi
> Mortales uritque animos et trudit in enses.[2]

There is in one of the *Seniles* the anecdote of a fool's reply on war between the Florentines and the Pisans. While others prepared for war he remained unconcerned: 'And will there be no peace to this war?' he asked. 'What, said his interlocutor, you think of peace, you fool, when there is now a great war?' 'I mean, said the fool, isn't there going to be a peace to this war?' 'But of course, said the other, no war lasts for ever, there will be a peace some time; only now it's war.' 'Then wouldn't it be better, said the fool, to make peace now before the war began, or before it proceeded further?'[3] The development of that anecdote in Rabelais is known to every one (and again, I shall not attempt to speak in terms of derivation); and Petrarch's comment that the *stultus* seemed *sapiens* to him fits the reflection

---

[1] Gerosa, *L'Umanesimo Agostiniano del Petrarca*, 15.

[2] *Africa*, VII. 982. 'Alas, what frenzy! and how much better that each people should have lived in peace within their borders! It is ambition will not allow this, the pride of the blind heart, and the thirst which inflames mortals with the everlasting hope of possession, sets their minds on fire and drives them to the sword.'

[3] *Sen.*, XIII. xvii. 1029. 'An non, inquit, belli huius pax erit? Quomodo, ait is qui loquebatur, pacem cogitas, ô demens, nunc maxime bellum incipit. Quaero tamen, inquit stultus, an non belli huius aliquando pax futura sit? Atqui, ait alter, nullum bellum sempiternum est, erit utique pax quandoque, sed nunc bellum est. An non igitur, ait stultus, satius esset nunc pacem facere antequam inciperet bellum vel procederet?'

in the *Africa*. It is a conception towards which Europe, in its moments of sanity, has tried to grope. What is Petrarch's reflection on the final battle that overthrew the power of Carthage? Not the glory of Scipio's arms: by the tragedy of Zama Africa vomits forth the spoils that it had won, and adds its own:

> Quid tot valuere rapinae?
> Raptor raptorem spoliat. Nunc ite per ampla
> Aequora, nunc validas prosternite turribus arces,
> Nunc insultet aratrum antiquis moenibus! Omnes
> Unus habet praedas hostis, mundique superbit
> Tot spoliis vestrisque simul.[1]

At the central point which might have acclaimed only the physical supremacy of Rome stands Petrarch's affirmation of peace, and a note of melancholy. After this it will not surprise that the first passage I quoted was closely followed by this counsel:

> Hoc etiam meminisse velim, nil gratius illi,
> Qui caelum terrasque regit, dominoque patrique
> Actibus ex vestris, quam iustis legibus urbes
> Conciliumque hominum sociatum nexibus aequis.[2]

The penitential attitude of the Middle Ages involved a renunciation of human activity, since that in its reality did not approximate to any pattern of virtue. Petrarch, as we have seen, hovered round that attitude: but he comes back to the idea of planning human life so that it may be fair and pleasing in the sight of God. Here is the same emphasis on law and liberty which we have found elsewhere; and with it goes the same affirmation of monarchy:

> nam rege sub uno
> Optimus est patriae status.[3]

There is still no recipe to civil discord but the *regia manus* to impose respect for justice:

> Tempus adhuc veniet, quum vix Romanus in urbe
> Civis erit verus, sed terras lecta per omnes
> Faex hominum: tamen et tunc se male sana cruentis
> Turba premet gladiis, et, ni fortissimus unus

[1] *Africa*, VIII. 28. 'What gain from so much plunder? A plunderer despoils the plunderer. Now go through the wide seas, now raze the citadel strong with towers, now let your plough leap on the ancient walls! One enemy has all the spoils of war, one lords it over all the plunder of the earth, and yours as well.'

[2] ibid., I. 490. 'Remember this as well, that there is nothing more welcome to Him who rules heaven and earth as lord and father in all your actions, than cities and the union of men knit in the bonds of equity.'

[3] ibid., III. 305. 'The best state of a country is beneath one king.'

Vir aliquis, dignus meliori tempore nasci,
Opponat sese medium frontemque manumque
Litibus ostendat, superest quodcumque cruoris
Pectoribus miseris per mutua vulnera fundant.[1]

Nor does that conflict with the congratulation to Rome on the
expulsion of the kings, and the indignation that it had obeyed impious
commands from a king instead of sacred laws.[2] Dante believed that
the justice of God would automatically fall on the Angevins at the
coming of the *Emperor* Henry VII (when instead it seemed to fall on
the latter as a fit punishment for the recklessness with which he
advanced, unarmed and uninformed, into the troubled state of Italy).
Petrarch thinks like Machiavelli in terms of virtue necessary in an
individual to transcend conflicting interests. The contrast, then, is
clear, as it was from the letters. Every reservation which Petrarch
made there on the status and the qualifications of a monarch obtains
in the *Africa*. It is liberty which is the gloss to monarchy, and both
are still to be defined in terms of justice: but lest that should seem too
Dantesque a programme, there is the reminder that there is nothing
automatic in its fulfilment.

It would be possible to develop parallels at greater length, but to
those which concern the body politic I will add only one which
reaffirms a personal relationship:

Rebus in humanis nil dulcius experiere
Alterno convictu et fido pectore amici.[3]

While I have attempted, then, before to show the reasonableness of
Petrarch's position, I am contented here to demonstrate its coherency,
and the extent to which the standards of the Middle Ages (lingering
as we have seen in Petrarch's mind) have been superseded by a return
to the experience of the ancients. The degree of Petrarch's dependence
on Cicero is obvious from what I have quoted; but it is his own
position which is expressed. We may ultimately decide to look for
these opinions in the letters rather than amongst the hexameters, but
that is a judgment which does not affect the opinions themselves.
And in making it we should be putting ourselves in the position (the

---

[1] *Africa*, II. 305. 'The time will come when there will be scarcely one true citizen in Rome,
but dregs of men from all the earth; yet even then this mob gone mad will turn with bloody
swords against itself, and unless one strong man, worthy of a better age, opposes brow and
hand to civil strife, there remains bloodshed alone from wretched breasts and mutual wounds.'

[2] ibid., III. 667.

[3] ibid., II. 515. 'Nothing sweeter in human life than the mutual intercourse and the tried
love of a friend.'

forced position) of Petrarch's contemporaries. Only thirty-four lines of the poem were available to the reader during Petrarch's life, and its publication after his death came, perhaps, too late for it to have a general influence. What of the opposing views of the first nineteenth-century examiners of the poem and the recent apologists? It is obvious that the charge of dead pedantry is untenable against a poem which embodies many of the ideas which were to fertilise the thought of the Renascence; it is equally clear that the new direction is not medieval. The Middle Ages often distorted antiquity, and medievalised its appearance out of mere ignorance. But Petrarch's attitude is a perfectly conscious one, and there is no distortion of historical fact. On the contrary, when we consider the slender bases in contemporary knowledge, or the lack of bases, his grasp of antiquity becomes astonishing;[1] and he remained true to the critical intentions expressed in the preface to the *De Viris Illustribus*. It is neither as a piece of medievalism nor as a piece of classicastry that the *Africa* fails, but simply as a poem and as a whole. Petrarch is so much more eloquent, so much more sustainedly eloquent, in the prose works.

The examination of the *Africa*, then, does not show Petrarch entirely trammelled by his medieval theory of poetry, or entirely successful in a classic *genre*. But it shows how firmly he holds to the positive elements which had intruded even into the *De Remediis*. That is not unimportant, especially when it is remembered that the penitential-renunciatory elements of the treatises play their part in the letters. The charge of being a medieval can (in spite of Saintsbury) be proved in some respects against Petrarch, but it is a charge which reveals both a contradiction and an affirmative. The charge of being a pedant receives no corroboration from the failure, the inevitable failure, of the epic. And the consistency of Petrarch's ideas through his very differing works is the proper note of ending here: had it been otherwise I should have been less sure of the foothold afforded by the positive side in his thought, or that his final conclusion for those who came after him was not *de contemptu mundi*.

---

[1] cf. Fracassetti, Prefazione, 68.

IV

THE REFLECTIVE TEMPERAMENT OF PETRARCH

THE preoccupation of Saintsbury with the value of beautiful words led him to acclaim the *De Vulgari Eloquentia* of Dante as an isolated peak of critical writing. In it the Ciceronian doctrine of persuasion (with its close connection with oratory) was ignored. Instead style, and the necessity for style to depend on a choice of words, was recognised. Saintsbury found himself therefore in accord with Dante when the latter put forward various grades of construction. *Petrus amat multum dominam Bertam* is insipid, and Saintsbury added a footnote on the insufficiency of clarity in writing: *twice two makes four* is clear enough, but who would assert that it has much literary merit? He did not find it quite as easy to determine the merits of the three other sentences which Dante quotes as sapid and most excellent;[1] but strong in this demonstration of the insufficiency of clarity, he did not allow himself to hesitate in declaring that the *principle* was right. One must use beautiful constructions and beautiful words (*vocabula pexa*, to use Dante's terminology) in order to command attention. In fact, no beautiful literature without beautiful words. I have already suggested that if Saintsbury had realised Dante's concern with the *canzone* in what he thus proposed, and not with the *Commedia* (in which, fortunately, Dante did not seek nobility of style), he might have advanced less incautiously; and it will be fairly obvious to readers of Dante that its strength more often lies in a pregnant concision, a nudity of expression, than it does in any elaborated rhetoric. But apart from this the tenets of Saintsbury are too reminiscent of the age of Swinburne to be of lasting value. It is true enough that the phrase *twice two makes four* has no merit: that is not the fault of its clarity, but of its insignificance. Clarity is a quality, it is not the thing in itself; and it should have been obvious even to Saintsbury that no elaboration of construction could render this particular phrase any more impressive. Petrarch, in one of his moments of bad taste, produced this jewel in the manner of Pietro Aretino or of James Elroy Flecker: 'Cease to scratch the itching of your ears with the nails of others' speech.'[2] *Twice two* could be so disguised without being made

---

[1] cf. *De Vulg. Eloq.*, II. vi.

[2] *Fam.*, III. v. 148. 'Desine tuarum aurium pruritum alieni sermonis unguibus scalpere.'

any happier. 'As truth is the goal, so unless I am mistaken, clarity is the felicitous quality of the mind.'[1] Behind the shop-window are the goods set out for sale; and we do ill to blame the glass if they are of little interest to us. Reflection on the formula *construction and beautiful words* will show that it includes the *Arcadia* and the *Hypnerotomachia Poliphili* at the expense of, let us say, the *Prince*, because it takes no thought of content. The observation of Petrarch which I have just quoted (had Saintsbury *read* Petrarch?) is not a piece of literary criticism: it is incidental to a recurrent theme in his letters, that we should aim at being what we wish to seem. But despite the lack of the intention to theorise it has a critical maturity which is lacking in the formal theory of the *De Vulgari Eloquentia*. Nor is it a single example in Petrarch's writing. In a letter to Francesco Bruni he combated the idea (later to prove a sterilising influence in Niccolò Niccoli and others) that the ancients had done all, and that there was nothing left to say. Solomon and Terence had maintained this first: yet look what had been done after the times of those two writers! Petrarch's conviction, apart from the idea of an unageing truth to be acquired and to be applied, was that there is nothing so polished or so complete that something cannot be added to it. And he added as a footnote: 'Doubt will make speech circumspect, cautious, sober and restrained; but confidence will make it happy, rich, magnificent, beautiful.'[2] Again, the remark is more or less incidental (that is why I quote its context); but the casualness with which it is delivered affects neither its own strength, nor the consequences of that strength on the relative positions of Dante and Petrarch as critics. It is Dante who insists on style; the cardinal points with Petrarch are truth, clarity and conviction. True, as with the contradiction between theory and practice with regard to poetry, it is possible to find Petrarch denying clarity. He answered a cardinal who urged intelligibility for everybody as the aim of style that this was vile and abject: that no-one should expect to understand without some stirring of the brain. The learned are always few (in his age, very few), and as for the vulgar, Petrarch did not wish to write for them.[3] That statement of a wilful complication of truth is the prose parallel to the theories of poetry we have seen in the *Africa* and the *Contra Medicum*. But the only sign of an approach to it in Petrarch's writing is the use of Latin. Meanwhile,

[1] *Ep. Sine Tit.*, Ep. Ult., 812. 'Nam ut veritas obiectum, sic ni fallor claritas est foelicitas intellectus.'

[2] *Sen.*, II. ii. 840. 'Dubitatio circumspectam, cautam, sobriam, ac modestam reddet orationem, fiducia vero laetam, uberem, magnificam, speciosam.'

[3] *Fam.*, XIV. ii. 279.

if we return to the remark on the origins of quality in writing, we shall see that we can consider the merit of the *Divina Commedia* in terms of it, while there is no inkling in the *De Vulgari Eloquentia* by which Dante's later achievement can be judged. Dante, like Lucretius, was perfectly convinced of the truth he had to proclaim; and the adjectives of Petrarch apply in almost equal measure to both their poems. Not only is this so, but outside these principles there is no genuine literature. Monti and Tennyson (whom Saintsbury should equally have approved of) are pseudo-poets. I do not mean that there is nothing more to be said in literary criticism; but the central points, the *sine qua non*, are here established. And it is, I think, obvious that the bulk of Petrarch's writing, and all his reading, is based on these criteria. The fact that this kernel of criticism is established where Saintsbury saw a lacuna suggests that the traditional values (or devaluation) set upon Humanisn and the Renascence must not be taken as absolute. The reversal of the rôles, by which Dante treats of form, while Petrarch insists that it is matter, and the attitude to matter, which create form, is no different from that which we have seen already in the case of the Doge of Venice. It is apparent—if we are on the look-out for the classicaster—that, although Petrarch does not mention in this context the word *persuasion*, the ideas of Cicero are not absent from his mind. But we have seen Petrarch's conviction of the necessity of persuading to virtue; that of persuading to truth is not less important. The weakness of Saintsbury's position was that he saw the Ciceronian persuasion as limited to oratory alone: in his advocacy of style he did not realise that it was the limitation and not the principle which was wrong. But what rests clearly on conviction and on truth has the greatest chance of impressing and persuading.

By the side of these casual, but operative, remarks the theory of poetry to which Petrarch subscribed seems clumsy, and even contradictory: it is hardly profitable to hide truth away when one is anxious to persuade to it. But there is little need to add again the reminder that this clumsy theory of poetry is the legacy of the Middle Ages in Petrarch, and that the contribution which he himself made to it forms its major interest. It need occasion no surprise that there is not a great deal else to add from Petrarch's writings which represents the direct criticism of literature *qua* literature. There is, for instance, no attempt at the criticism of separate works. But if we remember the meagre gleanings which form the first volume of Saintsbury's *History of Criticism*—and its field is from the beginnings in Greece down to the fifteenth century—it will be seen that there is nothing odd in Petrarch being concerned with literature as a criticism of life and as an aid to living; nothing odd, that is to say, for those who do not come to humanism with the preconception that it is a matter of imitation only. But we may legitimately expect a mind which is capable of reflections of this calibre to be critical in other directions in a manner which was not possible in the Middle Ages; and I have already stated my conviction of the novelty of this reflective procedure in Petrarch. While the house of civilisation lay in ruins, or was in the first tentative stages of reconstruction, reflection on its use was difficult, and could not in any case be very subtle: it was much easier to look up into the air and legislate completely for the whole of mankind than to draw reflections from observation of society. In so far as there is positive thought in the Middle Ages it is a *civitas Dei* which emerges, and not a *civitas hominis*; and I have already said that I regard this escape as to a large extent a liability. The sage reflection of Machiavelli is not irrelevant: a Christianity which insisted on suffering much rather than doing much would seem to leave the world a prey to scoundrels, who can handle it with ease when they see men seeking to enter Paradise by enduring their misdeeds, or even by provoking them, instead of avenging them. But that said Machiavelli, 'nasce più senza dubbio dalla viltà degli uomini, che hanno interpretato la nostra Religione secondo l'ozio, e non secondo la virtú.'[1] Machiavelli's language is blunt (though not the least interesting part is the possessive adjective), but that only shows the clearer how he and the fifteenth century before him have resolved the contradiction which we have seen in Petrarch, and this by the elimination of the medieval side and the development of the Ciceronian-Petrarchan principle of the acceptability to God of the organisation of human society in terms of virtue. In the *De Remediis* such things as unjust masters are to be endured as excellent tests of character; servitude, torture and the rest are similar instruments. But Machiavelli's reflection on this would be that a thing cannot be excellent in its effects, without being at the same time excellent in itself; and the idea of *remedies*, with that *de contemptu mundi*, implies logically a praise of disorder, and of injustice. Hence the importance of the passage from Medieval-Christian to Ciceronian-Christian ideas. Petrarch prepares for this elimination, though he does not take the final logical step. But there begins, nevertheless, unmistakably with him the possibility of an examination of man and of society: the era of reflective literature which has lasted till our own time.

---

[1] *Discorsi*, II. ii. One of the most important of Machiavelli's passages on religion.

Indeed, this is obvious from the contrasting attitude to literary criticism which we have seen in Dante and Petrarch: Dante legislating for the creation of literature (and so, quite logically, going wide of the mark, especially wide of his own performance in the *Divina Commedia*); Petrarch embodying an experience of literature not gained by preconception. That, if I may say so once again, is a sharp distinction between two types of mind, as also between two separate epochs; and it encourages me to attempt the difficult task of illustrating this reflective temperament of Petrarch from observations scattered throughout his letters and treatises. I do not intend to be exhaustive (*et utinam*!), since it is my intention to indicate a quality rather than to make a catalogue: and I shall inevitably be discursive. It is, I think, an essential attempt; it will illuminate to some extent themes already touched on, and it will serve to show the humanity of Petrarch—the degree, that is, to which he is concerned with life itself, and not merely with words and books.

Amongst the best-known anecdotes of Petrarch's life is the breaking of his leg by a horse's kick, the wound not being cared for till his arrival at Rome on the third day. There the doctors found the bone projecting and the flesh turned livid. Petrarch noted in his description of the incident the stench of the neglected wound, violent enough to revolt even himself; and although there is in each of us a certain innate familiarity with our own body which makes us bear in it, even with pleasure, what would cause distress in another's, yet this stench was strong enough to force on him, more than any corpse had done, the realisation how vile an animal is man unless the ignobility of the body is redeemed by the nobility of the mind. There is in this reflection a medieval tinge: Jacopone would have approved the recipe for a *salutary* valuation of the flesh. But by the side of the moral (and I hope it is obvious that Petrarch harboured no such unsavoury thoughts as Jacopone in Lauda XLVIII) there is an observation of a very different type: an observation, not a precept. This innate familiarity with our body, this ability to suffer from it willingly (*suaviter* even) things that would cause disgust in another, implies a recognition that all in human life is not vile. It has become possible to admit a pleasure in corporal existence (if in its humiliating aspects, then *a fortiori* in its better ones). The logical progression from this is

---

[1] *Fam.*, XI. i. 105. 'Odor neglecti vulneris tam molestus, ut me ipsum supra fidem impatientia sui saepe violenter averteret: et quamvis cum corpore nostro quaedam nobis innata familiaritas sit, per quam multa in suo corpore fert quisque suaviter quod in altero fastidiret, ego tamen raro unquam in alieno cadavere, ut nunc in carne propria, cognovi quam nihil, imo vero quam miserum et vile animal est homo, nisi ignobilitatem corporis animi nobilitate redemerit.'

to the attitude of Montaigne in the close of his last essay,[1] and it is not, perhaps, a coincidence that Montaigne there quotes St. Augustine on giving the flesh its due.[2] It has become possible to scrutinise this life, and make conclusions on it without reference to theology and without working *a priori*. It is an intimate and, in a way, a humble observation; but it is no part of greatness to ignore humble matters. Rather, the attitude to them may be taken as one test of greatness.

So much for the reinstatement of the body, what of the individual? In the *Divina Commedia* we find a simplification: Dido, for instance, suffers with the incontinent, not amongst the suicides. That tying of one label to one person is of course largely a question of convenience and economy: there are enough sinners not to complicate or repeat them! But it is also one of the approaches to the subject. Dante starts with capital sins and then sees instances of these: that is why he sees so clearly. If he had started with the individual his observation would have been more complex. As it is, Minos' task of judgment is not an intricate disentanglement of conflicting motives, contrasting sins and virtues, but a simple labelling of a single crime. Petrarch could not have written the *Inferno* without complicating the apparatus. For him it is not only true to say that there are as many opinions as men; but also that each individual varies within himself from moment to moment, and that there is therefore a multiplicity of opinions within the individual.[3] That is a complexity which the psychologists have since developed, though Petrarch would not have thought much of their habit of delving for the subconscious and encouraging its growth by the attentions paid to it. For him it is the victory of the conscious which matters: the first, the greatest part of virtue is the will.[4] There is at this point of the dialogue (it is in the *De Remediis*) a discussion reminiscent of the *Secretum* in one of its best-known passages. 'What if I desire virtue and cannot attain to it?' 'Many think that they desire a thing, and do not; that they do not desire a thing, yet do so; thus does each deceive himself, striving to persuade not only others, but himself as well, of his avidity for what is good. Nor is there an easier persuasion than of oneself, for as true virtue delights, so also does the false reputation of virtue, and thus it is sweet to deceive the people, one's friends, and to be deceived

---

[1] Essais, III. xiii. 446–451.   [2] ibid., 448, n. 3.

[3] *Contra Medicum*, IV. 1232. 'Verum est non solum illud: Quot capita tot sententiae, sed illud quoque: Cuiusque capitis, multas esse sententias. Unde saepe accidit, ut de una eademque re, aliud mane, aliud sero, immo et in eodem instanti, nunc illud uni et eidem ingenio videatur.'

[4] *De Rem.*, II. ciiii. 193. 'Quoniam prima et maxima pars virtutis est velle.'

oneself into the bargain.'[1] 'L'hypocrisie est un hommage que le vice rend à la vertu,' wrote La Rochefoucauld; and was it not he who added also that we are more ready to deceive ourselves than we are even to deceive others? It has been maintained that the distinction between Petrarch on the one hand and Aquinas and Dante on the other lies in this insistence on the necessity of willing virtue where the two rationalists think rather in terms of *knowing* it. I do not know if the distinction is entirely accurate:

> Se fosse stato lor volere intero,
> come tenne Lorenzo in su la grada,
> e fece Muzio alla sua man severo,
> cosí le avria ripinte per la strada
> ond'eran tratte, come furo sciolte;
> ma cosí salda voglia è troppo rada.[2]

And there are other passages in which Dante, at least, seems aware of the necessity for effort. But Gostanza's will, with the firmer ones of St. Laurence or of Scaevola, fights against an external force. Against this she pitted her will, but it was insufficient, and that is all. That may be a spur to our own effort, but it is not entirely an aid to our comprehension: the psychological reflection is lacking precisely because the external force, and not the internal forces, is the object of the will's attention. It is there that the analysis of Petrarch is both different and valuable. There is another side to this question of willing virtue: there are not only those who think they want it, when what they want is its reputation. There are also those who think they have it; and no-one strives to reach a point which he thinks reached already.[3] It is a very simple reflection, but a very useful one: the number of those who are uncharitable (for instance), not *although*, but *because* they profess charity is not inconsiderable. And if we are sure that our principles are right in general we often hold ourselves excused from the examination of our conduct in particular. There is a further observation in a very similar context to that of reputation desired, but not deserved: it is that often the strength of shame can do more than the strength of the mind itself. For the avoidance of cowardice a spectator may be more helpful than one's own virtue.[4] That

[1] *De Rem.*, II. ciiii. 193. Dolor: 'Quid quod virtutem volo, nec assequor.' Ratio: 'Multi se id putant velle, quod nolunt, id nolle, quod volunt, sic quisque se fallit, seque boni avidum non modo aliis, sed sibi etiam persuadere nititur, nec cuiquam facilius persuadet, quam delectabilis vera virtus, falsa virtutis opinio sic delectat, ut et populum, et amicos fallere, et falli insuper dulce sit.'

[2] *Paradiso*, IV. 82.   [3] *De Rem.*, I. xi. 8. 'Nemo studet agere, quod peregisse se putat.'

[4] ibid., I. xv. 13. 'Multis saepe quod vis animi non dabat, contulit vis pudoris, et ad ignaviam profligandam, saepe plus spectator valuit quam virtus.'

is a disinterested observation again; but the analysis of the elements of life is an essential preliminary *ad beate vivendum*, and it is only the ingenuous who will assert that what lies within oneself is always known, however poor the knowledge of the outside world, or of the accidents of fortune, may be. As Petrarch remarked elsewhere, external things are more easily foreseen than those which spring within ourselves: in every disease what is hidden is most dangerous.[1] From that we can deduce, I think, a reflection which is implicit in this as in most of Petrarch's thought, that the ills which others dismiss in us as *imaginary* can be more real than those which normally receive the adjective *real*. The first spring from our own character, and we must modify that before we can overcome them. The second are external, and as such can be overcome by character. The first spring from ourselves, and are therefore wedded to ourselves; the second can be separated from us. That is the sound part of the *De Remediis*; that is the point of the insistence on the will, and on the need for scrutiny and analysis; hence the insistence on the consciousness of the struggle. There are those, says Petrarch, who think to grow wise by growing old; it is as if the farmer spent seedtime in sleep and play, and hoped for a rich harvest in the autumn by the progress of nature's seasons. Those whom one sees as foolish old men (and there are not a few) were stupid youths.[2] There is no automatic process of conversion to wisdom: the years can only give back what has been given to them. Nor often do we learn what we should have been before we have become what we wished to be and cannot change to anything else.[3] Hence finally Petrarch's insistence on study, and his preference for a *docta pietas* over a *devota rusticitas*. That is Ciceronian rather than catholic: compare the answer of Bonaventure to the question whether a fool could love God as much as an educated man ('An old woman can do so more than a doctor in theology') with the insistence of a modern intransigent like Giuliotti on the virtue of analphabetism as an approach to God.[4] It is when the emphasis is shifted from loving blindly to the problem of living well that reflection finds its use: and for Petrarch ease without study is death, as it was for Seneca. What should the idle do other than watch the clock and count it round, first to supper and then to bed? For all the home-

---

[1] *Fam.*, XIV. v. 297. 'Facilius praevidentur externa quam quae nascuntur in nobis: profecto autem in omni morbo periculosissimum est quod latet.'

[2] *Sen.*, VIII. ii. 919. 'Quos igitur stultos senses videas ac deliros, stolidi iuvenes fuerunt.'

[3] *De Rem.*, I. i. 1. 'Nec prius quod esse debuistis advertitis, quam quod esse voluistis, effecti estis, fierique iam aliud non potestis.'

[4] Gentile, *La Filosofia*, 66. cf. Domenico Giuliotti, *L'Ora di Barabba*, *passim*.

liness of imagery in the *Divina Commedia* there would be no room
there for so intimate an observation of men's habits as this timeless
one of unlettered ease.[1] Is it any wonder, then, that Petrarch remarked
with scorn that there are those who accumulate books indeed (as
they do other things), not to be used in study, but from a mania for
collecting, not so much a garrison for their minds as an ornament
for their rooms?[2] And another insincerity was noticed by him:
'Have you observed those who are making dispositions for their
household? Scarcely one dares say: *When I die*, but *If I die*, as if
throwing doubt on one thing which is most sure of all. Nor even
does this *If I die* sound clearly, bur rather *If anything should happen to
me*. I wonder what this anything might be, unless it is the same thing
which has happened, and will happen, to all?'[3] To fools (and to the
analphabet) all things are unpremeditated[4] or disguised: it is the
wise man's duty to examine, and to be accurate. Place side by side
with this Petrarch's conviction on the fall of cities and the lapse of time,
the transference of empire, the change of customs and the innovation
of laws: but the things which exist *naturaliter* do not change. The
minds of men and the diseases of men's minds are the same now as
when Plautus (whom he had just quoted) wrote.[5] It is self-evident
what is Petrarch's object in the study of antiquity. He turns to
Plautus, as to Cicero, not to escape from life into literature, but in
order to pursue the examination of life which had been so long
interrupted. It is a new literature which will emerge, but it is the same
mankind; and we have once more, in general form, the fertile
reflection which Machiavelli was to apply to government.

We must foresee, then, and we must control:

> There's nothing ill but thinking makes it so

places the emphasis, as Petrarch had done, upon the thinker. In a
splendid passage of one of his letters to *Socrates* on being strong in
adversity he wrote: 'Fortitude is the shield against the onset of

---

[1] *Cont. Med.*, IV. 1227. 'Unde non miror, id tibi vitae genus invisum: quid enim hic ageras,
nisi numerare horas, et quaerere quando coenatum secundum regulas tuas, quando cubitum
ires. . . .'

[2] *Fam.*, III. xviii. 179. 'Sunt enim qui libros (ut raetera) non utendi studio cumulent, sed
habendi libidine, neque tam ut ingenio praesidio, quam ut thalami ornamentum.'

[3] *Rem.*, II. cxvii. 205. 'Observasti hos, qui domui suae disponunt, vix est qui dicere audeat,
cum moriar, sed si moriar, quasi in dubio ponitur, quo nihil est certius. Neque idipsum si
moriar clare sonat, sed si quid de me esset aliud: quid nam esset hoc aliud quaeso, et non potius
idem ipsum quod de omnibus fuit, eritve?'

[4] *Fam.*, VIII. i. 41.

[5] ibid., V. viii. 280. 'Quae vero naturaliter sunt, non mutari, et animos hominum et
animorum morbos prope omnes eosdem esse, qui fuerint dum Plautus ista fingebat.'

fortune. The timid are unarmed; those who fear most stand in most danger, the fugitive are pursued, the prostrate crushed. But those who stand cannot be trampled; the body may be prostrated against its will, the mind only if it consents. Nothing is unbearable to the man who wills, nothing can disturb the wise; nothing sad but what is thought sad, sweet and bitter a fiction of the fancy. All hangs on opinion: there is nothing hard to a brave mind, but all things seem hard to a feeble one.'[1] That is the stoicism of the *De Remediis* at its best. But with it there is a curiously different note. There is a sadness at times without apparent cause, either of sickness, loss or injury, of ignominy or error; without even a thought or sudden rumour of such things; but as it were a pleasure in pain which makes the mind sad—a plague all the more terrible in that its cause is unknown, and so its cure is more difficult.[2] The reader of the *Rime* will have no trouble in identifying this *dolendi voluptas quaedam*:

> Et a pena vorrei
> Cangiar questo mio viver dolce amaro. . . .
>
> Il mal che mi diletta e non mi dole.[3]

It is that love of melancholy which alone gives sincerity to these antitheses, and which alone is strong enough to transcend them. Petrarch, for this love of melancholy, has been compared (a little rashly) with Leopardi. But his reaction is still what I have indicated above: the progress of the *Rime* towards their closing sonnets, if not towards the *Canzone alla Vergine*, is genuine; and the advice of Cicero is to flee this melancholy as a rock on which the mind may suffer wreck.[4] It is neither the *noia* of Leopardi, nor is it inescapable; rather, the greater the difficulty, the more the struggle is internal, the greater the necessity for effort. Petrarch has often been accused of vacillation, and I have not refrained from pointing out what seem to me his contradictions; but the charge must not be exaggerated. He was always willing to change his opinion overnight, provided the truth prevailed. If I may

---

[1] ibid., XXI. ix. 79. 'Contra fortunae impetus fortitudinem esse pro clypeo, pavidos pro inermibus haberi, his qui plus metuunt, plus esse periculi, urgeri profugos, stratos obteri, stantes non posse calcari, corpus etsi nolit, animum nisi consenserit, non prosterni: nil volenti difficile, nil importabile sapienti: nil moestum nisi quod moestum creditur, pro arbitrio fingi vel amara vel dulcia, omnia ex opinionibus pendere, forti animo nihil durum, molli autem dura omnia videri.'

[2] *Rem.*, II. xciii. 183. 'Est autem quando nulla prorsus apparens causa, non morbi, non damni, non iniuriae, non ignominiae, non errorum mores neque ullus omnino rerum talium, et inopinus rumor, sed dolendi voluptas quaedam, quae moestam animam facit, pestis eo funestior, quo ignotior causa, atque ita difficilior cura est.'

[3] *Rime*, CXXIX. 20 and CCXXXIII. 11.   [4] *Rem.*, II. xciii. 184. 'Ceu animae scopulum.'

repeat a remark of Petrarch's which had the context of virtue, *nemo studet agere, quod peregisse se putat*. Petrarch is not necessarily weaker than Dante because he does not take his truths for granted. He was himself convinced that he might be more easily accused of obstinacy than of inconstancy.[1] It was the conscious effort towards truth and virtue which was to secure that constancy, and on this central point Petrarch remains firm.

Now it might seem that the insistence on the will, coinciding partly as it does with Dante's judgment on Gostanza, imposes an automatic guilt on the individual sinner. Gostanza suffered violence, but had her will been firm enough the violence would have broken before her purpose; and there the discussion might have ended. But in spite of this theoretic possibility Petrarch follows his statement of the multiplicity of the individual with the acknowledgment of the complexity of sin. In every fault or crime it is of prime importance to know what caused it, whether need, lust or pride.[2] Elsewhere he analyses ingratitude: it has three causes. Envy which finds injury to itself in benefits conferred on others; pride which thinks itself worthy of greater things, or is indignant at another's preference; greed, which is not assuaged by gifts, but kindled, and while it gapes after the things coveted forgets the things attained. And folly springing from ignorance lies behind these, as behind all other ills.[3] The putting of names to sins and virtues is a simple process: it is the delimitation of their frontiers and the anatomy of their essence which is the helpful process. The effort is demanded of the individual, of oneself primarily; the reflection on society as it is is not prejudiced thereby. And it is Petrarch who, with all his contempt for contemporary legal practice, established a principle of some importance. The degree of guilt depends on pressure of circumstances and unravelling of motives; but punishment is a different process, not expiatory, but preventive: not because sin has been committed, but to prevent it being committed again.[4] In the *Inferno* souls are punished eternally for their sin in eternal expiation. The theory is depressing, in Aquinas as in Dante.

---

[1] *Fam.*, XIV. iv. 286. 'Quasi non omnibus notum sit quibus ego notus sum, nullam minus maculam meis moribus convenire, aliquantoque magis, nisi ab iniquis rerum existimatoribus, pertinaciae suspicionem quam inconstantiae formidandam.'

[2] *Rem.*, I. xxx. 28. 'In omni sane delicto plurimum interest, utrum inopia, an libidine, seu superbia quis delinquat.'

[3] ibid., I. xciii. 77. 'Omnis autem ingratitudinis, triplex, nisi fallor, causa est. Invidia scilicet, quae dum impensa aliis beneficiis, suas ducit iniurias, in se collata non aspicit. Superbia quae vel se maioribus dignam censet, vel praeferri sibi aliquem indignatur. Cupiditas, quae muneribus non lenitur, sed accenditur, et dum quaerendis inhiat, quaesita non meminit.'

[4] *Variarum*, LIII. 451. 'Non quia peccatum est, sed ne peccetur inventa supplicia.'

Hell and damnation are good, but not for the damned: the good which emerges is not a preventive, it is the glory and completion of God's justice, and an enjoyable element in the beatitude of the elect, *ut de his electi gaudeant*.[1] Petrarch, again, stretches his hand back, ignoring this medieval theory; he does not claim originality for his own—it is *laudata sententia*—but, again, truth is not an invention or a monopoly, and a man's worth may be gauged by what he praises. Europe has not since Petrarch bettered the principle which he resurrects, any more than she has always observed the social assessment of punishment which he advances instead of the theological one put forward by St. Thomas Aquinas. But we must not ascribe our faults to Petrarch: the proof that he points the way from the Medieval-Christian world is plain enough in this divergence.

Perhaps before I pass to a further point about Petrarch I may put together a few observations which illustrate his eye for psychological generalisations without being otherwise linked. Only rarely is there the sting which we shall find in Machiavelli: 'perché li uomini sdimenticano più presto la morte del padre che la perdita del patrimonio.'[2] It is only with the spur of misogyny that Petrarch approaches this note: A brother lost is wept for calmly, parents more calmly, wives most calmly, often indeed most joyfully; only wealth is wept for bitterly.[3] That has the germ of Machiavelli's observation (and is obviously similar in procedure) without having quite the same weight. At other times Petrarch is in lighter mood in his observations. There is a rustic proverb on the great labour needed to make a dog's bed. If you ask the reason why, it is because the dog turns round and round before he lies down so that you don't know where to put the pillow. And there are men for whom you can do nothing right; your labour and attentions are all lost. Offer them the delights of the town, they praise the frugality of the country. Take them out of town, they desire company and loathe solitude. Begin to speak, and they are annoyed; but they are indignant if you are silent. They desire absent friends, and they despise those present: often they hate them.[4]

[1] Wicksteed, *Dante and Aquinas*, VII. 187-212, esp. texts 211-212 for Aquinas: 'Secundo ad hoc sunt utiles ut de his electi gaudeant, dum in his Dei justitiam contemplantur, et cum hoc se evasisse cognoscunt.'

[2] *Il Principe*, XVII.

[3] *Rem.*, II. xiii. 121. 'Lente flentur fratres perditi, lentius parentes, lentissime coniuges, saepe vero laetissime: solae opes flentur acriter.'

[4] *Fam.*, VII. ix. 375. 'Agreste proverbium, *lectum cani sternere magnus labor*. Dicti ratio si quaeritis; quia scilicet accubiturus, huc atque illuc in gyrum vertitur, ut nescias ubi pulvinar colloces. . . . Si urbanas illis offeras delicias, ruris frugalitatem laudent; si ex urbe deduxeris, frequentiam quaerant, solitudinem execrentur; si colloqui coeperis, fastidiant; indignenturque, i taceas; absentes desiderent, praesentes despiciant, amicos; saepe etiam oderint.'

s

That is elementary observation, but it is the path of the observation of society which leads to the century of the *Caractères*. The portrait of the young man at the university is light too, but entertaining: There comes a foolish youth to the temple, his tutors lecture him; they praise him out of love, or error; he puffs up, the populace is agog, his relatives applaud, his friends as well; when bidden he ascends into the pulpit, looks down on all things from on high, and mutters confusedly I know not what. Now his elders vie in raising him to the skies, as one who has spoken divinely. Meanwhile bells ring, trumpets blare, rings fly, kisses are imprinted; a round black hood is planted on his head. When all this is over, he comes down wise who went up foolish—a wondrous metamorphosis indeed, and quite unknown to Ovid. But so are wise men produced to-day.[1] Petrarch notes also the trick of language by which men clothe their faults, or disguise others' virtues: at Avignon simplicity is called *amentia,* and malice has the name of wisdom.[2] The latter is a philological distinction which has passed into the language, but it springs from the scrutiny to which Petrarch would subject external phenomena.[3] The tongue, or the pen, does not say everything: the face, the gesture, colour, accent, the foot, the hand, the eyes, the eyebrows —all speak as well.[4] Are not both these statements the foundation for a Proustian translation?

There is one social reflection of Petrarch of special importance, though not surprising, and decisive for European practice for centuries. Several times he meets the objection that poetry is ornament only, and nothing *necessary.* It is an objection which irritates Petrarch; and I may refer again to his concurrence with Cicero on gratitude for the passage from the necessary to the elegant arts, and to his anticipation of Montesquieu on virtues as something which raises above the general level. If it is necessity which ennobles, then the cobbler and the baker, with all the mechanical arts, will be the noblest of all. Philosophy, and all the others which make life blessed, polished and

---

[1] *Rem.,* I. xii. 10. 'Venit iuvenis stultus ad templum, praeceptores illum sui praedicant, celebrant seu amore, seu errore, tumet ille, vulgus stupet, plaudunt affines, et amici, ipse iussus in cathedram scandit, cuncta iam ex alto despiciens, et nescio quid confusum murmurans. Nunc maiores certatim, ceu divina locutum, laudibus ad coelum tollunt, tinniunt interim campanae, strepunt tubae, volant anuli, figuntur oscula, vertici rotundus et niger pannus imprimitur. His peractis, descendit sapiens, qui stultus ascenderat, mira prorsus transformatio, nec Nasoni cognita, sic fiunt hodie sapientes.'

[2] *Ep. Sine Titulo,* XI. 797. 'Ubi simplicitas amentiae, malitia sapientiae nomen habet.'

[3] And from Cicero, *Opera,* IV. 318.   [4] *Fam.,* IX. vii. 31.

adorned, will be ignoble.[1] The peasant is necessary; the domestic servant is often all the more necessary, the more ignoble is the task. The ass is more necessary than the lion, the hen than the eagle; are they then more noble? Instead of a utilitarian conception of society Petrarch stands boldly for an idealistic one; and we shall see the use that L. B. Alberti makes in the next century of the trilogy necessity, commodity, delight. Europe followed Alberti, as he had followed Petrarch, and antiquity. And when Europe abandoned that tradition with the nineteenth century it lost an important element in its civilisation: one that we in England have not replaced with anything of like value. It is not that Petrarch denies the commerce which was to form the life-blood of this same nineteenth century; he is the first, perhaps, to realise the value of circulation as the basis of prosperity. Gold, he says, has learnt to pass through my fingers, not to stick to them. It is not dug to feed the greed of men by accumulation, but to supply their necessities by transit.[3] But by the side of this realisation of exchange as the life-blood of the community there is the statement of the levels on which life can be lived. We have had our discussions on functional architecture (for instance), but Petrarch has already stated that ornament is a function in itself. If there is not this goal of delight above necessity we may find ourselves obliged (what else does Petrarch's warning state?) to consider a railway station as more noble, because more necessary, than the dome of St. Peter's or St. Paul's. *Saepe quo vilior, eo magis necessarius*, and it is only after the abandonment of standards which begins with Rousseau that we can be reduced to the possibility of this, and even of worse, logical absurdities. Before that the canon, suggested by Petrarch, established by Alberti with the assistance of Vitruvius, remained unchallenged. And it was not a medieval canon.

Petrarch's analysis does not stop at man in general: he begins to note racial differences. He noticed the urbanity of southern France, a people barbarous in origin, but now mild and humane, so that it

---

[1] *Fam.*, I. xi. 72. 'Ergo sutrina et pistrina, et vilissimarum mechanicarum artium (si necessitas nobilitare illas potest) nobilissimae omnium fient. Philosophia autem et reliquae omnes, quaecumque beatam atque excultam et ornatam vitam faciunt, si necessitatibus vulgi nil conferunt, ignobiles.'

[2] *Con. Med.*, III. 1215. 'Nescius quod servus domesticus, saepe quo vilior, eo magis necessarius. Clibanarius et lanista, quam necessarii, sunt quam viles. . . . Asinus magis est necessarius quam Leo, gallina quam aquila, ergo nobiliores. . . .'

[3] *Fam.*, XIX. xvii. 561. 'Aurum per digitos meos transire didicit, non haerere; placet equidem ac delectat. Ad hoc enim quaesitum, inventum, effossum, abstersum, consignatumque est aurum, non ut cupiditates hominum stando nutriat, sed ut transeundo necessitatibus medeatur.'

would seem that transplantation can change the nature of the plant.[1]
He quoted with approval the Emperor Frederick's judgment on the
difference between the Italian and German peoples: Reward both
equally for their merits, but do not punish them alike. Both are
spurred to virtue by encouragement, but the Italian mind grows
better when it is forgiven, and acknowledges both its sins and the
clemency of its ruler: on the contrary, the Germans are puffed up
by impunity, they impute mercy to fear, and the more you pardon
them, the more they will dare against you.[2] The merit of that
definition of difference may not be wholly Petrarch's; but at any
rate we owe to him a distinction which has not yet lost all its
vitality. And he looks across the landscape of Europe with clearer eyes
than any one who has come before him. There is a remarkable letter[3]
in which he sketches the political state of Europe in his time: his
information covers England, France, Spain, Germany, Italy, Greece;
the Balearic Islands, Sardinia, Corsica, Sicily, Crete, Rhodes and
Cyprus stand within his range of vision. The picture which he draws
is an unhappy one; but the possibility of its conception is the surprising
thing, not the darkness of its tints. The ability to see contours sharply
once again is no small achievement. There have been those who have
spoken with praise of Petrarch's geographical knowledge because of
his endeavours to find out the truth about Thule, and because of his
short essay on the itinerary to the Holy Land. But compared with this
advance by which the whole of Italy, and western Europe as well,
becomes open to his gaze these are matters of small importance. His
glance takes in securely the physical and the spiritual features of the
landscape, and in this even more than in his deciphering of the coins
which peasants brought him from the fields he is the forerunner of
the fifteenth century: Flavius Blondus only mapped in detail the topography which Petrarch knew. Nor must it be thought that this is an
irrelevancy, or a thing of small importance. I have said that when
we bear in mind the lack of apparatus Petrarch's knowledge of
classical antiquity is astonishing in its range and in its detail. But

---

[1] *Fam.*, XXI. xiii. 103. (On his life at Vaucluse.) 'Hic ipse populus tantus et tantarum
opum, cuius iam pene pars factus sum, haud dubie barbaram habet originem. Nunc (quid
non mutatio loci potest?) nihil moribus gentis humanius, nihil est mitius. Transplantatae
succos mutant herbae.'

[2] *Sen.*, II. i. 830. 'Esse has duas toto terrarum orbe praecipuas ac praestantissimas nationes,
inter se vero praelargiter differentes, utrorumque enim meritis aeque praemia deberi, sed
supplicium non ita. Nempe utrosque praemio ad virtutem erigi, verum Italos venia meliores
fieri, et suum crimen, et clementiam sui ducis agnoscere, Germanos impunitate tumescere,
misericordiam imputare formidini, quo plus ignoveris, plus ausuros.'

[3] *Fam.*, XV. vii. 329-34.

the apparatus was lacking just as much for the knowledge of the world around. No man before Petrarch had been easy in the possession of a country, let alone of Europe, and the limitation which Haskins placed on knowledge generally applies also to geography. Aeneas Sylvius was to travel further, and to have a more detailed knowledge of the Germans and the English, but Petrarch before him had travelled (like the Ulysses whose curiosity Dante damns) to observe the customs of men. Nothing in Renascence literature is more charming than the descriptions of Italy which Pius II left in his *Commentaries*, but their knowledge and their easy movement from place to place are anticipated by Petrarch. The examples are many and conspicuous, and I may content myself with a few references. In a letter on his proposal to live communally he sketches swiftly the picture of North Italy: with the cities, Milan, Genoa, Venice, Bologna, Lakes Como, Maggiore, Garda; with the lakes the rivers, Ticino, Oglio, Adda, Mincio. 'We shall see overhanging the lakes the airy, snow-clad Alps, a welcome sight in summer, forests reaching up towards the stars, murmuring streams in the hollows of the rocks, and rivers crashing down from mountain-tops; wherever one turns, the sound of birds and springing water.'[1] For Italy in general there is the letter to Philippe de Vitry on a Cardinal who thought of a journey there as exile. It dwells with pleasure on the route, notes the characteristics of Italian towns, and notes as well the scenery: 'So along the bay of Genoa, than which no other is more pleasant, through groves of cedars and palms, by the sweet-smelling and ever-sounding shore, he will come to the boundary of Italy and return to France.'[2] Not unconnected with this mood of observation is the tenour of Petrarch's life at Vaucluse or Arquà. Again, it is evidence both for himself, and for his time. There was no room for a Horace in the barbarian invasions, and the turmoil left by the ending of a civilisation must itself be ending before it is possible to speak of the country offering joy, simplicity and liberty, a state between riches and poverty, a sober rusticity in a peaceful region amongst harmless people. 'Here the air is mild and the breezes soft; the earth sunny, the fountains clear, the river fishy, the wood shady. Here are damp

---

[1] ibid., VIII. v. 433. 'Videbimus impendentes lacubus Alpes aerias ac nivosas, aestate gratis-simum spectaculum, et silvas astra tangentes, atque inter concava rupium querulos rivos, summisque de montibus magno cum sonitu cadentia flumina; et quocumque te verteris, avium murmur ac fontium.'

[2] ibid., IX. xiii. 51. 'Ita per Ligusticum sinum, quo nullus amoenior, per cedrinos ac palmi-feros saltus, per odoriferum atque undisonum litus, ad Italiae finem veniet, in Gallias reversurus.'

caves, grassy corners and smiling meadows; here is the lowing of cattle, the song of birds, the murmur of streamlets. It is hidden away, in name a Clausa Vallis and in reality; all around are hills rich with vines and olives.'[1] Dante names cities in order to condemn them, shows us places in the landscape to dramatise visually for us some detail of his poem; Petrarch ranges more easily over the whole (and his range is further than Dante's), but he sees things more for their own sake. In the *Divina Commedia* it is the *villanello* who represents the uncorrupted life of the country-side with its innocent appeal. Dante draws him with sympathy, and in obvious contrast to the occupants of hell; but there is no possibility of confusing Dante with the *villanello*, however attractive he may be. With Petrarch reappears the cultured enjoyment of Nature. And despite the visual intensity of Dante the picture of Italy emerges from Petrarch's letters rather than from the *Divina Commedia*. Petrarch sees things for their own sake, and for the sake of the pleasure which they give: and he, as Pius II, gives for the first time since Antiquity a picture whose elements we can recognise as substantially enduring.

There are those who have maintained that Petrarch lived in a shadow world of his own studies without contact with reality. Did he not call two of his friends by ancient names, write to many of the great names of antiquity, accept (*o vanitas vanitatum*, dreamed of in vain by Dante!) coronation on the Capitol? Did he not abandon the culture of his own time to plunge back into the past, resurrecting and imitating a dead tradition? To these, I think, may be fairly objected this sharp clarity of Petrarch's vision: if the picture which he drew, of men, places or Nature, was less real we might dismiss him as chimerical in his pursuit of Antiquity. But Petrarch had no thought of resurrecting an epoch. The idea that the Middle Ages is vegetable and the period of Antiquity mineral, and that therefore no cross-breeding can be possible between the two, would not have occurred to him. What he saw was that the plant Man is similar in potentiality in all ages, capable therefore of attaining to the same level of culture and virtue. For centuries the plant had been underdeveloped, and Petrarch sought its food where he thought it to be found, in the moralists of Antiquity. And, on the other hand, so far was he from snapping the continuity of the *Italian* tradition in

---

[1] *Fam.*, XVI. vi. 383. 'Aer hic blandus ac suaves aurae; tellus aprica, fontes nitidi, piscosum flumen, unbrosum nemus, antra humida, recessusque herbidi et prata ridentia, hic mugitus boum, avium cantus, murmurque lympharum, penitusque abdita et ex re nomen habens Clausa Vallis et amoena: in circuitu autem certatim Baccho grati colles ac Minervae. . . .'

literature that he handed on an inheritance which proved fertile, in more or less degree, until the eighteenth century. He has himself been often acclaimed, with some justification, as the chief glory of the Italian lyric; he can scarcely be blamed for the fact that the *Divine Comedy* (a work produced while he was still a minor) had such few imitators and so little continuation; or for the fact that Sacchetti is a lesser figure than Boccaccio. Instead of snapping the Italian tradition of literature Petrarch hands on what is only a modified version of Italian medieval lyric. The elements of his humanism are visible in the *Rime*, but it is not they which proved successful: that is why *petrarchism*, as distinct from the influence of Petrarch on humanism, proved almost as much a liability as a contribution to Italian, and European, literature. The Latin lyric, which springs at the end of the fifteenth century from the movement which Petrarch initiates, will act as a solvent to *petrarchism*: the lyric of Ariosto, that of Tasso, with the *Aminta* also, where they escape from *petrarchism*, owe some debt ultimately to Petrarch for this escape! There is not the same debit side to his humanistic contribution, and those who followed him rejected without hesitation the negative elements surviving in his thought. But it must not be imagined that the emergence of features which we can easily recognise as human, or as belonging to all ages, means that no advance has been made over the Middle Ages. Octavius talked of the love—

> which, left unshown,
> Is often left unloved;

and it is the consciousness of Petrarch which is significant. Truth is the object of the intellect, goodness that of the will; without the conscious effort attainment of either is difficult. Otherwise there is a necessary slipping away, since the nature of man is prompter in the imitation of bad examples than it is in that of good ones.[1] And Petrarch was constant, pertinacious even, in his determination to maintain that effort. His limitations are the result, not of an over-acceptance of Cicero, but of an under-acceptance; it is the continuation of the misanthropic Christianity of the Middle Ages which contradicts with the social ideals which he derives from contact with Cicero. But it was easy and inevitable for these contradictions to disappear in his successors. It is not a retreat from life into literature, but the achievement of a clearer view of life through literature. Life

---

[1] ibid., XVI. ix. 393. 'Ut est natura hominum ad imitationem exemplorum malorum promptior quam bonorum.'

must be faced, and experience is the best teacher: even more than that, Fortune is nothing, or rather it is only what happens without apparent cause, for without cause nothing happens.[1] That is an advance away from the Goddess of the medievals (or from the special conception of Dante), and it lays the basis for a positivist view of knowledge. Two ideas have been current on the ultimate value of the Renascence: on the one side, the idealists have maintained that the Renascence turned man's attention to what is purely human; that it is, therefore, an anthropocentric movement. On the other, the positivists have proclaimed it as a movement which turned man's attention to the rigid laws of Nature working without reference to man, and so producing at the end of the scale the scientist who thinks always of the universe as so many millions of years old, and of man as a transient and unimportant creature on it.[2] The truth is that Petrarch lays the foundation for a positive examination of the physical universe, but it is also true that by the side of the affirmation of nothing without its cause there is always the reference (if I may anticipate by quoting Filelfo's statement of the position which is Petrarch's also) *hominis bonum in eo quo homo est.*[3] The abnegation of the modern scientist re-establishes the position of Pascal, without the reason for that position: 'Que l'homme contemple donc la nature entière dans sa haute et pleine majesté, qu'il éloigne sa vue des objets bas qui l'environnent. . . . Qu'est-ce qu'un homme dans l'infini?'[4] Or perhaps one might say more reasonably that it is a different, and a less receptive, infinite on which the scientist bids us fix our gaze; but it is in both cases an exclusion which is foreign to Petrarch and the Renascence. He laid the basis for experimental knowledge, but he did not provide the excuse for divorcing it from its subordination to the proper study of mankind. Petrarch is midway between the two exclusions (for the position of Pascal is in reality close to that of the Middle Ages: they both recoil from man to fix their gaze on God, Pascal through a logical realisation of the physical unimportance of man, the Middle Ages through the impossibility of utilising virtuously man's physical inheritance). And it is he who establishes the active ideal, as against the contemplative one: a substitution which has been proclaimed as the work finally of Bacon, but in Bacon through the positivist influence of Machiavelli.[5] 'For good thoughts (though God accept them)

---

[1] *Sen.*, VIII. iii. 926. 'Sine causa enim nihil accidit.'
[2] A useful summary in Olgiati, *Anima dell'Umanesimo*, ad initium.
[3] Saitta, *Educazione dell'Umanesimo*, 173.   [4] *Pensées*, 347.
[5] For this thesis, v. N. Orsini, *Bacone e Machiavelli* (1936).

yet towards men are little better than good dreams, except they be put in act.'[1] Such a thesis, of course, rests on the hypothesis that Machiavelli is in contradiction with the stream of humanism that goes before him. But it is clear that Petrarch first establishes the social ideal of virtue, and will be plain soon how enthusiastically the fifteenth century follows his lead.

[1] *Essays*, XI.

V

THE SUCCESSORS OF PETRARCH:
HUMANIST EDUCATION

T. S. ELIOT has insisted on the value of tradition in the English Renascence, in that, by giving a common background, it lessened the demand upon the individual. The claim for Petrarch that he is the first modern man of letters means (if it is not merely a catch phrase) that his contact with Antiquity establishes some such tradition. With this in mind I have quoted from later writers in the European tradition, not always with the intention of showing a complete identity of thought with Petrarch, but with that of suggesting a similarity of attitude and procedure. Gibbon remarked on the long night of superstition which preceded the Renascence: 'The nerves of the mind, curiosity and scepticism, were benumbed by the habits of obedience and belief.' And in our own time it is Gentile who has spoken of Petrarch as the only sceptic of his time: one before whose gaze the various pseudo-sciences of his time, theology, dialectics, jurisprudence, alchemy and so forth are dissolved. The fundamental change is one from compilation to examination; there is nothing in Petrarch of the Jean de Meung, the Brunetto Latini or the Vincent de Beauvais (and how oddly against the Renascence the charge of imitation comes from the supporters of the Middle Ages—a period which copied more, and more hastily, than perhaps any other). The claim of the medievalists with respect to the vernacular literature of that period—that it has a *universal* appeal—may be taken as dangerous praise: a universal appeal represents quite often a near approximation to the lowest common denominator, and Petrarch, with his determination to please not many, but the few who desire virtue, is in a sounder position to advance. In medieval literature there is a pronounced declivity. The mystery play is born in the chancel, but it ends in the square with all the connotation of the farce. The *exemplum* is born in the pulpit (and Dante proceeds justly against its quality there[1]), and it ends in the *novella*, a metamorphosis this time which Ovid might perhaps have approved. But with Petrarch there begins the possibility of ascent. Dialogue XCIII of the second book of *De Remediis* may be taken as the first of the treatises on the dignity of man which fill

[1] *Paradiso*, XXIX. 103 ss.

the fifteenth century, and the insistence on virtue as a social thing, with the advance towards the elegances of life, is to be the dominant note of the age which accepts and develops the inheritance of Petrarch. These are general points, and I state them at the moment of transition from Petrarch himself to his immediate successors. Half the difficulty of considering the Renascence has been that the extent to which the fifteenth century is dependent on Petrarch's thought, rather than on Antiquity pure and simple, has often been pointed out in general terms and then obscured by the flood of information on the process of recovering Antiquity. Hence the contradictions implicit in Voigt's view of Petrarch and his influence. On the one side, an 'apparizione miracolosa'; on the other, a figure artificial, vain, incoherent and false; acclaimed as the father of humanism, and yet that movement dismissed as servile without any attempt being made to trace Petrarch's connection with its development. These contradictions were, it is true, noticed in a book from which much might have been hoped had its handling only proved equal to its inception.[1] But too often they have either been maintained, or else the position has gone by default, and the development of the Renascence been traced without reference to Petrarch.

In the consideration of immediate followers Boccaccio may, I think, be omitted. His personal veneration for Petrarch is well known, nor can his passage from creative to erudite works be entirely unconnected with that reverence. But the tendency to accumulated information on Antiquity was native in Boccaccio: does it not outrun discretion in the first of the romances, the *Filocolo*? The passage from the *Decameron* and the *Corbaccio* to the *De Genealogia Deorum* and the rest of the compilatory works may be taken to be, then, as much a personal development as the result of his admiration for Petrarch. In any case, the distance from Petrarch is obvious, and there is little evidence of a critical turn of mind in his works of reference, useful as these may have been as first instruments to the earlier generations of humanists. The real mirror for the attitude to Petrarch is Coluccio Salutati, Coluccio who wrote: 'The eyes of all are turned to you.'[2] Petrarch, for him, was to be preferred to the writers of antiquity. His success in verse puts him above Cicero; his mastery of prose over Virgil. 'For we have one whom we can, not only oppose, but even prefer, to Antiquity and to Greece herself:

---

[1] Benetti-Brunelli, *Le Origini Italiane della Scuola Umanistica*, which is unfortunately written at so exaggerated a length, and with such little clarity of expression, that little more than its direction remains to be praised.

[2] Coluccio Salutati, *Epistolario*, I. 83 (ed. Novati). 'Omnium in te oculi conversi sunt.'

this one man, Francesco Petrarca.'[1] Not only that, but in Italian he excelled, by the consent of all, his compatriot Dante and all other poets. These last remarks I have taken from his letter on the death of Petrarch, and in this he explains his reason for writing: 'For I should like you to keep before your eyes the life, the manners and the reputation of this man, by remembering whom (though you run swiftly towards virtue) you may be inspired to urge on your purpose.'[2] Not only Petrarch's writings, but his life also (o Voigt, where is thy sting?) emerge as an inspiration to virtue. In Coluccio there is another testimony as to what he expected from Petrarch. He was, it will be remembered, one of the most anxious to secure a copy of the *Africa* after Petrarch's death. But he was under no nineteenth-century illusion as to the nature of its contents. For him there was nothing pagan in the poem, or in its treatment, and his statement before reading it is an eloquent witness to the fact that humanism at its inception could not be considered as in any way anti-Christian. 'If ever a poet cultivated the muses and drank from the hidden fountain of Pegasus, it was this Petrarch of ours; not half a pagan drinking at the fountain of a horse, but drawing from the inmost lake all human qualities.'[3] That implies an acceptance of Petrarch's *distinguo* between the accidental faults of poets in antiquity, and the possibility of a pious poetry now. And later, when he had obtained the poem and read it all in the course of three nights (public business having taken his days) he admired its elegance, its majesty and its conduct, confessing that he had never read anything more weighty, better adorned, or more pleasing.[4] That this attitude should survive his disappointment at not being able to publish the poem (he wanted to spread copies systematically through the universities of Europe) is a proof of Petrarch's prestige for him, and is an earnest for many correspondences of thought between master and pupil. We may, if we like, take the panegyric also as evidence that Coluccio must not be expected to prove a critical mind of the first order: the grounds for superiority to Cicero and Virgil have an ingenuous touch, and this we

[1] Coluccio Salutati, *Epistolario*, I. 176. 'Nos autem habemus quem possimus et antiquitati et ipsi Graeciae, non dicam obicere, sed preferre: unum hunc Franciscum Petrarcham.'

[2] ibid., I. 187. 'In quo velim, comes egregie, istius hominis vitam, mores et famam ante oculos ponas, cuius memoria, quanquam citatissimo cursu ad virtutem anheles, ad urgendum propositum animeris.'

[3] ibid., I. 202. 'Si quis unquam musarum sacra coluit, qui abdito de fonte pegaseio biberit, hic noster Petrarcha, non semipaganus labra fonte proluit caballino, sed panigeros de penitissimo lacu quicquid humanum pertingere potest hausit.'

[4] ibid., I 252. 'Fateorque me nichil unquam gravius, nichil floridius nichilque denique gratius legisse.'

shall find reappearing in him. One other preliminary is worth noting: it is Coluccio's information with regard to Petrarch. It has been claimed that Petrarch's minor works were inaccessible to his public.[1] The *Africa*, as we have seen, remained unknown, except for thirty-four lines extracted from him under promise that they should not be divulged (one of those promises, as Petrarch observed, which are made easily in covetousness, and more easily forgotten in possession); the *De Viris Illustribus* was still not completed at his death, and was not published until last century, when it probably met with few readers; and there were other treatises which the prior of the Santi Apostoli, one of the most affectionate of Petrarch's Florentine correspondents, seems to have been ignorant of. If so, the letters, with Petrarch's personal conversation, represented the main channels of his influence; though if we bear in mind their bulk it does not seem as though the channels were inadequate. Nevertheless, the argument from Nelli alone is probably insufficient. It is true that the *Africa* and the *De Viris* were not available to any one till 1374; but Coluccio at least shows himself well acquainted with the range of Petrarch's writings. It is not, of course, a completely essential point: Petrarch has this in common with Voltaire, that he wrote on many occasions, and that the same ideas can be illustrated throughout the letters, the *Africa*, the invectives, and the various treatises. It is the constant preoccupation with similar ideas which I have tried to illustrate. There is no cause to deplore the repetition, for if he had not insisted so continually on those central ideas, and to so many correspondents, there was little chance of their acceptance. The effect, though, is that there is scarcely one of the treatises which is indispensable to a full realisation of the position of Petrarch; so that enquiry into their individual diffusion is not conclusive, even if there were sufficient grounds for generalisations.

I have said that the terms of Coluccio's admiration for Petrarch are an earnest for correspondences of thought. I might perhaps have said more, and asserted that much of what seems independent conclusion in him is derivative from Petrarch. The central position of Petrarch, with its concern for the first part of the path, is his also. It is not the length of life which is important, but the quality. 'He has not lived little who has reached perfection of life; it is not man's business to wish to live, but to wish to live well.'[2] And Petrarch had objected to

---

[1] cf. Cochin, *Un Ami de François Pétrarque*, Introduction.

[2] Sal., *Ep.*, I. 110. 'Non autem parum vixit, qui in vitae perfectionem evasit; nec hominis est velle vivere, sed bene vivere.'

the remark that a man lacked nothing but a longer life: 'I call no life short which has truly discharged the duty of virtue.'[1] From Petrarch comes also the acceptance of a purely Christian position of the same essential simplicity, and the authority for the belief in the divine governance of things in the world: 'We hold, as it seems right to believe, that all things are governed by the will of the godhead.'[2] It may seem a trivial coincidence with Petrarch's statement of Cicero's whole conclusion, but as a prelude to the statement of the goodness of things in this world it is not an unimportant derivation. His enthusiasm for the poets of antiquity receives Petrarch's justification, but the twist he gives it shows the inferiority at which I have already hinted. Who, he asks, is now so foolish as to give credence to Mars, Venus, Jove? But to his correspondent's imagined objection that the poets turn one aside from the scriptures Coluccio can only admit the truth of this, and that ideally it would be better to sweat without intermission over the reading of the sacred page. And yet the writings of the Gentiles, even the poets whom his correspondent abhors, if read high-mindedly can be of no small edification and profit to the things which concern faith.[3] Apart from the awkwardness of this, it is still substantially the thesis of Petrarch. But Coluccio weakens it immediately. By way of edification he descends to look for references to the Trinity, the unity of the Father and the Son, the eternity of the soul and the foundation of the Church, all hidden in the lines of Virgil. Petrarch had seen moral truths hidden, and had disclaimed theological ones; and this attitude of Coluccio stultifies his Petrarchan close ('So then I a Christian read Virgil, not as one who is going to remain always with him, or for long; but I search diligently if I can find, reading the works of Virgil, anything that helps character and right living [4]), and serves to throw up in relief the strength of Petrarch's rejection of the pseudo-prophecy in the IVth Eclogue. Coluccio's catalogue of those who have testified to the formative value of the ancients, with its inclusion of Jerome and of Augustine, is a mere echo.

As a symptom of the same inferiority we find that things which

[1] *Sen.*, XII. ii. 1013. 'Ego autem nullam brevem vitam dico, quae profecto virtutum munere functa est.'

[2] Sal., *Ep.*, I. 144. 'Nos autem, ut fas est credere, teneamus cuncta divini numinis arbitrio gubernari.'

[3] ibid., I. 302. 'Sanctius plane, fateor, et utilius lectioni sacrae paginae sine intermissione temporis insudare; sed haec inventa gentilium ac etiam, quos adeo horres, carmina poetarum, si quis ea alta mens libraverit, non parvum aedificant atque prosunt ad ea quae fidei sunt.'

[4] ibid., I. 304. 'Sic igitur ego christianus Virgilium lego, quod non sim ibidem semper aut aliquandiu mansurus, sed indagine diligenti perscrutor si quid ad honestatem et mores optimos, Maronica legens, valeam reperire.'

received—deservedly—a passing emphasis in Petrarch are often treated at exaggerated length in Coluccio's letters. Petrarch consistently abandoned the second person plural for the singular, without regard to the dignity of his correspondents; but once only, in all his extant letters, does he see fit to preach the innovation. Coluccio, however, inveighs quite frequently against the use of the plural (often repeating the dose to a recalcitrant correspondent, and writing over and over again to induce him to adopt the purity of the singular usage). Again, Petrarch remarked upon his brother's escape from the plague. Giovanni had insisted on remaining in his monastery, instead of escaping to some safer place. As a result, those who fled all met death by the plague elsewhere, while Giovanni tended all those who stayed with him until their end, and was the only monk to escape with his life. Petrarch added a sage conclusion on the impossibility of avoiding what God has in store. As Giovanni had answered to the counsel of flight: 'I like the advice, but there is no place inaccessible to death.'[1] It is an edifying reflection, but against its erection into a rule of conduct there are other (and perhaps more valuable) maxims in Petrarch: to offer oneself wilfully to danger is not magnanimity, but lack of prudence.[2] Coluccio had not the necessary circumspection, and he offered himself to a very grave danger. He indulges in wearisome arguments against running away from the plague, the burden of which seems to be that God will get you anywhere, if you are really marked down for it. This involves Coluccio in the doctrine of predestination (that Scylla and Charybdis of the prescience of an almighty God and the free will of man), and he has the strength, or rather the weakness, to plunge into a long discussion by which he seeks to prove that one may be predestined to salvation, but that one can only be foreknown to damnation. It is the departure from Petrarch's disregard for theological sophistry which shows up the strength of the one and the weakness of the other. Elsewhere he displays a curious inability to understand Petrarch's whole case. A correspondent writes expressing the desire to have some of Coluccio's own writings, and he replies (their number may suggest false modesty) that there is no point in seeking new writings when we have antiquity—the term,

[1] *Fam.*, XVI. ii. 366. 'Placere consilium, modo inaccessibilis morti locus aliquis usquam esset.'

[2] *Sen.*, XI. xii. 983. 'Sponte autem sese offerre periculis, non magni animi est, sed parvae prudentiae.' Petrarch .epeats in *Fam.*, XX. x. 36, this reflection on some modern talk of living dangerously, and cf. Cicero, *De Officiis*, I (*Opera*, IV. 307): 'Sed fugiendum etiam illud, ne offeramus nos periculis sine causa, quo nihil potest esse stultius.'

G

for him, includes St. Augustine. 'For, believe me, we invent nothing new, but as patchers sew up fragments from the rich garment
of antiquity, which we give out as new.'[1] To those who think of this
as a confirmation of Sabbadini's criticism it may be urged that, if we
take Coluccio at this word, we arrive at silence, not at humanism.
As I have said, Niccolò Niccoli wrote nothing, either in Latin or in
Greek, contented as he was with what the ancients had written.[2] But
that is a negation of Petrarch, if it is logically accepted, and it is best
taken as part of a vein of childishness which runs through Coluccio.
Thus he writes to ask for an explanation of the formation of images
in a mirror. He has taken up his pen in his right hand, yet the mirror
attributes it to his left. Pray, what is the reason for this?

I have insisted on the limitations to be found in Coluccio's mind
in order to differentiate him from Petrarch, but it is plain that we
cannot divorce them from his discipleship without doing him an
injustice. He has at times misunderstood or diminished his model,
and he has added little of his own; but in the main he is a most
efficacious channel for the spreading of Petrarch's influence. His life
was blameless, his advocacy of virtue unfailing, his position is obviously neither a rejection of what seemed true in Christianity nor a
leaping into the lap of antiquity. If he were taken by himself, and
without reference to Petrarch, it would be possible to rank him high.
And this has indeed been done. Saitta, who considered him without
noting his dependence on Petrarch (part of the tradition of ignoring
in practice the Father of Humanism), could write that the Middle
Ages with its partial, and therefore false, conception of man was
stricken to death by Coluccio.[3] That makes too great a claim for
originality in Salutati; placed in perspective, though, his *usefulness*
does not diminish. Nor is it of small importance that he begins the
series of humanists who held public position. As Chancellor of the
republic of Florence he initiates a tradition of good faith of which
Machiavelli could later be proud. With Petrarch he maintained that
truth derives from God, whether it is found in the Bible or in pagan
writers, whether uttered by theologians or by poets: where we find
it is indifferent, what we do with it, and that we should not despise
it, is the important thing.[4] It is the same practical concern that we
have found in Petrarch. And he formulated even a little more clearly

---

[1] Sal., *Ep.*, II. 145. 'Crede michi, nichil novum fingimus, sed quasi sarcinatores de ditissimae
vetustatis fragmentis vestes quas ut novas edimus, resarcimus.'

[2] 'Nihil tamen latine aut graece scripsit, scriptis veterum contentus.'

[3] *Educazione dell'Umanesimo*, 17.   [4] Toffanin, *Storia dell'Umanesimo*, 142.

than Petrarch the necessity for the study of history: 'I am glad that you have loved especially the historians, whose task it is to hand down the memory of past deeds to posterity, so that we by imitation of the example of kings, nations and illustrious men may exceed or equal the virtues of our forerunners ... since the knowledge of things past warns princes, teaches peoples and instructs individuals on conduct at home, with oneself, with one's family, one's friends and fellow-citizens, shows how one should behave both privately and publicly.'[1] There is nothing here, of course, which is foreign to the ideas of Petrarch on history as example and an aid to virtue: it is the inspiring note of Petrarch's own historical works. But, on the other hand, what else are the *Discorsi* than the fulfilment of this programme? 'Io ho sentito dire che la istoria è la maestra delle azioni nostre e massime de'principi, e il mondo fu sempre ad un modo abitato da uomini che hanno avuto sempre le medesime passioni. ...'[2] Where else had Machiavelli heard it said than by the humanists? The difference between Coluccio, who accepts from Petrarch this general truth, but is unable to do more than advocate it and repeat it, and Machiavelli, who can make use of it and of the past to illuminate the present, is that between the second and the first order of brains.[3] But Coluccio does not cease to be important as a link because of that, and his enthusiastic discipleship was necessary before the movement could make way. 'I could never moderate my appetite for books. ... Not only do I enjoy books and rejoice in them, but what is more, I feed on them and am perfected by them.'[4] And those who hold the thesis of Sabbadini must note not only the continued subordination of literature to virtue, but also the exercise of virtue itself by Coluccio.

In Leonardo Bruni we shall find the same enthusiasm, and we may expect also similar reflections of Petrarch's influence. Like Salutati he states explicitly that no-one is seriously disturbed by the old mythology as a body of belief; but there is much in it which reveals the praise of virtue, of faithfulness and self-sacrifice. Poetry is not literal

---

[1] Sal., *Ep.*, II. 290. 'Sed inter alios te praecipue dilexisse semper hystoricos, quibus rerum gestarum memoriam studium fuit posteris tradere, ut regum, nationum et illustrium virorum exemplis per imitationem possent maiorum virtutes vel excedere vel aequare ... quoniam rerum scientia monet principes, docet populos et instruit singulos quid domi, quid secum, quid cum familiis, quid cum amicis et civibus, quidque privatim vel publice sit agendum.'

[2] *Del Modo di Trattare i Popoli della Valdichiana*, II. 387 (*Italia*, 1813).

[3] cf. *Principe*, XXII.

[4] Sal., *Ep.*, II. 390 and 385. 'Nunquam in libris potui servare modum. ... Libris non fruor solum et exulto, sed quod maius est, perficior atque pascor.'

only, and there are many truths conveyed by figure.[1] That is the
doctrine of Petrarch, though Bruni occasionally weakens it as Salutati
had done. He cannot loose the IVth Eclogue from the Christian
grasp. Had not Lactantius thought that the Sybil was here alluding
to Christ?[2] He insists, then, first on the scriptures, and secondarily
on the classics, to draw from these what pertains to living well. And
when his interlocutor objects, But I am a Christian, and they perhaps
lived in their own way, he rejoins with fervour: As if character and
gravity of life were not the same then as they are now![3] Again, the
derivation is more than plain. Like Coluccio, and like Petrarch, he
insists on the practical side: literature without the knowledge of things
is empty; but the knowledge of things, though most important, lacks
something without letters.[4] 'I would prefer,' we have found Petrarch
saying, 'a man without letters, rather than letters without a man.'
Bruni's recommendation in studies is to think both of attainments and
of literary powers. Nothing has a more urgent claim than the
authors who treat of religion and of our duties in this world: that is
why he presses on the recipient of his treatise the poets, historians and
orators of the past.[5] In this central kernel, then, of his ideas Bruni is
the full heir of Petrarch: 'True learning, I say: not a mere acquaintance
with that vulgar threadbare jargon which satisfies those who devoted
themselves to theology, but sound learning in its proper and legitimate
sense, viz., the knowledge of realities.'[6] And wherever else we look
in Bruni we shall find confirmation of the dependence. Petrarch, as
we have seen, never preached the imitation of any single author for
purposes of style, and has himself been accused of savouring overmuch
of Seneca and Augustine to have a truly Ciceronian perfection.
Leonardo Bruni recommended for reading first Lactantius, Augustine,
Jerome, Ambrose and other Fathers of the Church, then Cicero,
Virgil, Livy, Sallust and the Latin poets; and these authors should be
taken as a test of correctness for vocabulary and construction.[7] It is
a fact which in itself, far as it obviously is from the conception of
the exclusive concern with antiquity attributed to humanism, gives
evidence against the idea of humanism resurrecting an epoch in the

---

[1] We are fortunate in having a book as admirable in its objective study and in its presentation
of essential texts for this part of my work as W. H. Woodward's *Vittorino da Feltre and other
Humanist Educators*. Its value has been recognised by an Italian translation as *La Pedagogia del
Rinascimento* (Firenze, 1923). For this, cf. Woodward, 213.

[2] ibid., 130.

[3] ibid., 182. 'Christianus sum, at illi forte suo more vixerunt.—Quasi vero honestas gravitas-
que morum non tunc eadem fuerit quae nunc est!'

[4] Bruni, *De Studiis et Literis*, 32 (Wood., 190).   [5] ibid. (Wood., 133).

[6] ibid., (Wood., 123).   [7] ibid., 125.

past to try and live in it. To make it plain that he does not reject the present Bruni takes up Petrarch's acceptance of cities with the specific praise of Florence. 'In the multitude of its citizens, the splendour of its buildings, the greatness of its activities, this city is most flourishing, and here have remained some of the seeds of the fine arts and of all our humanism, which seemed formerly extinct.'[1] It is plain how little the negative side of Petrarch's personal equation was listened to by his successors.

Petrarch had been very willing to accept from Cicero the view expressed in the *Tusculan Questions* on the relationship between Rome and Greece. Perhaps as a justification for his own ignorance of Greek (in spite of his own efforts and those of the redoubtable Leonzio Pilato) Petrarch kept firm hold of this belief in the improvement made by the Romans in what they had accepted from the Greeks. He did not renounce his longing for an acquaintance with Greek literature—his words on the Homer sent him are well known, and typical; he did not cry out on sour grapes. But while he recognised the abundance, and the brilliance, of the Greeks, he asserted that Varro and Cicero had dared to write after Plato and Aristotle, Virgil after Homer, Livy and Sallust after Herodotus and Thucydides. 'Finally, we have often surpassed and often equalled the Greeks in talent and in style, or rather, if we believe Cicero, we have always surpassed them where we have competed with them.'[2] In spite of the enthusiasm for all things Greek which is born of Petrarch's longing, and which flowered so rapidly at the beginning of the fifteenth century, Bruni retains this assessment; and he adds specifically: 'Look at philosophy (to take that first), which is the parent of all good arts and from which all our humanism is derived. It was brought from Greece into Italy by Cicero, and watered by him with that golden stream of eloquence.'[3] I am not concerned to argue the merits of the case; but it is important to point out that not only Bruni, but the whole of the fifteenth century also, follows Petrarch substantially in this judgment. Much has been made in the histories of the Renascence of the revival of Greek learning—a movement which, it is clear, traces its pedigree

[1] Bruni, *Dialogi ad Petrum Histrum*, 2. 'Nam cum frequentia populi, splendore aedificiorum, magnitudine rerum gerendarum civitas haec florentissima est, tum etiam optimarum artium totiusque humanitatis, quae iam extincta videbantur, hic semina quaedam remanserunt.'

[2] *Sen.*, XII. ii. 1010. 'Denique Graecos et ingenio et stylo frequenter vicimus, et frequenter aequavimus, immo, si quid credimus Ciceroni, semper vicimus ubi amnisi sumus.'

[3] Bruni, *Dial. ad P. Histrum*, 13. 'Vide, quaeso, philosophiam, ut eam potissime consideremus, quae est omnium bonarum artium parens et cuius ex fontibus haec omnis derivatur humanitas. Fuit olim ex Graecia in Italiam a Cicerone traducta, atque aureo illo eloquentiae flumine irrigata.'

also back to Petrarch. But in spite of the fervour with which the Greek tongue was studied, in spite of the Greeks in Italy and the Italians in Constantinople, the Renascence remains a Latin movement. What had remained most alive in the Greeks was a subtlety of dialectic; it was what the Renascence was least desirous of acquiring. The marked characteristic of the early fifteenth century is the abandonment of metaphysics for ethics:[1] that is the plain influence of Petrarch, and in spite of the impulse which he gave to the study of Plato (whom he conceived of as closer to the Christian position than Aristotle), in spite of the Platonic Academy which springs from that impulse, the direct Greek contribution to thought remains slight. Even the labours of Ficino, all his long task of translation and exposition, carries him more towards the Alexandrines than to any valuable discovery. Pico della Mirandola passes through these to occult learning, and ends in a frustration of the Renascence. On the other hand, despite the heroic efforts of Aldus, the diffusion of Greek recedes from the beginning of the sixteenth century; and in the meantime, it was without influence on the course of Italian literature. The connection of Machiavelli with Livy, of Ariosto with Virgil, is plain to see: but there is no similar connection to be made between writers of the Italian Renascence and the poets or the historians of Greece. Even if we invoke the *Moscheidos* of Folengo it will be a case of *lucus a non lucendo*. I repeat that this is a statement of what happened, and not a comparison of the merits of Greek and Roman literature in themselves. But I may add that this attitude which Petrarch bequeathed to the fifteenth century, and which dominated it unconsciously, still finds its echoes in the eighteenth. 'Les inventeurs ont toujours la première place dans la mémoire des hommes; mais quelque respect qu'on ait pour ces premiers génies, cela n'empêche pas que ceux qui les ont suivis ne fassent souvent beaucoup plus de plaisir. On respecte Homère; mais on lit le Tasse; on trouve dans lui beaucoup de beautés qu'Homère n'a point connues.'[2] This in its substance cannot be divorced from the attitude of Bruni to the golden stream of eloquence. And the importance attached to eloquence by Petrarch we have already seen; that of other humanists we shall see shortly. Closely related to this is Bruni's attitude to Aristotle. The philosophers who claim to derive from him, but who know no letters, produce more solecisms than words when they speak. What they say is harsh, inept, without eloquence. The *ipse dixit* of Aristotle is for them

[1] Wood., 221 (on the General Purpose of Humanist Education).
[2] Voltaire, *Essai sur la Poésie Epique.*

identical with truth, as if he alone had been a philosopher.[1] It is not that Bruni wishes to attack Aristotle: but his books have suffered such a transformation that he could no more recognise them now than the dogs could know the stag Actaeon. Cicero vouched for Aristotle's eloquence, but now he is as obscure as the Sybil, and his books have become tedious to read.[2] The partial dismissal of Aristotle in the *De Ignorantia* had been conducted in no other terms. It was the translators, and the Averroists, who had marred him. But also, 'he teaches more attentively what virtue is, this other urges more powerfully that virtue should be cultivated,' said Petrarch[3] on the distinction between Aristotle and Cicero; and Bruni looked to the same personal profit. He requires an erudition which shall join the knowledge of letters with that of things. Study is to be wide, scrutiny is to be close, 'so that some utility may derive to us from our studies.'[4] It is the utility of this last distinction of Petrarch in favour of Cicero, and marks an essentially practical outlook.

It will be clear, I think, at this point how close we are to a theory of education—a theory, and a practice, and how small was the step from Petrarch to the first generation of humanistic educators. Petrarch abandoned speculation as unprofitable, and he turns men's attention to conduct: for him if true philosophy is to love God, virtue is both to feel rightly about God, and to act rightly among men.[5] Those who called themselves philosophers before him dealt in questions and words, and neglected the problems of conduct for speculation.[6] Petrarch reverses the attitude, and his reversal leads directly to the humanist ideal of education, and remains in European currency until the eighteenth century.[7] Has not the eighteenth century been called scantly philosophical because it thought of philosophy in Petrarchan, rather than in speculative terms? Gibbon, for instance, scarcely thinks of philosophy in any other context. What more

---

[1] Bruni, *Dial.*, 15. 'Quasi vero aut ille solum philosophus fuerit.'

[2] ibid., 18. 'Molestos in legendo et absonos.'

[3] *Apol. cont. Galli Calumnias*, 1194. 'Ille docet attentius, quid est virtus, urget iste potentius, ut colatur virtus.' cf. Gentile, *La Filosofia*, 184.

[4] Bruni, *De Lit. et Stud.*, 64. 'Eruditionem . . . legitimam . . . et ingenuam, quae literarum peritiam cum rerum scientia coniungit.' And 78. 'Unde nobis ad studia nostra aliqua sit proventura utilitas.'

[5] cf. *Fam.*, XVII. i. 411 ss., and XI. iii. 111. 'Recte sentire de Deo, et recte inter homines agere.'

[6] ibid., XVII. i. 411. 'Sollicite atque anxie circa questiunculas et verba versari. . . . Ita penitus oblivioni veritas datur, negliguntur mores boni, res ipsae spernuntur, in quibus philosophia illa nobilis est, quae neminem fallit.'

[7] cf. *supra*, 44, n. 3. Voltaire's conviction of the futility of metaphysics is expressed very frequently.

natural than that the successors of Petrarch should be dominated by his attitude, and should take the logical step forward? For them, then, philosophy is ethics, a practical guide to living. Hence their Petrarchan insistence on Cicero, who had absorbed the best elements of Greek ethics, and combined them with the practical temper of the Romans.[1] Logic, which had preoccupied the medievals, is for Vittorino da Feltre merely a means to clear and precise expression: Petrarch had spoken in no other terms.[2] Eloquence (that is, style) is of supreme importance: it is for philosophy to point out canons of excellence in thought and character, for history to illustrate them; but it belongs to eloquence alone, by fitting stimulus, to enforce their application.[3] If the fifteenth century is, as Sabbadini claimed, the century of insistence on *form* it is clear for what practical purpose this concern began. This is recognised by Woodward: 'No doubt that the Humanists as a body were profoundly convinced of the practical character of classical studies.'[4] And Woodward quoted one of them, Ticozzi: 'Soleva dire, non tutti i suoi discepoli aver bisogno per vivere onoratamente, di professare filosofia, legge, medicina . . . né tutti essere ugualmente da natura favoriti . . . essere bensí tutti a vivere in società destinati ed a professare la virtú.'[5] That depends very clearly on Petrarch.[6] Vittorino quoted with approval Cicero's remark that the whole praise of virtue consists in action: Petrarch, as much as Cicero, had taught him this.[7] Even Voigt noted of Vegio that his aim was not mere learning, but practical citizenship.[8] Similarly with Vittorino the aim was citizenship. Woodward noticed that it was a co-ordination of Christianity and the classical ethic, as both essential to the development of complete manhood: and that there was no sense in Vittorino's mind of any contradiction between the two.[9] The reason for that is clear from Bruni's exclamation above: As if character and gravity of life were not the same then as they are now! It is Petrarch who is responsible for this lack of contradiction; Petrarch who had pointed out the lacuna in medieval Christianity

---

[1] Wood., 57 (though, of course, here there is no reference to Petrarch).

[2] For Vittorino and Vegio, Wood., 231; *Fam.*, I. vi. 57. 'Tu ergo senis tui discipulos meis verbis excita; neque deterreas, sed hortare, non quidem ut ad dialecticam, sed ut per eam ad meliora festinent.'

[3] Wood., 230.   [4] ibid., 182.   [5] ibid.   [6] *Fam.*, XIX. xvii. 562, etc.

[7] *De Ign.*, 68. 'Etsi enim non sit in virtute finis noster, ubi eum philosophi posuere, est tamen per virtutes iter rectum eo ubi finis est noster; per virtutes, inquam, non tantum cognitas, sed dilectas,' etc. For Cicero, cf. *Op.* IV. 299. 'Virtutis enim laus omnis in actione consistit.'

[8] *Wiederlebung*, II. 461 (Wood., 182). 'Der berühmte und im Staate tüchtige Mann ist sein Ziel, nicht allein der Gelehrte.'

[9] Wood., 67.

which the humanist educators strove to fill. 'I study much that I may be an educated man, but more that I may be good and free. The one makes one feel rightly, and the other makes one live rightly.'[1] Had not Petrarch insisted that we must philosophise in actions if we wish to be safe in reality?[2] 'We call those studies *liberal* which are worthy of a free man; those studies by which we attain and practise virtue and wisdom; that education which calls forth, trains and develops those highest gifts of body and mind which ennoble men, and which are rightly judged to rank next in dignity to virtue only.'[3] On the one side a social conception of virtue; on the other the rising sentiment of the dignity of man, or of his capacity for dignity. Matteo Palmieri makes it clear that by solitary virtue 'divengono gli uomini beati, e veri conoscitori delle cose divine; ma in uomini oziosi, viventi in solitudine, e rimossi da ogni pubblica azione, sono senza alcuna utilità del comune vivere degli altri mortali solo intenti alla propria salute. Di questi si legge ne'libri sacri: la semplice santità solo a sé fa pro.'[4] That is not very far from Petrarch's implied mistrust for the *ocium* of the monks; and the title of Palmieri's book, *Della Vita Civile*, goes some way towards showing us that the reversal of the contemplative ideal attributed to Bacon and Machiavelli has already been achieved under the aegis of Petrarch. The *bonum communionis* as against the *bonum suitatis* is plain in Palmieri. Plain also in others of the same school. Pius II speaks the same language: 'Nor will I have you solitary. . . . For I know what profit it is for men to prove in experience what they have learnt in education. Nor do I praise those men who give themselves so to letters that they despise other things.'[5]

Alongside the theory, the practice. I do not think I need to illustrate it, in spite of its obvious importance for my theme. There are few more respected names in the history of education than Guarino Veronese and Vittorino da Feltre, while to come upon *Casa Giocosa* after the Middle Ages is to experience the same exhilaration that Saintsbury felt (misguidedly) on meeting with the *De Vulgari Eloquentia* after the critical blank since antiquity. But information, for precisely these reasons, is not very hard to come by on their

---

[1] Vergerio, *Epist.*, CVI. 'Curo multo studio ut literatus sim, sed magis ut bonus et liber. Hoc enim recte sentire, illud recte vivere facit.'

[2] *Sen.*, I. ii. 815. 'Philosphandum nobis et rebus est, si re ipsa salvi esse cupimus.'

[3] Vergerio, *De Ingenuis Moribus*, tr. Wood., 102.   [4] M. Palmieri, *Della Vita Civile*, 24.

[5] E. S. Piccolomini, *Opera*, 604 (1551). 'Nec te solitarium esse volo. . . . Scio namque frugi esse quae homines litteris didicerunt experimento comprobari. Nec ego hos homines laudo, qui sic se literis dederint, ut res caeteras parvi faciant.'

schools, and it is not my intention merely to repeat, even though I should myself find pleasure in the repetition. One particular I may underline: the old opposition by which the body is the enemy of the mind (Petrarch, as I have said, adhered to it in his negative moments) finds little trace in the ideals of Guarino and Vittorino. It is true that in Petrarch the tinge of reprobation for the flesh was not of the same nature as Jacopone's crying out for the 'grande malsania'.[1] Petrarch recognised the desire in all to be happy, nor did his dislike of doctors imply any corresponding dislike for being healthy. Maffeo Vegio recommended the hardening of children physically by exposure to the climate instead of coddling them. Vittorino employed gymnastics and bodily exercise generally as indispensable equally with the improvement of the mind. The innovation was a logical one: it was part of the cultivation of the whole man, part of the establishment of a pattern of education which was to remain sound for centuries. So far is the Italian fifteenth century from being an epoch of flagellants that even the enemies of humanism speak a different language from that of Jacopone, or of Passavanti. The author of the *Lucula Noctis* thought of the study of antiquity as harmful, in that it was unnecessary, and might turn aside from the consideration of the scriptures—the arguments which we have seen Coluccio and Bruni refuting as had Petrarch, and which continue the old theme:

> Tale qual'è, tal è:—non c'è religione.
> Mal vedemmo Parisci—c'hane destrutto Ascisi:
> con la lor lettoría—messo l'ò en mala via.[2]

But Dominici reproved the soul's anxiety to free itself from the body, and when penitence desired an indiscreet abstinence from food he sanctioned disobedience to it: eat and drink what is needful.[3] If that is the position of a recalcitrant it is not surprising that the humanists set forward a programme of physical education; and it was quite in accordance with their practical nature that this should begin with infancy, and not disdain minutiae. Vegio desired education from the beginning, one *a la* Rousseau, of example rather than precept, reason rather than beating. Mothers were to feed their children at the breast, and not to hand them over to the stupid minds of maidservants. Reason especially was to be used as soon as possible: Vegio opposes the New to the Old Testament, which had an over-

---

[1] *Lauda* XLVIII.   [2] Jacopone, *Lauda* XXXI.

[3] Dominici, *Regola del Governo di Cura Familiare*, 75 (1860). 'Da questo detto impara, se l'anima avendo fretta di sciogliersi da te . . . si privasse del cibo necessario, e tenesseti in penitenza non discreta, non l'ubbidire; ma tu mangia e bei quanto bisogna a te per lei.'

salutary respect for the rod as an instrument of training for children. He graded the reading of the scriptures for every age, and added classical texts as well; but the Bible was the milk for the children's minds their first nourishment.[1] In this connection I cannot resist quotation of two contradictory remarks of Voigt. He recognised that the Bible was always Petrarch's favourite book, a predilection which increased with age, and he observed that it was easy to understand why, in spite of his cult for antiquity, the Church could later count the Father of Humanism among her defenders. Yet he added: 'Au fond, la Renaissance, d'après les idées mêmes d'alors, n'est que l'expression de ce qu'il y a de purement humain dans l'esprit et dans le coeur de l'homme, de l'humanité prise dans le sens grec et romain du mot, et par conséquent en contradiction flagrante avec les idées du christianisme et de l'Eglise.'[2] That is the contradiction which Vittorino, with his ideal of Christian citizenship, did not see. It is clear enough that if these humanistic ideas on education are to be regarded as imitation, it will be an imitation of Petrarch much more even than it is of antiquity. The debt of the theorists to Quintilian may be plain to see; but just as it was Petrarch who made the first discovery of the text of Quintilian, so it was he who rendered first its application possible. It is true that the terms *Christian* and *citizen* in Vittorino's ideal are co-ordinated and equal, so that the first is not the illustration, but the companion, of the second. That follows from all that has gone before; and medieval Christianity is inevitably rejected in this marriage. There could be no room for the stupidity of Jacopone in any theory of education. But that rejection was a gain for Christianity, rather than the loss of Christianity; and it is only if we hold to some chimaera of a unity in the history of Christianity that we can reach the conclusion of Voigt set out above. Or rather, perhaps Voigt himself reached it another way. Much of the difficulty in the evaluation of the Renascence has been precisely that the labour of mapping out the physical process of recovery of the works of antiquity (and the magnitude of this task must give pause to those who think there was no intermission in the knowledge of antiquity) has obscured the question as to what use was made of them. Petrarch recovered Quintilian here, the letters of Cicero there, and an oration of the latter in Liège: there was scarce enough ink in Liège for him to copy it out, and what there was was yellow. In the retailing of such scraps and anecdotes (are they not a staple of Burckhardt's study of the Renascence?) it has often been taken for granted that Petrarch and his

[1] *De Educatione Liberorum*, summarised B–Brunelli, 374.　　[2] Voigt, 4.

successors wanted the works they found merely for some reverent labour of imitation, and that they were themselves but ciphers to this great accompt. How else is it possible to explain the contrast between Voigt's statement and the clear position of the humanists who derive from Petrarch? That is why I insist upon the evidence that they, where they imitate, imitate Petrarch more plainly even than they imitate antiquity; but that if their position derives logically from his, it is as well a development of it. They advance from his position, and build practically on his foundations, without any thought of denying these. But since their practice has been illustrated (and I may refer cursorily to Burckhardt and to the valuable compendium of Woodward) it is my business to make as plain as possible the connections with Petrarch, and, since advance involves departure, the divergence from him.

In this what we must expect (and it is what we have seen so far) is Petrarchan principles by the side of practical advice. Thus Vergerio declares: 'If we hold it our first duty to live honourably and bravely, whether in peace or war, we shall not overrate the blessing of long life as so many do.'[1] Petrarch and Coluccio had encouraged him in this belief. But when he advises us not to attempt too much at once, to limit the number of subjects we have in hand so that daily revision may make our acquisition sure; when he counsels us to put our heart into one subject at a time, and to repress a superficial curiosity, then he is playing his part in the advance from Petrarch. 'There is an order in studies which should be obeyed. A habit of irregular reading, or dipping into books, here the beginning, here the end, here the middle, is responsible for much useless study.'[2] That is admirable; and it is not Petrarch. But if that is the general pattern it is possible to find, by the side of striking agreement, equally striking independence. For Enea Silvio Piccolomini character is the essential: 'Our one sure possession is character: the place and fortune of men change, it may be suddenly, profoundly; nor may we, by taking thought, cunningly hedge ourselves round against all the chances of life.'[3] And literature still for him is essential for the establishment of this essential, character: 'Literature is our guide to the true meaning of the past, to a right estimate of the present, to a sound forecast of the future. Where letters cease darkness covers the land; and a Prince who cannot read the lessons of history is a helpless prey of flattery and intrigue.'[4] SINE LITERIS OMNIS AETAS CAECA EST—it is a magnificent declaration of

[1] P. P. Vergerio, *De Ingenuis Moribus*, tr. Wood., 113.   [2] ibid., 110.
[3] E. S. Piccolomini, *De Liberorum Educatione*, tr. Wood., 140.   [4] ibid., 141.

faith in the practical value of literature. Doubtless, it contained the seeds of danger: Woodward noted that history did not become a field of critical enquiry, while medieval history was ignored (or almost so: the merit of Flavius Blondus lies in his examination of the Middle Ages as an era that had closed; but he stood alone, and his means were inadequate to his attempt). Hence the sources of history were fixed and literary: does not Platina speak of Vittorino's indignation when confronted with scepticism as to the accuracy of Livy, a sound Latinist, an elegant narrator, and a Paduan![1] It is a danger which existed, and in some proved fatal. They, in their turn, have often proved fatal to the critics of the Renascence: the period is so vast, the criteria for dealing with it have been so few, or so unitarian (as in Burckhardt) that there has not always been the possibility of deciding what is live and what is dead weight. If all who wrote in Latin in the fifteenth century are humanists, it is easy to pick on many whose worth is slight and judge from them as to the whole. If it is all humanism, indeed, what need to pick and choose? But Valla and Machiavelli both assent to the claim of Aeneas Sylvius (which writes large what Petrarch thought); and few will venture to assert that their minds are uncritical. Nor will the career of Pius II suggest that he kept his head entirely in thin or ancient air. 'It is the sign, said Petrarch, of a degenerate mind to insult inferiors, not to be able to endure an equal, to await the opportunity, not the reason, for doing harm.'[2] And there have been too many critics of humanism ready to use any stick to beat it with; nor has any stick come readier to hand than the trailers after a great movement. But it is a queer criticism which sees the stragglers, and ignores the movement.

Let us return to Aeneas Sylvius,[3] since it is with his views that I am concerned. He also limits Logic to a preliminary which is of no profit except in enabling us to recognise in our reasoning the fundamental difference between certain, probable, and manifestly false steps in argument. 'But beware of logicians who waste time and ingenuity in mere verbal subtleties, in whose hands Logic is a thing, not of living use, but of intellectual death.'[4] He meets the objection of the shallow churchman who objects to wasting precious time in studying such sources of corruption as the pagan poets. Indeed, he adds a defence

[1] Wood., 217.

[2] *Fam.*, VI. vi. 347. 'Degeneris animi signum est insultare minoribus, non posse comitem pati, nocendi, cum possit, occasionem expectare, non causam.'

[3] I quote him by all his names, which I give to avoid confusion: Enea Silvio Piccolomini = Aeneas Sylvius = Pius II.

[4] Aen. Syl., *De Lib. Ed.*, tr. Wood., 135.

of his own: if one is to exclude the great writers of antiquity for the errors which we know them to contain, how are we to treat the masters of theology, from whom proceed the heresies?[1] He also prescribes a list of authors to be read which includes the Old and New Testaments, the writers of antiquity, but with these he prescribes as well such modern writers as Leonardo Bruni, Guarino Veronese, Poggio and Ambrogio Traversari.[2] This again is perfectly in accordance with tradition. But it is not idle to insist on it. The treatises of Bruni and Vergerio belong to the opening years of the fifteenth century; that *De Liberorum Educatione* is of 1450. Thus the blind preoccupation with Cicero, for purposes of style, and style alone, is still lacking half-way through the century, and when the predominantly Latin period (in language, I mean) is drawing rapidly to a close. It is Aeneas Sylvius who wrote that all needless imitation should be avoided.[3] That is consonant with what we have seen of Petrarch's attitude; and there is evidence to show that the humanist educators were at pains to avoid mere imitation. 'It is of importance to remember that in comparison with intelligence memory is of little worth, though intelligence without memory is, so far as education is concerned, of none at all. For we are not able to give evidence that we know a thing unless we can reproduce it.'[4] Doubtless the memory was stronger then than now when it is vitiated by the abundance of books, and feats of memory abound among the pupils of the humanist educators. But the emphasis on intelligence is not camouflage. Guarino Veronese, for instance, in his teaching insisted on full understanding, and not a repetition of words: 'Express a passage, not word for word, but in its sense, so that you may seem to grasp the body rather than the limbs.'[5] If there had been a concentration, as alleged, on style it would seem reasonable that they should have attained to something more correct in their latinity. Petrarch, we have seen, was tainted in his Ciceronianism with Seneca and St. Augustine, Valla pointed others to elegance, but achieved an individual vigour of his own, Aeneas Sylvius writes a fluid Latin which is almost at times a spoken language, Pontanus later is so unshackled as to be almost Neapolitan in his Latin, while Politian (a scholar, perhaps, rather than a humanist) professes imitation indeed, but an imitation which seeks out its vocabulary from all the corners of the Latin language. Bembo

[1] Aen. Syl., *De Lib. Ed.*, tr. Wood., 149.   [2] ibid., 151.

[3] Aen. Syl., *Op.*, 989. 'Fugienda artis est omnis supervacua imitatio.'

[4] Vergerio, *De Ing. Mor.*, tr.Wood., 109.

[5] Guar. Ver., *Epist.*, II. 270. 'Nec verbum ex verbo sed sensa tantisper exprimes, quasi corpus non membra circumscribas.'

is the triumphant purist in Ciceronianism, and it is a doctrine which belongs to another century. There it deserved the castigation which Erasmus gave it, but in its origins it was not wholly unsalutary: the followers of Politian found rancid words enough in the crannies of Latin literature, and a reaction against this *embarras de richesses* was the result. But neither action nor reaction belongs to the period of Petrarch or of humanist education. Enea Silvio, then, is so far in the tradition we have seen, and laudably so. But he is not afraid of independence. Thus he maintains that when the employment of metaphors obscures plain discourse it ceases to be an ornament, and becomes a weariness. 'If long drawn out, this affectation of figure tends to allegory or to mere verbal puzzles.'[1] His concrete mind, that is, rejects the theory of poetry which Petrarch had inherited from Dante and the Middle Ages. For Petrarch, in theory at least, allegory represented the fair veil of poetry, and the verbal puzzle was to ensure that the best mind reached the prize, and found satisfaction in the effort of so doing. That was inevitably a doctrine which the practical mind of the fifteenth century was to abandon. It is not surprising that the word is spoken by a man of action such as Pius II. No quality distinguishes him more than that of common sense. There is another passage in the *De Liberorum Educatione* which might have distressed Petrarch in spite of its studied moderation. Aeneas Sylvius begins by considering the need for restraint in eating and drinking. Wine is to be avoided for children (and this concern with the welfare of the child is the same that we have found in Maffeo Vegio); but Plato allowed its moderate enjoyment as tending to mental relaxation, and, indeed, temperance in the true sense is hardly consistent with the absolute prohibition of all that might seduce us from our virtuous resolutions.[2] It is the temper of that reflection, even more than the substance, which shows that we are swinging forward from the position of Petrarch. I have been concerned with Aeneas Sylvius here mainly as a member of the group of writers on the practice of education; but even in this connection it is clear that he is the contemporary of Valla. It is significant, though, that the author of the phrase *Pium respicite, Aeneam respuite* (nor was there so much to reject)[3] puts the emphasis still on virtue. Petrarch prepared the way for a conception of Christianity which should not be incompatible with the enjoyment of this life, and the independence of Valla and Pius II is quite logical. I have referred to the common sense of Aeneas Sylvius, and one practical

---

[1] Aen. Syl., *De Lib. Ed.*, tr. Wood., 146.   [2] ibid., 139.

[3] On his election to the Papacy in 1458. 'Look to Pius, forget Aeneas.'

detail from his treatise may be added here. He is the first (so far as I
know) to recommend the learning of modern languages: that he does
so on the authority of antiquity is a piquant sauce for those who
maintain that the fixing of the gaze upon the past destroyed the sense
for the present. Mithridates had known the language of all his various
subjects, and Aeneas Sylvius preaches his example to Ladislas of
Bohemia. He should seize every opportunity of learning to converse
in the vulgar tongues spoken in his realm, because it is unworthy of a
prince to be unable without an interpreter to hold intercourse with his
people.[1] We may take the detail as a reminder that the humanists were
not mere theorists any more than they were mere imitators. The
beginning of the fifteenth century is dominated by the full gospel of
Petrarch. So far there is development, and a crystallisation of his ideas
which involves some change, but they are still plainly recognisable;
and for the establishment of the foundations Europe owes a debt to
Petrarch greater than to any other single figure since. His was not
only the scepticism which dissolved the Middle Ages, it was also the
affirmation which made possible the modern epoch. The conviction
of Dante as the supreme poet may at times carry with it the conviction
also that Dante is the first modern man; but even where Dante has
ideas and aspirations which are close to those of Petrarch he remains
a medieval in his complex mentality; the subtle mesh of his treatises,
even, romanticism apart, of the *Vita Nuova*, fatigues and baffles the
reader more than it encourages. The poem retained its appeal into
the Renascence, even though it affected subsequent literature less than
we might expect; but the treatises of Dante disappeared fairly
thoroughly from view until the scholarship of the nineteenth
century revived them. That was not a casual disappearance: it was
the heritage of Petrarch which proved fruitful. After him it is the
whole man whom the humanists will try to educate, and the time
when education ceases to have that concern, and offers natural knowledge for its own sake, will be one of abdication. I have in front of
me a brochure advertising the *World of Science*, a digest of 'the mass of
knowledge which a great army of the finest brains has fashioned into
Science.' As baits to trap me into further examination it offers samples
of what I may be glad to know: 'The air in an average living-room
weighs as much as a small woman. The pressure on a fish the size of
a cod at sea-bottom is equal to the weight of a locomotive. If all the
people in Europe talked at once the energy would just run a motor-
cycle.' Unlike Petrarch, in his reaction to the assorted (and possibly

[1] Aen. Syl., *De Lib. Ed.*, tr. Wood., 142.

Aristotelian) natural history of the young man in the *De Ignorantia*, I have an implicit faith in the accuracy of all these statements. But what then? The conclusion of Petrarch on their supreme irrelevancy still holds good: *nichil penitus ad beatam vitam.* The *medieval* nature of the scientist would be easily recognised by the humanists, who might well apply to the achievements of Science the phrase of Petrarch on the Church possessing wealth: 'It is good if she possesses it, but most bad if she is possessed by it.'[1] *Bene si habet, pessime si habetur.* Without a centre in a humanism of some sort all external knowledge becomes a passive balance.[2]

[1] *Fam.*, VI. i. 307.

[2] cf. Voltaire, *Dialogues d'Evhemère*, VIII. 'A quoi me servira s'il vous plaît, de savoir qu'une planète pèse sur une autre, et qu'on peut disséquer la lumière, si je ne me connais pas moi-meme?'

VI

THE AUDACITY OF VALLA

THE humanist educators, then, are on ground which is irrefutably Petrarchan; but the very fact of their building where Petrarch only laid foundations suggests the inevitability of a development away from him. The temper of a casual reflection of Aeneas Sylvius which I quoted will have hinted which way the change would come. Petrarch had said that nothing which went against Nature could be good; he had expressed the opinion that Nature would be a stepmother if she hid poison in honey (which is attractive to us).[1] But we have seen that he did not always draw the logical conclusions from this premiss. By the side of the affirmation there still stood part of the medieval-Christian denial. 'What is a father, but vile seed? What a mother, but a filthy dwelling? God gave the soul, life, intellect, the appetite for good, the freedom of the will.'[2] That sharp distinction reminds us that, for Petrarch, Nature does some things wrong. Again, he affirmed not only Nature, but the man-made arts as well; and to these also he gave partial denial. In his praise of rural life there is this renunciation: 'Those who love an honourable poverty should not so much hate as despise riches. Gold neither frightens them nor keeps them in suspense. They look on pictures, statues, Corinthian vases, oriental jewels and Sidonian purple not as an ornament to their possessors, but as the glorious handiwork of Nature, and with the same mind use them or do without.'[3] The arts, according to this valuation, are not a contribution of man to life, but a gift of Nature to man. Where he speaks of the arts as inventions Petrarch distinguishes between the liberal arts (which concern the mind) and the mechanical ones (which concern the body).[4] It is his preoccupation with the first which dictates the passage quoted on doing with, or

[1] cf. esp. *Sen.*, XII. ii. 1004-6. For the honey, ibid., XII. i. 991.

[2] *Fam.*, X. v. 93. 'Quid enim pater, nisi vile semen? Quid nisi foedum mater habitaculum? Deus animam, Deus vitam, Deus intellectum, Deus appetitum boni, Deus arbitrii libertatem dedit.'

[3] ibid., XIII. iv. 224. 'Qui ingenuam diligunt paupertatem, divitias non tam oderint quam contemnant: quos nec terreat aurum nec suspendat; qui pictas tabulas ac statuas et vasa corinthia et eoas gemmas ostrumque sidonium, non ut possidentium ornamentum, sed ut naturae decus aut artificium aspiciant, eodemque animo illis utantur et careant.'

[4] *Con. Med.*, III. 1224. 'Constat autem liberales propter animam, mechanicas propter corpus inventas.'

without, the second. The flowering of beauty is brief, the taste of pleasure is bitter in its leaving: it is virtue which is the most amiable of all and the most attractive[1]—and virtue is an aim of the mind, not of the senses. Dante had made, in the *Commedia*, one solitary reference to Epicure:

> Suo cimitero da questa parte hanno
> con Epicuro tutti i suoi seguaci,
> che l'anima col corpo morta fanno.[2]

Petrarch also held no truck with Epicure for this denial of the soul's immortality, but he insisted sharply on another cause for quarrel. For him the *summum bonum* was *honestas*; for Epicure it had been *voluptas*. 'Let it be far from me, says Petrarch, to place, not the *summum bonum*, but (since in this matter also I am a Stoic rather than a Peripatetic, though in everything I would sooner be a Stoic than an Epicurean) any good at all in riches or pleasure. These are the conveniences and props of human life, and so they call the one the goods of Fortune, and the other the good of the body. But the good which we seek is in the mind, dependent neither on the body, nor on Fortune. I admit that the others are called *good*, but I contend that they are not. And don't think that I say this inadvertently, or through some slip. I am not ignorant of what Aristotle says, or Epicure, upon this point; but the authority of the philosophers does not prevent liberty of judgment.'[3] As Petrarch himself remarked, what we have learnt by long usage, must be unlearnt by a long dis-usage; and although he gives Epicure at one point the credit for moderation personally in such matters as food, the very rare references to him in Petrarch's letters attack him contemptuously on these grounds, or in the terms of Dante. 'Except for Epicure, and I know not how many others of his infamous flock, there is nobody who denies the immortality of the soul.'[4] Nor, since the bridge by which Cicero could become, to a

---

[1] cf. *Fam.*, IX. xi. 37 for praise of Cicero's observation, 'Virtute nihil amabilius, nihilque quod magis alliciat.' And *Africa*, II. 477.

[2] *Inf.*, X. 13.

[3] *Fam.*, III. vi. 148. 'Absit a me, non modo summum, sed (quoniam et in hac opinione Stoicus quam Peripateticus, etsi in omnibus Stoicus multo quam Epicureus esse malim) ne aliquod quidem bonum in divitiis, aut in voluptate reponere. Commoda sunt haec, et adminicula vitae mortalis; itaque illud fortunae, hoc corporis bonum vocant. Bonum vero, quod quaerimus, in animo est, nec corpori serviens, nec fortunae. Caetera vocari bona fateor, sed non esse contendo. Neve me forsan, errore lapsum, putes inadvertenter hoc dicere. Non sum nescius quid de hac re Aristoteles, quid Epicurus sentiat: sed philosophantium auctoritas non impedit iudicii libertatem.'

[4] *Fam.*, IV. iii. 208. 'Praeter Epicurum enim, et nescio quot ex illo infami grege, immortalem esse animam nemo est qui neget.'

Christian, a minor revelation consisted in his lack of elements in conflict with the Christian revelation itself can there be any wonder that
Epicure should be rejected out of hand. Of Cicero Petrarch could
say: 'I admit that he says different things: I deny that he says opposite
ones. Christ is the word, the virtue and the wisdom of God the Father:
Cicero said much on the art of words, on virtues and human wisdom,
things that were true, and therefore without any doubt most pleasing
to God.'[1] There was obviously no likelihood of his writing about
Epicure in such a vein. Montaigne, then, could write: 'C'est une
absolue perfection, et comme divine, de jouyr loïallement de son
être,' but Petrarch, although he approaches this affirmation on one
side, could not avoid strong reservations in connection with it. Nature
must be followed as a goddess, but only within limits; and virtue is
still by definition a matter of the mind against the body. It remained,
then, for the question to be asked whether virtue could not be of the
body as of the mind; it still remained to make the enquiry whether in
giving attractions to the body Nature was any more a step-mother
than in the provision of honey. And in the matter of the arts, it
remained to make full use of Petrarch's adherence to the goodness of
the passage from the necessary to the elegant. It remained, in short, for
the fifteenth century to adhere to the whole conclusion of Cicero as
Petrarch had stated it, and to more than that conclusion. It goes without saying that the fifteenth century could not have done this had
Petrarch not preceded; and moreover some of the physical factors
which rendered the process more easy were also set in motion by
Petrarch. Parallel with the discovery of codices went the discovery
of the physical remains of Rome, and of Greece also to a lesser extent.
Petrarch himself had been much less informed on the art, than on the
history and thought of Rome. In Rome itself, despite his walks,
despite his vantage-point on the roof of Diocletian's Baths,[2] he
acquired no accurate topographical knowledge of the ancient monuments, and no trained visual appreciation. He reduces very largely
the fables of the *Mirabilia Urbis Romae*, but he could still think of the
Pyramid of Caius Cestius as the tomb of Remus; and in Provence
he failed to recognise Roman monuments under their medieval
names. The fifteenth century applied itself with patience and enthusiasm to the recovery of ancient monuments, and to their understanding. Where Petrarch had waited for peasants to bring him coins or

[1] *Fam.*, XXI. x. 86. 'Diversa fatear: adversa negem. Christus verbum est et virtus et sapientia
Dei patris: Cicero multa de verborum arte, deque virtutibus et humana sapientia loquutus est,
vera utique et idcirco veritatis Deo absque ulla dubitatione gratissima.'
[2] cf. *Fam.*, VI. ii. 310.

gems for identification when they dug them up in their fields, the new
generations searched far and near. There are still slight errors in
Poggio's topography of Rome, but his lament on the reversal of
Virgil's line about the Capitol[1] is a sign that before long Raphael will
be inspector of monuments in Rome, enquiring into the principles
of beauty in ancient buildings. From that enquiry there had already
come, anticipatorily, the unity of classical building, as against the
multiplicity of parts in Gothic architecture. But it is not only architecture which changes its appearance in the fifteenth century: the re-
discovery of classical art brings with it the revolution by which the
ascetic principles of Byzantine painting are finally forgotten. Mâle
observed that the medieval tradition was killed by the art of the
Renascence. The Middle Ages had expressed in the visual arts all the
humble sides of the soul: suffering, sadness, resignation, acceptance
of the divine will. The art of the Renascence had as its highest
expression the nude human figure, its hidden spirit was pride.[2] The
antithesis of Mâle is not quite accurate, and I have noted already that the
grotesques and the misericords of medieval art echo the contradiction
between life and theory, between action and reaction. In art, as elsewhere, the Middle Ages is a compound of blind reverence and disrespect for reverence. But the tendency upwards in Renascence art is
visible enough; nor can the wriggling of neo-scholastics alter it.
'Senza paura di sbagliare, si può asserire che gli artisti, i quali hanno
talvolta dipinto certi Crocifissi spaventosi, avevano nell'anima più
letizia, che non gli Umanisti e gli uomini redenti e sghignazzanti della
Rinascenza.'[3] That is the old procedure, by abuse on the one hand,
and by a proposition proved by reference to itself on the other.
Does the *sghignazzanti* describe the Michaelangelo of the Adam, the
Raphael of the Galatea, or the Giorgione of the sleeping Venus? It is
instead the result of relying too much on ready-made opinions about
the Renascence, an echo of De Sanctis or Gregorovius.[4] The spirit
of Renascence art is a serious one, in spite of, or because of, its pride
in the human form. And it is also plain, I think, that such a movement and so vast a production cannot depend on imitation of a past
epoch, but must be intimately connected with the realities of the
present outlook. It is not possible to divorce the artistic expression

---

[1] 'Aurea nunc olim silvestribus horrida dumis
  Aurea quondam, nunc squalida spinetis vepribusque referta.'
[2] E. Mâle, *L'art religieux de la fin du moyen âge*. V. discussion in Olgiati, *op. cit.*, 188.
[3] Olgiati, 203.
[4] It is the latter perhaps who sees the leer appearing most often on Renascence faces. cf.
Storia di Roma, tr. Manzato, VII-VIII.

of the Renascence from the movement of humanism from which it sprang. The two names to which we are coming—Lorenzo Valla and Leon Battista Alberti—are there, each in its own way to forbid any attempt at separation. And it must be equally clear that the signal for the change had been given by Petrarch. He had not only spread the enthusiasm by which antiquity was explored, and its message accepted; but without coming into any opposition with the Church (indeed, while trying to hold fast to a medieval asceticism) he had provided the sanction for the enjoyment of one's being. Once more the attitude of Montaigne depends ultimately on that of Petrarch, and in the fifteenth century the rehabilitation of Epicure was inevitable. So inevitable was it that it springs simultaneously in more than one writer,[1] while all shades of Epicureanism, genuine or spurious, can be found. We have seen the link that unites Pius II to the humanistic educators, and we have seen how he does not wish to banish either pleasures in moderation, or temptation, its resistance being another element in character. That hint of a changed atmosphere may make it less surprising that Aeneas Sylvius could declare of Epicure that he was great once, and now reproved in words rather than in deeds by the philosophers of the present time. 'For how many are there, even among the theologians, who do not serve pleasure?— Since there are two ways, within which all human life is contained, one of virtues, the other of pleasures: the one deserted, uncultivated, shut in by leaves and bushes, the other always full of men, nor is there anyone who does not yield to pleasure.'[2] That is the moralist taking an exaggerated view of a movement in which he is himself a part, but it will serve to inform us as to the strength of the movement itself, and to warn us of the dilemma which was to arise. In the meantime, we have, as we might perhaps expect, an ambiguous work, in which we cannot quite be sure whether the extreme or the moderate statement of Epicureanism is to be taken as valid: the *De Voluptate* of Valla. But in approaching Valla we must not forget that the acceptance of Epicure was prepared by Petrarch himself, in spite of his denial personally of Epicure and all his infamous flock. And once the gate had been opened for Epicure the means of exclusion have been hard to come by.

---

[1] For a survey, and especially for Cosmo Raimondi, cf. Saitta, *La rivendicazione d'Epicuro nell'umanesimo* in the book *Filosofia Italiana e Umanesimo* (1928).

[2] E. S. P., *Op.*, 725. 'Nam quotus est obsecro, vel theologorum qui voluptatibus non inserviat?—Cumque duae viae sint, quibus humana vita continetur, altera virtutum, altera voluptatum: illa deserta, inculta atque interclusa frondibus et virgultis: haec semper hominum frequentia, nec quisquam est qui voluptati non obsequatur.'

To connect Valla, who may seem to be a contradiction, rather than a continuation, with Petrarch needs, perhaps, some preface, or some excuse. The *Dialogi ad Petrum Histrum* had had as interlocutors Coluccio Salutati, Niccolò Niccoli and Leonardo Bruni himself; the *De Voluptate* is put into the mouths of Bruni,[1] Panormita and Niccoli, and this small detail may suggest that the search for continuity of thread in humanism is not, at least, illegitimate. And Valla also was one of the first to hold a chair of rhetoric and eloquence, the establishment of which in the universities by the side of the former chairs of medicine, law, astronomy, was an innovation due to the new ideas on education. We have seen the reasons for insistence on eloquence in Petrarch and his continuators. Valla is so closely linked to them that he can deny the possibility of separating books good by their moral content from those that are beautiful, because there can be no good books written badly. 'Thus either eloquent books, or none at all, are to be read.'[2] As with his predecessors, that does not mean that he attaches no importance to content, but that he attaches so much that the form must be consonant. Without elegance and Latinity, that is, without the studies which Petrarch initiated, all learning is blind.[3] It is an affirmation comparable to that of Aeneas Sylvius. Valla adds the specific assertion that without the new humanities no branch of studies can be pursued.[4] That suggests in him a Romanity which is, indeed, one of his most prominent characteristics. I have emphasised only very casually Petrarch's belief in Rome, partly because it has been insisted on time and time again (it was one of the few ideas which could bring Petrarch close to insipience, as when he once spoke of other peoples preferring a harmful and ambiguous liberty rather than embrace the safe and salutary rule of the universal Mother[5]). Valla shows considerable independence. He reverses often the ranking of individual Greek and Latin authors, not hesitating to rate the first above the second now that he has with Greek literature the acquaintance Petrarch lacked,[6] and he spiritualises the empire of Rome even more than Petrarch had done. Rome gave laws, the path to all wisdom, and the transformation from barbarity to civilisation. Who is there impartial in his judgments who will not prefer the nobility of

---

[1] For Bruni's attitude to Epicure, cf. Saitta, *La rivendicazione d'Epicuro nell'umanesimo*.

[2] Toffanin, *Che cosa fu l'umanesimo*, 90. 'Ita aut eloquentes aut nulli libri legendi sunt.'

[3] Valla, *Elegantiarum*, III, Proem. 80. 'Latinitatis atque elegantiae sine qua caeca omnis doctrina est.'

[4] ibid., 'Persuadeamque sine studiis humanitatis non posse, quam cupiunt assequi facultatem.'

[5] *Sine Tit.*, IV. 790. 'Tutum et salutare publicae matris imperium . . . amplecti.'

[6] Nor (cf. Tommasini, II. 656) to rate St. Paul's eloquence above that of Demosthenes.

those who cultivated letters to that of those waging horrid war?[1] Petrarch did not divide the activities, or the qualities, of the Romans quite so sharply.

Petrarch had rejected the legal studies of his time because of their aridity and insufficiency. He had tilted against their exponents, who were concerned with law only as a means of gain; but he had expressed the opinion that a true legal science, in other conditions, might exist. His procedure was, here as in other places, to illumine by his intuition what was bad, and then to excise that branch of knowledge from his consideration. Those who built on Petrarch's foundations (if I may mix my metaphors) had time to demolish piecemeal the edifices which he marked down for attack. Thus Valla moves against the lawyers (he had, perhaps, as an additional incentive the inferiority of his own emoluments as a professor of rhetoric to those carried by the older chairs). They derive their power from their practical acquaintance, in the dissolution of society, with the labyrinths of the legal code, a superiority not of intelligence, but of experience and vested interest. From the code of Justinian down to the law-books of the fifteenth century is a record of constant accretion, gloss upon gloss, in which the spirit of the law had long since been suffocated. Ulpian and Sulpitius—the last of the swans—had handled the law with ease and equity; but the geese of the present, Accursio, Baldo, Bartolo, use it with harshness, iniquity and injustice. Their books in volume seem designed to be borne by pack-horses rather than by men: in worth they are to be despised openly.[2] Against this perversion of practice Valla sets a principle, none the less valid in that it derives from Quintilian: 'All law consists either in the interpretation of words, or in the distinction between what is just and what is unjust.'[3] That is Valla's own method of approach, the practical reason for his conviction that without an accurate knowledge of the Latin tongue the accretions could not be cut away. Valla is a philologist, but he is so because it seems to him that he can best proceed from the interpretation of words to the distinction between what is just and unjust. The Romans had admitted an admixture of Greek, but these moderns have admitted an admixture of *Gothic*. Hence the necessity for the minute examination of the Latin language. By some this has been accounted the chief contribution of those pedants the

---

[1] Valla, *Eleg.*, Proem. 3. 'Quare quis aequus rerum aestimator non eos praeferat qui sacra litterarum colentes, iis, qui bella horrida gerentes clari fuerunt?'

[2] Barozzi, *Studî sul Panormita e sul Valla*, 180. For Voltaire, cf. *supra* 46, n. 2.

[3] Valla, *Eleg.*, III, Proem., 80. 'Omne ius aut in verborum interpretatione positum est: aut aequi pravique discrimine.'

humanists: the establishment of the principles of orthography, the rules of grammar, the laws of rhetoric and elocution.[1] But as before with eloquence, so here with Valla's philology, the reasons for his attitude are explicit: 'I do not speak thus to carp at study of civil law, but rather to exhort to it; and to persuade men that they cannot obtain that command of the subject which they desire without the study of the humanities.'[2] Valla's constant procedure is from the concrete to the abstract. It is one which has been formulated as philosophical questions arising from philological decisions; and it would be only if the *Elegantiae* were the sole constituent of Valla's work that strictures such as Monnier's would have any meaning when applied to him. In the matter of the law his attack, which I have sketched in lightly to show the connection with Petrarch's standpoint, is purely destructive, and purely literary: that is, it involved no creation of a legal system. But it has been asserted that a comparison of the barbarous medieval jurists with Budé and the great legal reformers of the sixteenth century leaves no explanation of the vast gap other than the merit of Valla. At least, Petrarch and Budé might equally have subscribed to Valla's statement of the humanities as the essential background to the study of law.

Petrarch, with his conception of the primacy of Plato, had attacked the dominating position of Aristotle. As we have seen, in face of all the philosophers of Antiquity he reserved his liberty of judgment, and his Christianity. But in view of the complete ascendancy of the authority of Aristotle accepted by so many of his time he spoke his mind about him often and explicitly. 'I think that Aristotle was a great man and of much learning, but that he was a man, and therefore ignorant of some things, even of many. . . . I believe without a doubt that he went wrong not only in little matters, where error is not very dangerous, but in great ones also, and that in those pertaining to salvation he was wholly off the track.'[3] This authority of Petrarch for the scrutiny, at least, of Aristotle was seized on by Leonardo Bruni; and Valla attacks Aristotle in similar terms. The commentators and translators through whose hands the texts of Aristotle had passed

---

[1] cf. Monnier, 212. 'Le style fut, en effet, leur préoccupation dominante. On peut même affirmer qu'il fut leur préoccupation unique,' and what follows.

[2] Valla, *Eleg.*, III, Pr. 'Veteres admiscebant linguae suae Graecam. Isti admiscent Gothicam Neque vero hoc dico ut iuris studiosos carpam: immo ut adhorter potius: persuadeamque sine studiis humanitatis non posse quam cupiunt assequi facultatem.'

[3] *De. Ign.*, 40. 'Ego vero magnum quendam virum ac multiscium Aristotilem, sed fuisse hominem, et idcirco aliqua, imo et multa nescire potuisse arbitror. . . . Credo hercle, nec dubito, illum non in rebus tantum parvis et ubi minime periculosus est error, sed in maximis et spectantibus ad salutis summam aberrasse tota, ut aiunt, via.'

were ignorant: Averroes, Avicenna and the rest knew no Latin, and little Greek, though it is precisely from the value of words that philosophical questions spring. But who after Boethius knew any Latin, who was not wholly barbarous? And on the other hand, Aristotle himself was not the Hercules of the heroes, since though he wrote much, he also compiled from others without citing them, or even while he was deriding them.[1] Again, the terms are very close to Petrarch's: 'I know that much can be learnt from his books, but I think that something can be learnt outside them as well, and have no doubt that before Aristotle wrote, before he learnt, before he was born, much was known to others.'[2] But this derivation from Petrarch must not mislead us with regard to the originality and the independence of his mind. Although the beginning of the fifteenth century derives, willy nilly, from Petrarch there is some possibility, in Valla's estimation, of Petrarch being engulfed in the trough of barbaric Latin after Boethius. Nor did Valla show any inclination to deny the sovereignty of Aristotle in order to establish that of another; and signs that the liberty of Valla's judgment is not impeded by the authority of Petrarch are not hard to find. He has neither the fervid admiration of Petrarch, nor the formal reverence of the sixteenth century, for Cicero, and is not afraid to place him after Quintilian in his estimation. He is among the first to prefer Demosthenes to Cicero, to place Pindar and Homer before Horace and Virgil, Sallust before Livy, Thucydides before Herodotus, Dionysius before Cicero. With more information, he has no longer Petrarch's need of the general affirmation of Roman superiority. In fact, for an admirer of Rome, he shows himself at times iconoclastic: after the Brutists and the Catoists he rises to assert the superiority of Caesar over Scipio. Cato, for Valla, killed himself out of envy. If we are to divide between Petrarch and Valla the two nerves of the mind proclaimed by Gibbon, then Petrarch's will be curiosity and Valla's will be scepticism. So acid is his mind that not even Lucretia does he accept without a query.[3]

It is for reasons such as these that Valla has been recognised as the first critical mind of his time. It has been asserted that he was the first to ask himself the question: Is this fact possible? Does it agree with what the writer says elsewhere, and with what others say?[4] And thus he denied the authority of Livy with regard to the Tarquins, showing

[1] Barozzi, 180.

[2] *De Ign.*, 72. 'Scio in libris eius multa disci posse, sed et extra sciri aliquid posse credo, et antequam Aristoteles scriberet, antequam disceret, antequam nasceretur, multa aliquos scisse non dubito.'

[3] cf. Barozzi, 203.   [4] ibid., 223.

him at variance with himself, and with Dionysius. 'Is any man better than reason? Or is the authority of reason worse in any way than that of a man?'[1] It is not a remark that suggests any servility in its author towards any period, or any single author; and we may put it against the remark of Vittorino quoted earlier on the reliability of Livy. But again Valla is not quite first in inventing a historical criticism. The preface to the *De Viris Illustribus* already suggested the necessity of some such labour: 'Some details which were lacking in one author I have supplied from another, some I have shortened, some made more clear; some, where brevity made for obscurity, I have put at more length; some which were scattered in various authors I have pieced together, and from the account of several made one narrative.'[2] And apart from that general, and somewhat elementary, statement with regard to the *De Viris* there is one particular instance of Petrarch anticipating clearly the method of Valla. It is in the letter to Charles IV on the falseness of the privilege by which Austria was claimed to be outside the jurisdiction of the Empire.[3] What are its terms? 'Nos inquit Iulius Caesar Imperator, nos Caesar, et cultor Deorum, nos supremus terrae Imperialis Augustus et reliqua. . . .'[4] Petrarch objected to the plural *nos*, to *Augustus*, first used by Julius Caesar's successor. He rejected as spurious the date, 'datum Romae die Veneris, regni nostri anno primo.'[5] A date without the consul and the month? And what of *regni*? 'Caesar, as you have heard, styled himself Imperator, Pontifex and Dictator. Never King.'[6] Doubtless, the forgery was a clumsy one; but the merit of the essay in demolition lies in its novelty. It is in accordance with the formula that was to be Valla's that it was carried out, and the letter to Charles IV is the prelude to the examination of the Donation of Constantine.

The minute scrutiny of the Latin language was undertaken by Valla in the *Elegantiarum Linguae Latinae*, a work which filled so important a place that Erasmus said one must take account of it as of the nails and fingers of one's hands.[7] It was a work sufficiently competent to hold its place throughout the next century as well as in its own. Erasmus epitomised it at the age of eighteen, and it sold in Paris faster than Erasmus' own *Adages* even when Erasmus himself was in Paris. And Erasmus retained his admiration for the mind of Valla, consider-

---

[1] Barozzi, 232. 'An melius ullus homo est quam ratio? Nunquid deterius est rationis quam hominis ratio?'

[2] 'Quaedam enim, quae apud unum absunt, ab altero mutuatus sum, quaedam brevius, quaedam clarius, quaedam, quae apud alios carptim dicta erant, conjunxi, et ex diversorum dictis unum feci.'

[3] *Sen.*, XV. v. 1055 ss.   [4] ibid., 1056.   [5] ibid.   [6] ibid.   [7] Mancini, *Valla*, 273.

ing him the author of the resurrection in criticism and humanism. His intentions in the *Elegantiae* were clear: to destroy the old edifice, sweep out the barbarous Latin, and return by means of grammatical studies to purity. He was convinced that such a study was not to be despised, and that something new could be added even to the work of the ancients (remember Petrarch's answer to the idea that all had been accomplished in Antiquity). But one must go back to Priscian, Servius and Donatus, and abandon the medievals who make the learner more foolish than he was before: 'the first of these is Isidore, most arrogant of the unlearned: one who, since he knows nothing, teaches everything. . . . People teaching you to know nothing at a huge price, or making their pupils more stupid than when they took them on.'[1] The grandiose edifice of learning had been supported by one language, which diffused the light of civilisation to all peoples; and while it flourished there flourished with it the liberal arts, law and wisdom, so that it was the vehicle of thought in the same way as money is the medium of exchange. The pacific temper of Petrarch is inherited by Valla, even, as I have suggested, accentuated. He does not lament over the fall of Roman domination, or desire to resurrect it. The restoration that he desires is the basis, in the Latin language, of learning; and it is a piety towards Italy, but also towards all mankind as well, which prompts his desire.[2] The culture of Rome deserved more fame than the arts of war, and the fruits of the Latin language were more noble, as of the mind rather than of the body.[3] Petrarch had been at times a little more dazzled by the military ascendancy of Rome. There is another modification to be noticed in this preface to the *Elegantiae*: the liberal arts appear, as with Petrarch, as the concern of the mind, and the mind is still by definition more noble than the body. But there is not the sharp opposition to them of the mechanical ones. The humanities will allow the resurrection of those arts which come next to the liberal ones, as painting, sculpture, modelling, architecture. All these have been degenerate: they died with Letters, and in humanistic times they will be roused and resurrected.[4] This return to an intellectual

---

[1] Valla, *Eleg.*, II, Pr., 41. Only stammerers after trio above: 'quorum primus est Isidorus indoctorum arrogantissimus: qui cum nihil sciat: omnia praecipit . . . alii . . . magna mercede docentes nihil scire: aut stultiorem reddentes discipulum quam acceperunt.'

[2] *Eleg.*, Pr., 4. 'Pro mea in patriam pietate: immo adeo in omnes homines.'

[3] ibid., 3. 'Optimam frugem et vere divinam: nec corporis, sed animi cibum.'

[4] ibid., 4. 'Illae artes quae proxime ad liberales accedunt: pingendi: scalpendi: fingendi; architectandi: aut tan diu tantoque opere degeneraverint: ac pene cum literis ipsis demortuae fuerint: aut hoc tempore excitentur ac reviviscant.'

interpretation of the ideas of Vitruvius[1] heralds the change in the status of the artist, as much as it announces the revolution in his practice. Henceforth he stands with the humanist, and the *proxime accessit* of Valla will change by the end of the century to a position of equality. That raising of the artist's status[2] was inevitable from the moment that Petrarch turned men's attention to the remains of antiquity; but it is not idle to insist how quickly and how clearly it is announced by Valla. This, on the one side, is the forward prospect, and the programme. In retrospect, it is significant that Valla does not minimise the merit of the Church, when with the fall of the Roman Empire the vehicle of thought had failed, and with it had failed also the whole light of civilisation. Any survival was due to the Church, which took the Latin language to itself; and the renascence of learning was only possible inside Christianity.[3] It is especially to be noted that Valla does not think in terms of a hostility between Christianity and humanism: there is no surer proof of the origins of humanism in the thought of Petrarch. Petrarch introduced Cicero (that is, moral philosophy) to fill the blank in the ideas on this world in medieval Christianity. Valla will go further still, and propose the absorption of Epicure into the system of Christianity. But since the steps forward are logically dependent on the initial impulse given by Petrarch Valla will not be conscious of opposition, any more than Vittorino was.[4] Rather he will be irritated by those who anticipate the celebrated anecdote of Bembo repudiating the missal as dangerous for one's latinity. Fazio, one of the many whom Valla attacked, objected strongly to Valla's quotation of St. Jerome, as one unworthy of *imitation*. 'Have you ever read him? I asked.—Indeed no, I shouldn't want to have read an African and a Barbarian.—If you haven't read him, I said, how can you condemn him?'[5] This attitude can be confirmed elsewhere, and in people whom one might not suspect of it. Thus Filelfo expressed his amazement at the insipience of some, who when they hear a saying or an example aptly taken from a Christian text change countenance or look away, as if offended; the same people exult and show pleasure if they hear something taken

[1] cf. Vitruvius, *De Architectura*, I. i.

[2] cf. Blunt, *Artistic Theory in Italy*, 1450-1600 (1940), and *Modern Language Review*, XXXVII. i. 99-100.

[3] Barozzi, 161.

[4] I stress the point because of the common view, for which cf. Monnier, 90: 'L'humanisme qui est né en dehors de l'Eglise, qui, à tout prendre, est né contre l'Eglise. . . .' V. *supra*, 40.

[5] Mancini, 60. 'Facius insanire coepit et Hieronymum carpere tamquam indignum quem imitemur. An eum lectitasti inquam? Ne vellem quidem, inquit, Afrum et Barbarum lectitasse. Si non legisti, inquam, quo pacto damnare potes?'

from the fables of the poets and the gods of the Gentiles.[1] Meanwhile, in devoting himself to a task which is in itself something of a sacrament[2] Valla has no thought of destroying the major revelation. The business of the *Elegantiae* is to prepare the way for progress on every side: it is a work of abnegation and devotion, but for a practical purpose. As Valla says himself, others will write history, orations, poems, translate from the Greek. These are things worthy of praise, but they will not drive the enemy away from the land. Camillus is wanted to bring back the standards and restore the fatherland. 'I go into battle . . . to make others more eager in other pursuits as well.'[3] It is not philology an abstraction from, a renunciation of, life; but philology which is to be the liberator from barbarity and the prelude to the activity of the Renascence. That is why it is essential to remember that the arts (in our sense of the word) have advanced from being mechanical to being next to poetry, history, oration: they also are to be liberated by the work of humanism.

Valla's merits are not limited to the devotion which inspired the *Elegantiae*, and the originality of his mind is best illustrated elsewhere: in destructive criticism, the treatise on the Donation of Constantine; in positive contribution, that on Pleasure as the True Good. Before examining these, there are several minor points which will suggest the quality of Valla's mind. He had all Petrarch's contempt for prejudices and superstitions (he laughs at the wasp's nest in Vespasian's nostrils, the frog to which Nero gave birth—hence *Laterano*), and the progress of knowledge made it possible for judgment to rest on more than on the intuition of irrelevancy. Valla rejected the Bible which was attributed to the hand of St. Jerome himself with the aid of palaeography, by which he proved its ascription to a scribe of King Robert of Naples. He dismissed the legend of the images of Peter and Paul which had been shown to Constantine by Sylvester with the remark that more than ten thousand of them were revered. These are specimens of the alertness of his mind, and of its quickness to criticism.[4] Where he uses his own method of distinctions arising from words he can be disconcerting. Petrarch had praised the retirement of the monks, but for Valla the vow of the religious was a misnomer. It is,

---

[1] Mancini, 60. 'Soleo nonnunquam mirari quorumdam inscitiam, qui cum aliquod aut exemplum aut dictum e fidei christianae religione vel tempestive apteque depromptum audierint, tamquam offensi et mutant vultum et avertant faciem, iidem si quid e poetarum fabulis atque gentium diis exceperint laeti exhilaratique exsultant.'

[2] *Eleg.*, Pr., 5.

[3] ibid., 'Ibo in aciem . . . ut redderem alios quoque ad caetera prosequenda alacriores.'

[4] And cf. Tommasini, II. 654-5 for the influence of Valla's criticism on Erasmus and Luther.

in effect, an oath, a thing, that is, which, far from adding to the merit of human actions, had been specifically condemned more than once by the Church. And as for obedience to poverty and chastity, if these are virtues, yet one must remember that so also is the power to command wisely, the right use of riches, and the sanctity of marriage. Rather, those who reach a goal to which they are not pressed by a tie have more merit than those who are forced throughout their progress.[1] Of two men who were ill, one needed four men to hold him in an operation, the other none: whose courage shall we praise? The staff is for those who slip, medicine is for those who ail; those who fear dig camps to guard themselves, the bold go forth to battle.[2] Besides, as he reminded Eugenius IV, this insistence on obedience is derogatory to the Holy See: for if only those who obey can be safe, what then is the position of the Pope? The praise for the social, as against the solitary, ideal goes back to Petrarch; but Petrarch would have been the first to be embarrassed by the sharpness of Valla's logic. Similarly, where Valla derives from others in the same tradition, he does other than echo their words. In the *De Libero Arbitrio* he makes, like Coluccio Salutati, an attempt to reconcile the prescience of God with the free will of man. It is a reconciliation which does not differ materially from that of Salutati: to foresee is not to produce the evils which come from demerits. But the opuscule advances more interesting opinions *en passant*. Could Sextus Tarquinius alter his destiny by prayer and the promise of amendment of his conduct? No. Why? Because, just as God created the wolf rapacious, the lion bold, the hare timid, the ass stupid, the dog ill-tempered, the sheep mild, so with men he made the hearts of some hard, of others soft, some inclined to wickedness, others more to virtue. That has nothing to do with Coluccio's lame conclusions, and will prove on examination, I imagine, incompatible with a Christian standpoint. Apart from the fact that Valla places the responsibility on God—since He is the creator of the minds and inclinations—while the behaviourists place it on a complex resulting from race, organism and milieu (the same things, that is, without a Creator), conduct is equally reduced to a necessity. That conclusion is a by-product in Valla's thought, and I do not think that he sub-

---

[1] Valla, *De Professione Religiosorum*.

[2] Valla, *Contra Calumniatorem Apologia*, 799. 'Etenim via a Christo tradita nulla est tutior, sicut nec melior, in qua nulla professio nobis iniungitur. At vita ipsorum, inquiunt, ab illa Christi non discreptat. Sane vero, sed ne aliorum quidem, nec enim in solis cucullatis vita Christi custoditur. Et vestri duces, atque autores istius disciplinae, sapienter illi quidem existimarunt, tutius esse uti baculo, sed lapsantibus, et medicina, sed aegrotantibus, et ad tutelam confodere castrorum, sed in aciem prodire metuentibus.'

scribed fully to it. Rather, he adheres to the very opposite ideas of Petrarch on the importance of the will. He says, for example: 'Doubtless, evil is not to know evil things, but to will them,'[1] a distinction which the English have often been accused of forgetting. And is not the labour of the *Elegantiae* an effort of the will towards improvement? But Valla's mind is rich enough to light the sparks of heterodoxy where it passes. And what is important is the freedom to express such opinions. Petrarch, in the *De Ignorantia*, exclaimed on the pitfalls represented by the number of the sects, the waywardness of opinions, the ambiguity of things and the perplexity of words: 'Truly, in this great dearth of knowledge, when human pride opens its unfeathered wings to the wind, how frequent and how hard are the rocks!'[2] But he supported his general lament with particular examples, and although he concluded modestly that it is enough to know as much as suffices for salvation, he opened the gate for speculation and heterodoxy. For the first time, perhaps, since the suppression of the Schools of Athens it had become possible for the Western mind to dispute freely on the important problem of human existence and the universe. The possibility for the flouting of authority which appears with Valla rests on two things: the strength afforded by an increasing erudition, which had fortified the judgment by offering to the eye of the critic a larger store of materials (and Petrarch's list is after all prophetic as much as it is retrospective); and secondly, the fact that humanism grew up under the aegis of the Church. From Petrarch to Valla humanism is not concerned with speculation; but with Valla the shift from the ground of Petrarch is clear enough for an element of speculation to be creeping back. Indeed, it is with Valla, at one point, that the split seemed inevitable. Blamed by Eugenius IV for the expression of his opinion in the *De Voluptate* he made bold to defend himself in apology addressed to the Pope. In this he protested vigorously against the use of theological weapons in a philosophic dispute: are not all the philosophers equally condemned by the Church? 'If I proposed a philosophic disputation is it not against the rules of the argument to attack me with the weapons of theology, that is, from the back, not from the front?'[3] From that statement he goes on to a very sure rehabilitation of Epicure, but in the meantime it is to be observed that if we took him at his word we should see re-estab-

---

[1] *Cont. Cal. Ap.*, 798, bis. v. 'Haud dubie malum non sit mala nosse, sed velle.'

[2] *De Ign.*, 58. 'Sane in hac tanta scientiae inopia, ubi implumes alas vento aperit humana superbia, quam frequentes et quam duri scopuli!'

[3] *Cont. Cal.*, 797. 'Quid si de philosophia certamen proposui, nonne praeter legem certaminis est aggredi me Theologiae armis, idque a tergo, non a fronte?'

lished what had been out of sight since Petrarch—the doctrine of the two truths ('Nothing here of the miracles of God, since I am discussing natural things naturally'—as opposed to the idea of 'all true things true from the Truth').[1] That possibility of a divorce between Truth and truth—and it means ultimately, of course, the imputation of false-hood to the first of these two terms—is significant of the boldness of Valla's mind. Barozzi will maintain that the divorce, an emancipation frustrated in Italy by the Council of Trent, would have permitted giant strides in the science of thought. That, again, may be true; though if it is, it is clear also that it involves the rejection of Chris-tianity itself. But, once more, we must not exaggerate, or we shall miss the focus of Valla's main position. I have suggested the cleavage for the benefit of those who may find distasteful his contribution to the Ciceronian conception of Christianity which was the legacy of Petrarch.

It is time to exemplify the originality of Valla in his main contribu-tions, where both the destructive and the constructive side is of importance. The common charge against the humanists has been that they lived outside the real world, in an imitative one of their own. The riddling of the false privilege by Petrarch and the demolition of the Donation of Constantine by Valla are part of the case for humanism as a return to realities. When criticism, and criticism alone, can destroy a fabric that has lasted for centuries in spite of its falseness, then the nerves of the mind are not only functioning in individuals, but have received some general recognition. It was claimed for the Papacy that Constantine, having the intention to found a new capital in the East, had no further use for the western portion of his empire, and renounced its temporal dominion to his converter, Sylvester. Dante (and the reasons are well known) deplored this donation, though it did not occur to him to suspect the Church of forgery, and it remained essentially unchallenged till Valla's treatise. This, in the brilliance of its language, and the clarity of its arguments, is one of the most remarkable documents of its century. But if Valla had Petrarch as a predecessor in the method he employed, he had him as a predecessor also in the conception of the Papacy which inspires the *De falso credita et ementita Constantini donatione Declamatio*; and it is a different conception from that of the *De Monarchia*. There is a chapter in the *De Remediis* on the Papacy, which I might have adduced earlier as evidence for that institution before it was affected by humanism or

---

[1] Toffanin, *Storia dell'Umanesimo*, 19, for Siger de Brabant: 'Sed nihil ad nos nunc de Dei miraculis, cum de naturalibus naturaliter disseramus.' For Petrarch, cf. *supra*, 39, n. 1.

the Renascence. The first popes were called from that office to their martyrdom, but now they think themselves called to enjoyment. 'You will be styled Servant of Servants, beware lest you should wish to become the Lord of Lords.'[1] The vigour with which Valla insists on this conception is witness against the divorce whose possibility I have mentioned; it is also, I think, to be connected with Machiavelli's views on the Papacy.

Valla's beginning is bold, and would be astonishingly so if one did not remember that he was under the protection of Alfonso of Naples when he wrote. He recalls his many writings, and his differences of opinion with many approved authors, so that already to some he had seemed rash and sacrilegious. What will happen now when he is writing, not against the dead, but against the living, not against private individuals, but against the Pope himself, armed not only, in the fashion of kings, with the temporal sword, but with the ecclesiastical one as well? There is nothing in this double terror to frighten Valla, or to make him quit his purpose. The Pope cannot bind or loose unjustly, and to sacrifice one's life in the defence of truth and justice is praiseworthy.[2] The cause of truth (*causa veritatis, causa iusticiae, causa Dei*) demands courage: nor is a man worthy of the name of orator if he knows how to speak well, but only if he dares to speak.[3] For a private fault, a private rebuke; but a public one for those who admit no private counsel, just as Paul reproved Peter. 'But I am not Paul to be able to reprove Peter. Or rather, I am Paul if I imitate Paul.'[4] These are blunt words: consonant, indeed, with the freedom of tone which Petrarch used towards Urban V on the long continuance of the Babylonian captivity of Avignon, and to be observed by those who think that after Dante no-one dares to raise his voice above a servile whisper.

These are the preliminaries: what of the argument? The claim of the Donation was that the whole of the Western Empire, Rome itself, the two Sicilies, all Italy, France, Germany, Britain, were handed over to the temporal jurisdiction of the Popes. 'But I think that it would be permissible rather for the rulers to strip you of all the

---

[1] *De Rem.*, I. cvii. 90 (*De Pontificatu*). 'Solebant primi ex hoc statu ad martyrium peti, nunc ad delitias vocari credunt. . . . Servorum Servus diceris, cave ne dominorum dominus fieri velis.'

[2] Valla, *De donatione*, 761. 'Et in defendenda veritate et iusticia profundere animam summae virtutis, summae laudis, summi praemii est.'

[3] ibid., 762. 'Neque enim is verus habendus orator, qui bene scit dicere, nisi et dicere audeat.'

[4] ibid., 'At non sum Paulus, qui Petrum possim reprehendere. Imo Paulus sum, qui Paulum imitor.'

dominion that you possess,' said Valla to the Pope by way of statement of principle.[1] The donation is unlikely both from silence and
from human nature (*cupiditas regni*); but this latter may have been
changed in Constantine by his conversion. If it was, then Constantine
should have given liberty to his cities, not changed their ruler; and
is it more religious to lay down rule than to administer it for the
benefit of religion?[2] On Sylvester's side, the example of the prophets
and of Christ barred the way to his acceptance of the gift. Elijah
would receive nothing for the cure of Naaman. Christ spurned
the temptation in the wilderness (*Freely thou hast received, freely give*).
Valla puts into Sylvester's mouth the words a Christian Pope should
have used at such an offer: 'And do we so renounce earthly goods in
order that we may attain to them in richer measure? Have we cast
away private possessions, so that we may possess what belongs to
others, and to the public? . . . Of what use to me are riches and
wealth when I am bidden by the voice of the Lord to take no care for
the morrow? . . . I fear, Caesar, that you will make me, from Peter,
into Judas. . . . My kingdom, he said, is not of this world.'[3] I have
quoted Voltaire before, to show that he has something of the same
concern as Petrarch: but Voltaire combines that concern with the
polemical ability of Valla, and on this point he speaks with a complete
identity of terms: 'N'est-ce pas encore une plaisante contradiction de
se faire petit à petit cent mille écus de rentes précisément parce
qu'on a fait voeu de pauvreté?'[4] Or, at least, the method is identical
if the point at issue varies slightly: Voltaire was attacking the wealth
of the convents rather than the rule of the Church. There is, then,
a *prima facie* case why the donation should not have taken place, both
sides having reasons urging them against it. But suppose it nevertheless to have taken place: where is the taking of possession, where the
handing over? Did Constantine never lead Sylvester in triumph to
the Capitol? or to the Senate? did he not lead him through Italy,
or into Gaul? If not in person, at least by proxy? And when he
went away, what governors of provinces and cities did Sylvester
appoint? and who cast him from his possession? Name the date, name

[1] ibid., 762. 'At ego contra existimo, iustius licere principibus spoliare te imperio omni quod
obtines.'

[2] ibid., 764. 'Quasi religiosum sit magis, regnum deponere quam pro tutela religionis illud
administrare.'

[3] ibid., 768. 'Ideone terrenis renunciamus, ut eadem uberiora assequamur? Et privata
abiecimus, ut aliena possideamus, et publica? . . . Quo mihi divitias ac opes, qui domini voce
iubeor nec de crastino esse sollicitus? . . . Itaque vereor Caesar, ne me ex Petro facias Iudam.
. . . Regnum meum, inquit, non est de hoc mundo.'

[4] Voltaire, *Conversation de M. L'Intendant des Menus avec M. L'Abbé Grizel.*

the person who despoiled the popes of their new dominions? 'O wonderful, says Valla, the Roman Empire, born in such struggles and with so much blood, is won and lost so quietly, so placidly, by the Popes that no bloodshed, no war, no quarrel intervened.'[1] And what is no less to be wondered at, the who, the when, the how, the how long is all unknown. What? We know the consuls of ancient Rome, the dukes of Athens, the kings of the Medes, Persians, Chaldeans, Hebrews; no name escapes us. Yet we are ignorant *in* Rome *of* Rome? The laws of the ancients were inscribed on metal and stone: is this unheard of donation a scrap of paper only, and a scrap inserted at some date in the Decretals of Gratian? There is the silence of the codices, and of Jacopo de Voragine, an archbishop. Yet the author of the *Golden Legend* was not lacking in credulity! Again, in this triumphant argument from silence there is a plain parallel with an attack of Voltaire: 'Je ne vous conseille pas de parler des miracles de Moïse devant des gens qui ont de la barbe au menton. Si tous ces prodiges avaient été opérés, les Egyptiens en auraient parlé dans leurs histoires. La mémoire de tant de faits prodigieux qui étonnent la nature se serait conservée chez toutes les nations. Les Grecs, qui ont été instruits de toutes les fables de l'Egypte et de la Syrie, auraient fait retentir le bruit de ces actions surnaturelles aux deux bouts du monde. Mais aucun historien, ni grec, ni syrien, ni égyptien, n'en dit un seul mot. . . .'[2] Is Voltaire more chimerical, or Valla (and with him humanism) more real than had been supposed? On the other side Valla asserts that the conversion of Constantine took place before the pontificate of Sylvester, and in the reign of Melchiades, to whom he gave the Lateran and a few private gifts. There is extant a medal of Constantine, still Emperor, and yet already Christian—a practical detail, like the appeal to palaeography before. But more especially, what of the text? Its Latin is corrupt, its sense is even more spurious. It gave supremacy to the Pope over four sees—Alexandria, Antioch, Jerusalem, Constantinople, as well as over all other churches. Is it not odd that it should talk of Constantinople as a metropolitan see, when it was not yet either metropolitan or a see; when it was not a Christian city, neither so named nor founded, nor destined to be founded? Since it is claimed that the privilege was granted immediately preceding Constantine's formal conversion, was not Byzantium the name to use? 'If he wished to transfer the empire elsewhere, he

[1] Valla, *Don.*, 771. 'O admirabile casum. Imperium Romanum tantis laboribus, tanto cruore partum, tam placide, tam quiete a Christianis sacerdotibus vel partum est, vel amissum, ut nullus cruor, nullum bellum, nulla querela intercesserit.'

[2] Voltaire, *Le Dîner du Comte de Boulainvilliers*, II (Pendant le Dîner).

had not yet transferred it. If he wished to establish his empire, he had not yet established it. And if he wished to build a city, he had not yet built it.'[1]

Magna animi paupertas ignorantia, qua nihil maius praeter vitium. Sine literis omnes aetas caeca est.[2] Nothing, I imagine, can persuade more convincingly of the truth of the proud boast than these blows of an awakened criticism against an usurped authority resting on ignorance. Nothing, I hope also, could show more revealingly the falseness of the assertion that humanism was a mere literary cult, something divorced from any sense of reality. Nor was Valla's conclusion far removed from Petrarch. It contained the threat to proceed more truculently if the Pope proved obstinate (and had not Petrarch expressed his intention of speaking more sharply to Urban V if the latter's death had not intervened?); but it contained also the appeal to all princes and peoples to constrain the Pope, so that he might once again become the vicar of Christ only, and not of Caesar as well; the hope that the horrible news of the Church, or rather the Pope, fighting against the Perugians or the Bolognese might no longer be heard. 'Then he will be called pope, and will be as well the holy father, the father of all, the father of the Church: nor will he stir up war amongst Christians, but those stirred up by others he will check by apostolic censure and with the majesty of the Papacy.'[3] The cause of truth, of justice and peace was Petrarch's own, and the connections are not hard to see. Is it the fault of either, or of the new learning generally, that Julius II fought both against the Perugians and against the Bolognese? Perhaps his career especially can be taken as proof of the falseness of such assertions as those of Monnier and Voigt: the reversion of Julius II to a policy akin to that of Innocent III is in spite of humanism, and not because of it. It represents the Church's failure to absorb humanism, except as the individual achievement of a few Popes, and not a perversion of the Papacy or the Church by means of humanism. Machiavelli will condemn Julius II, and his reasons might well be summed up in this closing appeal of the *De Donatione*. Since Valla wrote in the middle

---

[1] *Don.*, 777. 'Quae nondum esset, nec patriarchalis, nec sedes, nec urbs Christiana, nec sic nominata, nec condita, nec ad condendum destinata. . . . Si ille alio transferre volebat imperium, nondum transtulerat. Si ille volebat constituere imperium, nondum constituerat. Sic si volebat aedificare urbem, nondum aedificarat.'

[2] cf. *supra*, 25 and 110.

[3] *Don.*, 795. 'Ut papa tantum vicarius Christi sit, et non etiam Caesaris: nec amplius horrenda vox audiatur, partes contra ecclesiam, ecclesia contra Perusinos pugnat, contra Bononienses. Non contra Christianos pugnat Ecclesia, sed papa. . . . Tunc papa et dicetur, et erit pater sanctus, pater omnium, pater ecclesiae: nec bella inter Christianos excitabit, sed ab aliis excitata censura apostolica, et papali maiestate sedabit.'

of the fifteenth century (the treatise was begun apparently in 1440) there are not the same external factors as in Machiavelli's time to emphasise the vicious rôle of the Papacy in Italian history. That does not lessen the merit of Valla in reacting against it. It was the appearance of a mind capable of looking sufficiently broadly at political phenomena to classify them, which impressed Barozzi, and he mentioned the name of Machiavelli as most akin to Valla in his practical manner of considering things. In particular, he noticed the similarity in their classification of the causes of war. Valla maintained that what is won by arms is lost by arms. It is the Christian principle of Petrarch (*Raptor raptorem spoliat*). From that he went on to state the causes of war, which he saw as follows: to revenge one's own injuries, or those of friends; to blunt a power which in the future might become pernicious; love of conquest; love of glory. Of these, the first has some colour of honesty, the second less, the last two none at all.[1] The pacific temperament of Petrarch has been carried to its logical conclusion. Barozzi went further than the suggestion of Machiavelli as the heir to Valla: 'Il quale col rigettare il diritto di conquista e la prepotenza delle armi, coll'inneggiare invece alla rivoluzione e al diritto popolare su cui fondasi la società moderna, parve precorrere quelle larghe idee di libertà e quasi diremo quel sentimento dell'umanità, che sorsero potentissimi nel secolo XVIII.'[2] By the side of such merits the blemishes in Valla's character appear insignificant: his violence in invective against his personal enemies, as for instance Poggio, with whom he exchanged full-blooded diatribes, a detail which has unduly disturbed the historians of literature. We can forgive Voltaire and Valla for their weaknesses.

Such, on the one side, is the development of the nerves of the mind; and the advance, as I have constantly suggested, is less far from the position of Petrarch than is usually supposed. But there is also the positive contribution, the rehabilitation of Epicure. The words of Aeneas Sylvius will have already made it clear that this was not limited to Valla only, and as a matter of fact there were others contemporary with him who moved in the same direction—a proof, if proof is necessary, of the extent to which Epicureanism was latent in the positive contribution of Petrarch. I shall, however, content myself with the examination of the *De Voluptate*, and leave on one side the general inquiry into the return of Epicure.[3] For Petrarch, as we have seen, the good of the body, as the goods of fortune, represented

---

[1] Barozzi, 260.   [2] ibid., 264.
[3] For this, cf. Saitta, *La Rivendicazione d'Epicuro nell'umanesimo.*

a misnomer. He insisted on the necessity of following Nature, and yet he denied her in this most important particular. Therefore for him the Stoic ideal was often closest to his conception of Christianity. But if honey is sweet and we must not suspect Nature of cheating us in offering us that sweetness it will follow to a logical mind that other sweetness in Nature is equally legitimate. Such a development is inevitable with the acceptance of a social conception of virtue, such as that prepared by Petrarch. Thus, as the medieval-Christian denial of this world disappeared from view, it was logical that the inclusion of Cicero and moral philosophy into a Christian outlook should be succeeded by a further step: the inclusion of Epicure himself. Such a step may seem to some revolting, or impossible; but that judgment must not lead to distortion in the view of the procedure. It is not that the new Epicureanism of Valla represents a substitution of pagan for Christian sentiments: it is simply that the Petrarchan formula of a major and a minor revelation, the second of which lies within our sphere of vision, and admits of our scrutiny, allows of this evolution by which what was in the Middle Ages a blank is filled first with the aid of Cicero, and then with that of Epicure. It is this which accounts for the connection, and for the opposition, with Petrarch that we shall see in the *De Voluptate*.

The work begins, inevitably, with a defence of stoicism, given to Leonardo Bruni as one of the immediate successors of Petrarch. This is short, is evidently not Valla's own position, and is speedily demolished by Panormita. Here it is more difficult to decide how far Valla subscribes personally to the bold opinions of Panormita, who substitutes a strong, and rather terrestrial, Epicureanism for the Stoic ideal. Panormita was at one time amongst Valla's adversaries,[1] and the ideas ascribed to him may be wilfully exaggerated. Niccolò Niccoli comes in at the end to contend that the true good is in Christianity, and to reproach the two former speakers with having spoken as pagans. 'Why have you who are a Christian spoken almost as one not a Christian? . . . And why finally did you bring Nature herself into your argument, rather than Jesus Christ?'[2] But his defence of Christianity involves a reconciliation of Epicure with Christ. Both Epicureans and Christians place in beatitude (=happiness) the supreme end of life. Let the followers of Epicure believe in the life to come, and propose to themselves the attainment of an enjoyment

---

[1] Tiraboschi, VI. 1553 (ed. 1824).

[2] *De Vol.*, 975. 'Cur tu cum Christianus sis, locutus es quasi non Christianus? . . . Cur denique ipsam naturam potius in tuum colloquium deduxisti, quam Iesum Christum?'

which continues after death. As a natural corollary to this, Niccoli draws the picture of a heaven which holds also enjoyment for the senses. He shows, as against the ascetic principles of medieval Christianity, which offer future enjoyment only to such as will deprive themselves of any now, that it is lawful to enjoy within the necessary limits the goods bestowed on us by Nature. If beatitude without end is our final goal, how can we logically reject a limited beatitude now? Petrarch's conclusion from Cicero that all we see with our eyes and understand with our minds is divinely ordained for man is receiving its application. For Valla Epicure is a man of many personal virtues: 'Was Epicure a bad man, given up to the pleasure of the palate and the belly? Rather, who was more frugal, more continent, more modest than he? and indeed in not one of all the philosophers do I find there to have been less vices than in him.'[1] The pleasure which he set up as a goal to be pursued was good, not bad, consisting of the health of the body and the quiet of the mind. 'I say that good pleasure is to be sought after, and not bad.'[2] I think, and it seems generally accepted, that Valla's own position is more that of Niccoli than it is that of Panormita (apart from the fact that it is Niccoli who holds the close of the book itself), but the full gospel was not without effect in the second half of the century, and I have no desire to minimise it. Thus, after these general outlines, we can return to the detail, and the precise position of Valla can be left to the conclusion and to the individual judgment.

Bruni's picture of life is depressing. We have drunk in the love of vices with our mothers' milk, the fault of Nature rather than of ourselves. From earliest infancy one can see children inclined to greed and pleasures, instead of lifting themselves towards what is dignified and honourable: they hate rebuke, they love blandishments; they flee precept and follow wantonness. Compel the bat to seek light rather than shade; persuade the mole to use the surface of the earth and not its bowels, this common air rather than a perpetual grave; ask the deaf to hear, the dumb to speak, the lame to run swiftly; expect virtue of the many.[3] In face of this corruption Bruni

---

[1] *Con. Cal.*, 797. 'Malusne vir Epicurus fuit, gulae ventrique deditus? Imo vero quis eo parcior, quis continentior, quis modestior? et quidem in nullo philosophorum omnium minus invenio fuisse vitiorum.'

[2] ibid., 798 bis. 'Bonam enim sequendam dico voluptatem.'

[3] *De Vol.*, IIII. 902. 'Videre enim licet a primis statim annis pueros defluere potius ad vitia gulae, lusus delitiarum, quam tollere sese ad decus atque honestatem, odisse castigationes, amare blanditias, fugere praeceptiones, sectari lascivias.' And VI. 903. 'Coge vespertilionem, ut

sets up the ideal of virtue, and the stoic necessity of suffering. The development is slight, and it is evident that Valla is as little interested in the stoic ideal as Bruni. Panormita, however, has a freer range, and Bruni has scarcely finished stating the difficulty of virtue, and its rareness, when Panomita calmly asserts that the *summum bonum* lies in *voluptas*. He deplores the long faces of the stoics, sneers at Diogenes (rightly called a cynic) who lived many years in a barrel, as if his mother had been a tavern.[1] Nature is good, and it is only to perverted palates that she will seem bad. She offered pleasures, and at the same time she formed the mind inclined to those pleasures. It is a disease and frenzy in the stoics which prevents them giving thanks to Nature, and makes them choose to live a sad and solitary life. If only they knew, they could live most happily by following Nature, as a most indulgent mother.[2] 'Le plus simplement se commettre à nature, c'est s'y commettre le plus sagement.'[3]

What is pleasure, then? It is a good wherever it is sought, consisting in the delight of the mind and of the body. The arbitrary definition accepted by Petrarch is thus broken down, and, correspondingly, *honestas* is devalued: it is in the stoic definition a good whose reason derives from virtue, to be sought, not for any external reason, but for itself.[4] 'We who follow the laws of Nature say that delights are to be sought for. They offer gratuitous labour, we enjoyment. They torments, we pleasures. Finally, they death, we life.'[5] It is following the laws of Nature to preach the pursuit of pleasure; and man consists both of mind and of body. The good of the body consists in health, then beauty, then strength and so on (many can be well without beauty, no-one beautiful without health). If, then, the gifts of Nature, strength and beauty, are placed in man, is he to think so

lumina quam tenebras malit. Persuade talpae, ut facie terrae potius quam visceribus, et hac communi aura quam perpetua sepultura uti velit. . . . Roga surdum ut audiat, mutum ut loquatur, loripedem ut velociter currat.'

[1] ibid., XI. 908. 'Qualis ille Diogenes, qui apposito nomine vocatus est Cynicus, hoc est Caninus, qui multos annos vixit in dolio, tanquam matrem cauponam habuisset.'

[2] ibid., XII. 909. 'Nempe quod natura tibi voluptates in medio posuit, simulque animum ad illas tibi propensum dedit atque formavit. Tu nunc non illi gratias ages, sed nescio per quem morbum ac frenesim . . . praeeligis solivagam ac tristem vitam degere, et . . . naturam incessitis, sub qua, velut indulgentissima matre, si quid saperetis, felicissime possetis vivere.'

[3] Montaigne, *Essais*, III. xiii. 391.

[4] *De Vol.*, XVII. 912. 'Voluptas . . . est bonum undecunque quaesitum, in animi et corporis oblectatione positum. . . . Honestas est . . . bonum cuius ratio ex virtutibus constat, non propter aliud, sed propter seipsum expetendum.'

[5] ibid., XVII. 912. 'Nos ipsius naturae iura retinentes, dicimus appetendas oblectationes. Illi labores gratuitos, nos iucunditatem. Illi tormenta, nos voluptates. Denique illi necem, nos vitam.'

badly of her as to suspect a deception, and not an honour? The question is none the less shrewd because Petrarch had asked it in a different form, and answered it without realising its implications.[1] Nature, for instance, gives many women an honest and open countenance. For what reason?—that it should be an ornament to them, or for them to take no care of it? Panormita answers emphatically, that they should enjoy it and rejoice.[2] Otherwise there was no reason why Nature should take such trouble, for even in heaven it must be difficult to find anything more beautiful than a lovely face. But beauty is not restricted to the face alone: it may exist in the whole body. Hence statues with an arm, a leg, or a breast naked; hence others without any veil (as Diana on Monte Celio). And if it is lawful for women who have beautiful hair, a beautiful face or bosom to show their beauty, why should it be forbidden to those whose beauty lies elsewhere? Such is Panormita's enthusiasm for the idea that he is led on almost inevitably (and it is not an accident that these sentiments are put into Panormita's mouth) to suggest that it would be better for women to go about naked or semi-naked in summer because it would give more delight to the men.[3] What more? The man who does not praise beauty is blind either in soul or body, and if he has eyes deserves to lose a faculty whose possession he does not feel.[4] Measure with this the bitter remark of Petrarch on avoiding temptation, *dum in animum redit quid est femina*, and the progress is obvious. Measure what follows with the chapters of the *De Remediis* which advise sighing as better than singing, proscribe painting, sculpture, architecture as vanities, and the same progress appears. For what is true of physical beauty is true elsewhere: why did Nature produce gold or gems, if not for adornment? What need to mention the things made by the hand of man, as statues, pictures, magnificent things, public spectacles? Are we to despise the pleasures of the fields, the vineyards or the gardens?[5] Must we prefer weeping to singing? Rather, Nature has formed the ears of men to pleasure in the songs of birds as well, and such is the antiquity of music that *musici, vates,*

[1] *De Vol.*, XXI. 914. 'Quare si hoc naturae munus est in homines collatum, quis tandem erit tam iniquus rerum aestimator, ut arbitretur illam non honorasse nos tali munere, sed decepisse?' For Petrarch, cf. *Sen.*, XII. i.

[2] ibid., XXII. 915. 'Natura foeminis multis dedit faciem, ut inquit Terentius, honestam atque liberalem, quam ob causam quaeso, ut ornamento illas afficeret, an ut contumelia, ut hoc munere illae fruerentur, an nihil curarent? Certe ut fruerentur atque gauderent.'

[3] ibid.

[4] ibid., 916. 'Quid plura? Qui pulchritudinem non laudat, hic aut animo aut corpore caecus est, et si oculos habet, illis orbandus, quos se habere non sentit.'

[5] ibid., XXIII. 916.

sapientes were originally synonyms. Wine also is praised—and very warmly—on the same principle, with a little tilt against the sour teetotaller: 'It is easy to abstain from things one does not like, as some object to wine, and so are called abstemious. It is not who does what that is to be noted, but why he does it.'[1] It is a remark which implies the same interest that Petrarch had in psychological observation. Such is the virtuosity of Panormita, and so much is he fired by the ardour of advancing across open land that had long been fenced away from thought, that he does not stop here. He defends adultery, and the philologist Valla is able to make his point by means of a pretty pun.[2] He appeals to Plato for the doctrine that women should be in common, or rather, why Plato, he asks, since it is an obvious law of Nature; and think of the benefit to the human race if it had always been honoured! There would have been no war for Helen, and no ten years' siege of Troy. Such a judgment involves a more serious pendant: the rejection of the monastic virtue of continence. That was implicit in any movement which set up a social, as opposed to a solitary, ideal; and Panormita, as might be expected, is downright in his condemnation. For him the prostitute deserves more of society than does the nun.[3] The institutions of monasticism he dismisses as a vanity invented by certain old, cold men, poor or avaricious so that they would not or could not pay a dowry. Thus although temperance is an essential part of pleasure, since it prevents any blunting of the appetite, yet the stoic system, with the suffering it involves, must be a *summum malum*, not a *summum bonum*. The door unlocked by Petrarch has been thrown open wide by Panormita, wider perhaps than Valla intended to keep it; but it is the hatching out of this new element which is responsible for the trend to hedonism—whether we applaud or condemn that trend is another matter—of the second half of the Renascence. In its causes there must not be forgotten the contemporary discovery of statues attributed to Phidias and Praxiteles (and most statues received some such complimentary attribution), which helped in placing the emphasis on physical beauty. 'L'ansia dei

[1] ibid., XXV. 917. 'Facile est enim eo abstinere quod displicet, ut quidam vinum aversantur, unde abstemii dicti sunt. Non est itaque notandum quis aliquid faciat, sed qua causa faciat.' Again, note the origin in Cicero of this idea of observation: 'In quibus videndum est, non modo quid quisque loquatur, sed etiam quid quisque sentiat, atque etiam qua causa quisque sentiat' (*De Officiis*, I, in *Opera*, IV. 315).

[2] ibid., XXXVIII. 922. 'Maritus quoque quid aliud quam marem significat? An non et adulter mas? Vide ne forte sit ipso interdum marito marior.'

[3] ibid., XLIV. 924, and cf. XLVI. 'Nullum in rebus humanis intolerabilius virginitate tormentum est.' For the anatomy of this, v. Diderot, *La Religieuse*.

codici e del passato non creò l'umanesimo, ma ne fu l'effetto,' wrote
Toffanin in a different context,[1] and the principle is equally true here.
The enthusiasm for Greco-Roman sculpture follows, and does not
direct, the movement which begins with Petrarch. And to condemn
(apart from the extravagances of Panormita) is to renounce much
that is most serious and most valuable in the production of the
Renascence.

There is not much to add on Niccoli's conclusion in the third book,
but one or two points are of interest. The children whom Bruni had
seen as examples of human corruption he exonerates: they seek the
good of the body, which is alone within their ken. Later, with the
development of the understanding, they will seek the good of the
mind. But for both mind and body the aim is happiness or pleasure
sought by natural instinct, and Epicure judged preferable in the
various sorts of pleasure the health of the body and the peace of the
mind. But there is no question of the honest to be loved for its own
sake only, nor is it right even to love God without the hope of any
reward. Genesis, Ezechiel, Psalms offer *voluptas* (*Ex torrente voluptatis
potabis eos*—a text quoted, as it happens, by Petrarch), and beatitude
—the aim common to the Epicurean and the Christian—is not identical with God himself, but the delight which derives from union
with him. All things are loved from one of two reasons: either that
they offer joy (as things we see or hear), or because they receive it (as
the eye). 'For our beatitude is not God himself, but descends from
God, as the joy which I experience in clarity of vision, or in hearing
a sweet voice, is not the same as clarity or the voice, but these things
cause my enjoyment.'[2] The two attributes co-exist in God; but for
the creature the means of receiving pleasure must exist, and the
heavenly *voluptas* is to include the pleasures of the senses, and is not to
consist in mere contemplation. I do not think that this conception of
heaven has been accepted in theology, either at the Council of Trent,
or in any other assembly. But since the sixteenth century neither
mankind nor the Church has been wholly able to deny Epicure his
place; and when we have stripped the thesis of Valla of the exaggerations of Panormita the establishment of the claim of 'l'homme moyen
sensuel' is no mean contribution to the modern epoch. It is a departure from Petrarchan humanism, but it is a departure by the suppres-

---

[1] *Che cosa fu l'umanesimo*, 24.

[2] *De Vol.*, III. xii. 979. 'Nam beatitudo nostra non est ipsemet deus, sed a deo descendit, ut
gaudium quod capio ex videnda claritate, aut audienda suavi voce, non idem quod claritas aut
vox, sed illa faciunt ut gaudeam.'

sion of the negative elements in Petrarch, and a logical development of the positive ones. And it remains, for all its exaggerations, a humanism. With its accomplishment (and from the middle of the fifteenth century Italy is at peace, and at the height of her prosperity) Italy was ready for the admitted achievements of the Renascence.

VII

THE ITALIAN VITRUVIUS

VALLA was born in 1405, Leon Battista Alberti possibly a year, possibly a few years, earlier. I should, then, have considered him before his junior. But there were other reasons than the fact that Alberti outlived Valla by fifteen years to induce me to ignore the niceties of chronology. Valla devoted himself to criticism that others might create better: Alberti's creative activities range over half a dozen literary genres, and outside literature into the arts as well. In the forefront of Valla's theory stands the ambiguous figure of Panormita with the excessive emphasis on anarchic pleasure; behind Leon Battista stands the moral solidarity of the Alberti family, rich with the good faith and the moderation of the Florentine merchant class. Valla hurled his invectives at Poggio a little extravagantly: Alberti endured misfortune and misuse with fortitude. Valla stands uncompromisingly as a Latinist: Alberti uses Latin and Italian, not indifferently, but according to the quality of what he has to say. Valla's *Elegantiae* help to a more critical purity in writing Latin: Alberti's unequal Italian prose—at its worst suggestive of the *Hypnerotomachia* or the *Ecolier Limousin*, at its best a clear and attractive Florentine—points the way forwards to Machiavelli, still, perhaps, Italy's greatest writer of prose. At least, that of Alberti is outstanding in the fifteenth century, and there are tricks of style and vocabulary which it seems probable Machiavelli inherited from him. Machiavelli's interest (a dominant one) in a *vivere civile* is an echo of the humanist's concern; and the phrase itself, which is to be one of the burdens of the *Discorsi*, is already to hand in the *De Iciarchia*. Along with ideas which Machiavelli reproduces there is exemplified in Alberti's style that casual slipping into the second person singular by anacoluthon which is so often instanced as a characteristic of Machiavelli's procedure: 'Cosa scellerata non resistere alla disonestà ove tu possa reprimerla: e chi permette in altri la ingiustizia, in sé non è giusto.'[1] In the universality of his interests Leon Battista has been acclaimed as typical of the early Renascence, and as the precursor of Leonardo: in his essentially practical goodness, and in his robust common sense, he has quite often

---

[1] Unless otherwise indicated I quote Bonucci for Alberti's Italian works. *De Iciarchia*, III. iii. 150 (= Bonucci vol. III, *De. Ic.*, Bk. III).

been accounted a strange phenomenon in the fifteenth century. Mancini was not slow to express surprise that Alberti was not pagan in his ideas like the most illustrious writers of his time.[1] A recent writer who endorses Mancini's view sees him as necessarily distinct from cynical despisers of Christianity and professors of the most shameless Epicureanism such as Valla and his companions.[2] All this surprise is comparable with that expressed by the editor of Castiglione's *Cortegiano*, when he saw fit to remark upon the fact that what Castiglione said was inspired by a high morality, and that Castiglione himself was a pattern too of that.[3] Castiglione has affinities in outlook with Alberti, and it is an interesting commentary on the strength of the preconception that the influence of humanism must be degrading that it is necessary to pluck, with every appearance of surprise, here a brand, and there a brand, from the burning. It is because of this that it is necessary to insist on the pattern and the development of humanism. And again, I hope that not only the exposition of Valla's thought, but also the connection with one admittedly so good as Alberti, may help to stay the flames.

I have used the word *humanism* to include Alberti, and there are some to whom it will seem an offence so to have used it: did not Leon Battista write in *Italian*, and sponsor, in the 'certame coronario,' the claims of the vernacular as a literary vehicle? How, then, can he be set up as a humanist? It is, of course, well known that a humanist is a person who ignores reality, and the time and place to which he is born, in order to write in Latin, a language which died its death some centuries before. It is not frivolous in me to raise a protest against the definition: we have only to remember Petrarch's *Africa* to know what happens. Humanism is dead pedantry, therefore if Alberti is alive and not pedantic how can he be a humanist? To such chop-logic there is only one answer (unless, like Diogenes, we begin the other way round); and because of the certainty of the answer, and the frequency of the admission that this is the century of the humanists, distortions have often crept in, and to the most carefully official of compilations. Thus, the rather dreary catalogue of contents which is Rossi's history of the *Quattrocento* gave twelve lines to a work *De Re Uxoria*, written by a boy of eighteen years of age (a suitable subject for the school prize essay), and well stuffed with passages compiled from a galaxy of classical authors. On the contrary, one of the most important works of Alberti (and indeed of the whole century) went at a couple

---

[1] Mancini, *Vita di L. B. Alberti*, 204.   [2] Semprini, *L. B. Alberti*, 119.
[3] *Cortegiano*, ed. Cian, 103 n.

of lines, while a treatise of Aeneas Sylvius in which Rossi himself confessed he saw the breath of a modern reality got merely a mention.[1] That is an odd procedure in the examination of literature. Recently there has been an attempt to put back on the map of French literature all the background of French classicism in the seventeenth century. 'I have smiled, says Prof. Lancaster, to see certain scholars present us with three names, isolated from those of their felllows and supposed to represent the whole dramatic life of the seventeenth century in France. . . .'[2] He smiled because he knew with Corneille, Molière and Racine of scores of other playwrights, and hundreds (for aught I know, thousands) of other plays forgotten in the light of the central achievement, as the moon sweeps away the lesser stars. Few such smiles of superior erudition can light the faces of Italian scholars: a tradition of painstaking mummification has retained the names of all those who wasted ink and paper in the fifteenth century. The perversity of the method is plain from this example of Rossi's handling: the children and the failures stand almost more chance of recognition in the history of literature than those who wrote with competence and can represent the essential achievement of their century: for by an initial prejudice the latter are regarded as less typical of their times. Three names at the summit are sufficient to establish the greatness of French classical drama, and the lustre of its name will not easily be dimmed by the awareness that there were hosts of camp-followers of scant or no importance. It is what is significant that demands a place in the histories of literature, and to be exhaustive (after so many centuries in which so many names have been so conveniently, and so suitably, forgotten) can rarely be other than to be exhausting. To write of what was merely because it was, and not because of what it was, is a form of asceticism that is more understandable than praiseworthy. There are, in the vast accumulation of books which we inherit, as in those we add to the accumulation, two sorts: those which give some constituent to our mind; those which take our time. And similarly, there are two sorts of reader: those who look in literature for what concerns themselves, and those who give themselves to literature (that is, to literary research) without the hope of any reward, and as a substitute to being themselves. It is to these that the *De Re Uxoria* by right belongs: give them time, and they will analyse its sources and appraise its syntax. What rare reading in a lad of

[1] Rossi, *Il Quattrocento*, 87.

[2] H. C. Lancaster, *A History of French Dramatic Literature in the Seventeenth Century*, 9 vols. cf. review by L. A. Bisson, *M.L.R.*, July, 1941, 414.

eighteen, what skilful compilation! But prominence in the genuine history of literature belongs to merit. If there is no other literature in the fifteenth century than the *De Re Uxoria* and its like, let us forget the century and spend our time more worthily. If there is other metal of a better composition, then let us look to that.

It is because I attach importance, then, to Leon Battista Alberti that I have left him till after Valla, and in some ways to be a corrective to Valla. My first business, in view of the definitions of humanism against which I have protested, is to make clear his connections with what has gone before. Since humanism is an attitude of mind, and not a trick of writing Latin, there is nothing criminal in imagining that Alberti might be more humanistic even in his Italian works than Barbaro in the *De Re Uxoria*. Alberti's written work is large, unsystematic and varying in mood. It still lacks a complete review, and even the canon is not completely certain,[1] though we in England can congratulate ourselves on a recent contribution to the study of the man.[2] The fluctuation in Alberti is one both of style and of thought: there is, for instance, so much difference between the texture of the prose in the *Tranquillità dell'Animo* and the third Book of the *Della Famiglia* that they might seem from different hands (and the Pandolfini theory had a superficial justification in the difference in prose style between the various books of the *Della Famiglia* itself). In thought also there are fluctuations, ranging from the pessimism of his youthful misfortunes to the optimism of his later years. It is not surprising, then, that there are connections to be seen with Petrarch in his ascetic moods, but also, and equally important, with Valla and the humanist educators who precede Valla. In the broken facets of Alberti's writings much of contemporary thought is reflected; in the most valuable of them all the development away from Petrarch is accepted and powerfully promoted. Naturally, it is the correspondences with Petrarch which need stating first. Firstly, perhaps, there is the insistence on the will, especially in the matter of virtue. It is not what happens by chance that matters, but the predominance of reason and the will. And if one seeks and loves it, there is nothing easier to be had than virtue. Only those who will it have it. 'Chi adunque ben consiglia, ben può quanto e'vuole. Vuolsi adattare l'animo a virtú.'[3] Moreover, his conception of virtue is in the Petrarchan tradition: it is a Stoic complement, that

[1] Unpublished mss. exist; Bonucci printed an incomplete version of the *De Re Aedificatoria* in Italian as Alberti's own draft. I have not noticed a discussion of the attribution.

[2] Blunt, op. cit. This has naturally a specialised interest in Alberti, and it begins conveniently where I intend to stop.

[3] *Della Famiglia*, II. iv. 14, Proemio. And *Tranq. d. An.*, I. i. 19.

K

is, to the Christian revelation.[1] Alberti has with this the general
aversion for speculative philosophy, and especially also for the logicians. These waste time in their theories and their subtle distinctions,
neglecting practice, or what is worse, leaving a gap between their
lofty principles and the conduct of their life. He excepts Socrates
from his attack on ancient philosophers, both for having the most
excellent opinions of all, and for his practice of virtue.[2] In words
which echo Petrarch very closely, and which he emphasises by
repetition, Alberti stresses the need for conformity between principle
and practice: 'E sempre ti sia proposto in animo che al bene adoperarsi
niuna cosa piú giova, quanto se tu al tutto delibererai essere quello,
il quale agli altri vorrai parere.'[3] Despite acquaintance with Greek
philosophy in the original texts there is no trace of their influence on
him in any speculation, nor is there much in him of the neo-platonism
which ran like measles among his fellow-citizens of Florence. In his
youth he had all Petrarch's bitterness in his views on women: no
animal more wicked than the female, all of them mad and full of
fleas; from them nothing but displeasure, hindrance and disgust.[4]
Flee Love is the burden in the *Intercoenales*; *flee woman* is still the motto
for the Tranquillity of the Mind.[5] The mind is infinite and immortal,
the gift of a Being infinite and immortal, it must not be left to rot in
pleasures: 'Questo intelletto, questa cognizione e ragione e memoria,
donde venne in me, sí infinita e immortale, se non da chi sia infinito
ed immortale? Ed io lascerò io me simile a un ferraccio macerare e
marcire in ozio, sepolto in mezzo'l loto delle delizie e voluttà?'[6]
Petrarch would have understood such language, which perhaps helps
to explain why the *De Ocio Religiosorum* could never be a whole-
hearted document: the sense of the necessity for the development of
the mind prevented in Petrarch any complete acceptance of the passive
obedience of the monk. Shun ease and pleasure: it is advice to which
Alberti still clings long after, in his last work, the *Iciarchia*.[7] But the
statement on pleasure in the *Tranquillità*, though it might perhaps
have satisfied Petrarch in certain moods, or been inspired itself by the
De Remediis, could not satisfy Alberti for long. Man takes pleasure
in house, villa, ornaments, ampleness of life, dignity, power; in wife,
fatherhood, good nature of offspring. All these things are part of the

---

[1] Semprini, 165. Mancini, 204.   [2] Sempr., 156-7.

[3] *Famigl.*, II. ii. 196. For Petrarch, cf., e.g., *Fam.*, III. xii. 167, which echoes Cicero, *De
Officiis*, II (*Opera*, IV. 323): 'Quanquam praeclare Socrates hanc viam ad gloriam proximam et
quasi compendiariam dicebat esse, si quis id ageret, ut qualis haberi vellet, talis esset.'

[4] *Tran.*, I. i. 43.   [5] Sempr., 53 and 64.   [6] *Tran.*, I. i. 31.

[7] *De Iciarchia*, III. i. 9.

ineptitude of man, a flouting of his reason. These are the poisons of the mind, by which true and worthy virtue is corrupted in our bosoms.[1] Such statements as these may have brought tranquillity of mind to the youthful Alberti, comforting himself in his own distress with the idea that all things depend upon opinion. But they do not hold validity for long; and already in the sharpness of the attack on idleness (*ozio*) there is discernible the passage from Petrarch to the humanist educators.

If idleness is the worst enemy of virtue, then there is an ethical value to work, as much as to mental activity; and man is born to be useful to his fellows. As with Petrarch, not all are born for letters, and goodness is the common goal. If I had children, says Lionardo in the *Della Famiglia*, I should not waste melancholy over their calling. It would be my business first to see that they grew up with honest ways and virtue, and whatever calling pleased them would be welcome to me, so long as it was not shameful.[2] Letters are still both pleasing and useful, even most necessary, but they do not stand alone. Alberti insists on the interdependence of man. Man is born to be useful to man, and Nature (who constructs all things well) has placed man in the open midst of other men. Alberti uses almost the words that will be Bacon's to express the practical goal of humanism: 'Da' buoni pensieri seguitano buone operazioni grate a Dio, accette agli uomini, onde tu conscendi in grado onoratissimo fra primarii cittadini.'[3] Virtue, then, is social virtue, and Alberti stands in complete accord with the theorists and the practitioners of humanist education; with whom, of course, he has such obvious links as precepts for the exercise of the body, and the setting forth, in the first book of the *Della Famiglia*, of ideas on the upbringing of children. And if man is born to be useful to man, so are the arts. Alberti has Cicero's, and Petrarch's, gratitude for the inventors of so many and so convenient aids to living well,[4] and he is more thorough in his logic than Petrarch was. Why so many arts?—all to serve man. Knowledge for its own sake, no; but for the sake of man. That was the attitude of Petrarch, and it will still be something like it which dictated, for example, the method pursued by Buffon in the *Histoire*

---

[1] *Tran.*, I. ii. 62.

[2] *Famigl.*, II. i. 112. 'Solo in me saria prima opera fare, che i miei venissero crescendo con buoni costumi e con virtú; e qualunque esercizio loro gustasse, piacerà ogni esercizio che sia senza infamia.'

[3] *Ic.*, III. ii. 72. cf. Bacon, *Essays*, XI as quoted *supra*, 93.

[4] ibid., 101. 'E quanto siamo noi obbligati a'primi inventori di tante utili e commodissime cose a vivere bene.'

Naturelle. The authors of the *Encyclopédie* unwittingly instituted the revolution by which Europe abandoned that conception of *scientia* for the modern one of science—an unfortunate development. It was still possible in the eighteenth century for Montesquieu to prophesy that if anything more lethal than gunfire was invented the united conscience of mankind would drown the invention, as Orlando drowned the gun itself in a hopeful moment of the poet Ariosto.[1] Who would venture to make such a prophecy of science now? *Scientia,* for the humanist, was the servant of man; but man has for a long time been the servant of science. It follows logically from the acceptance of society and of the interdependence of man that other forms of activity than letters become praiseworthy. Petrarch's division into liberal and mechanical arts we have seen nibbled at by Valla, who gives to what we call the fine arts (or more simply, art) a *proxime accessit.* Alberti goes the whole way, and obliterates the distinction: to be a musician, a painter, an architect or the like is to be concerned with 'le buone arti.'[2] Elsewhere he makes the acceptance even wider, and the term *arts* covers merchants, argonauts (shipowners or sailors?), architects, doctors, craftsmen, as well as painters, sculptors, musicians. 'Tutti questi modi del guadagnare, i quali sono in noi, si chiamono arti.'[3] It is, I think, clear that this logical progression from Petrarch represents the impact of humanism on the practical mind of the Florentine merchant class. Leaving the youthful pessimism of the *Intercoenales,* he does not deny wealth as an object of activity. He would have denied his family if he had. But he attaches it to virtue, and to magnificence.[4] And with it goes the interdependence of man, and the abandonment of the superiority asserted for purely mental activity.[5] It is a maturer conception of society than was possible in Petrarch; and it is a practical development of the social ideals of the humanist educators which had important consequences for the standing of the artist in the Renascence.

Alberti, then, has very definite contacts with Petrarch and his immediate successors. But he is also the contemporary of Valla, and though he does not discuss the *De Voluptate,* though, as we have seen,

---

[1] *Orlando Furioso,* IX. xc-xci.   [2] ibid., III. i. 58.   [3] *Famigl.,* II. ii. 208.

[4] ibid., 213. 'Se la fortuna vi dona ricchezze adoperatela in cose magnifiche e onestissime. . . . Non pertanto si pregino le ricchezze, ma signoregginsi le cupidità, e nel mezzo della copia e abbondanza delle cose, cosí vivremo liberi e lieti.'

[5] ibid., 194. 'Non fece la natura gli uomini tutti d'una confessione, e d'un ingegno, e d'un volere, né tutti a un modo atti e valenti: anzi volse che in quello in quale io manco ivi tu supplisca; e in altra cosa manchi, la quale sia appresso di quell'altro. Perché questo? perch'io abbia di te bisogno; tu di colui; colui d'un altro; e qualcuno di me.'

he puts *voluptas* with *ocium* as the nurse of vice, he does not escape the influence of Valla. That he did not escape that influence, and that it proved beneficent, is perhaps some evidence as to the weight we need attach to Panormita's contribution in comparison with Valla's own position. In the proem to the most famous of the four books on the Family (*Il Padre di Famiglia*) Leon Battista writes of the habit of Messer Antonio Alberti, who often used to pace the gardens disputing which was the greatest loss—the Roman empire or the Latin language. He had no doubts about the conclusion of the argument: it was the language that was the main loss, the language in which so many noble writers had set forth 'tutte le buone arti a bene e beato vivere.'[1] For when it failed the light was out. The end of the Roman Empire saw also, and immediately, 'accecato quasi ogni lume e notizia della lingua e lettere latine.[2] That, I need scarcely remind the reader, is the language of the proem to Valla's *Elegantiae*. Alberti, it is true, has one important particular which differs from the conclusion of Valla. Like the latter in the explicit statement of this same proem, Alberti writes for all men, not for himself alone.[3] That is a part of the conception of usefulness both of virtue and of knowledge. And that being so he writes in Italian (is it any less difficult to write it correctly than it is to write Latin?) in order to reach the many. Again, the ease with which the independent position is established suggests that Valla's influence will be no more shackling than that of Petrarch. Already in the *Tranquillità* a voice was raised against those strong minds which feel nothing of the accidents of life, but remain securely trenched within themselves: to be alone insentient to the things which infinite men feel is to be alone in not being a man. If there is charity or love in human minds, there must be room there also for anger, indignation and the like.[4] That is a claim for the normal man, and elsewhere Alberti sets out a thesis on the nature of man which partakes both of Petrarch and of Valla: 'Diciamo a nostro proposito, che l'uomo sia posto in vita per usare le cose, per essere virtuoso, o diventare felice; imperocché colui il quale si potrà dir felice, costui agli uomini sarà buono; e colui il quale ora è buono agli uomini, certo ancora è grato a Dio. Chi male usa le cose, nuoce agli uomini e non poco dispiace a Dio; e chi dispiace a Dio stolto è se si reputa

---

[1] *Famigl.*, II. iii. 218.   [2] ibid., 219.

[3] *Sempr.*, 153. 'Sappia che le cose da me scritte le scrivo non solo per me solo, ma per l'umanità.' (Letter to Bishop of Aleria.) And for difficulty of language, cf. *Famigl.*, ibid., 221.

[4] *Tran.*, I. i. 24. 'Chi non sente le cose che senton gli altri infiniti uomini, costui solo non è uomo. Se negli animi umani abita la carità, se vi ha luogo l'amore, convien che vi cappia l'ira e la indignazione e simili.'

felice. Adunque si può statuire cosí: l'uomo da natura essere fatto a usufruttare le cose, e nato per essere felice.'[1] Petrarch set virtue first, and as he saw it in the mind could not put the use of things as important, although he proclaimed the goodness of Nature and, in theory, the goodness also of the *adminicula vitae*. Alberti remembers that man is a compound of body and of soul. Instead of denying the former for the sake of the latter he asserts its validity, and retains the order which Valla gives: first health, then strength, then beauty. But the body, like other things, is made for use. Alberti is as close to Montaigne as he is to Valla here.[2] He admits the cogency of Valla's reasoning on finite and infinite beatitude, and links it with the ideals of the humanist educators: in a definition immediately following the passage on use, virtue and happiness, just and good works are those which harm none, but are of benefit to others.[3] That is the gloss to the 'buono agli uomini,' and the check on a merely selfish view of happiness. There is an equally important definition to virtue, and one which illuminates the *or* which links virtue and happiness in the quotation above: 'Non è virtú altro se non in sé perfetta e ben prodotta natura.'[4] That provides a different answer from that which Petrarch might have given to his own questions in the *De Ignorantia* on the nature of man: the answer which, as I have said, was inevitable in the development from Petrarch's thought. It is the answer dictated by the practical common sense of Alberti. The author of the *Della Famiglia* is himself the representative of a family which embodied all that was most sturdy and honest in the Florentine character, and the contact with contemporary life makes Alberti's views more important than the neo-platonism which has attracted so much more attention. The inclusion of Alberti in the movement of humanism lessens the possibility of considering this as unrealistic.

In fact, so strongly is Alberti's writing contemporary that no better picture of the Florentine merchant class of his time can be found, and that at times the general value of his views may seem limited by the particular nature of the society he represents. The Alberti, even in the misfortune of exile, have their mercantile establishments in London, Bruges, Cologne, Venice, Genoa, Rome, Avignon, Paris, Valencia, Barcelona, 'ne' quali tutti luoghi i nostri Alberti sono piú anni stati

[1] *Famigl.*, II. ii. 192.

[2] *Sempr.*, 204. 'Il corpo è una cosa bona e grande, adoperolo in cose oneste, utili, lodate e grate e cerco conservarlo quanto piú posso, lungo tempo sano, robusto e bello; tengolo netto, pulito e civile e cerco adoperare cosí le mani, la lingua e ogni altro membro.'

[3] *Famigl.*, ibid., 193.

[4] ibid., II. i. 93. It is no accident that this is Cicero's definition, *De Legibus*, I (*Op.*, IV. 274).

integrissimi e onoratissimi mercatanti.'[1] They can look back to the time when they imported enough raw wool for all the cloth manufacturers of Florence, and for a good part of Tuscany as well.[2] They have a robust independence which suits with the Florentine character, as much as with their position. Giannozzo, the patriarch of the dialogues on the Family, speaks for them all: 'Sempre a me piacque piú tosto servire altri, che richiedere; piuttosto farmi altri obbligato, che obbligarmi. . . . Voglionsi i buoni tutti riputare amici: e ben che a te non siano conosciuti, i buoni e virtuosi voglionsi sempre amare e aiutare.'[3] The background—the substantial background—of Florentine stability to the humanist ideas of Leon Battista is a necessary corrective not only to the often-expressed view on the divorce between life and literature, but also to that of the essential corruption of Italy in the fifteenth century.[4] Giannozzo frankly put life before literature: 'Tu sai, Lionardo, che io non so lettere. Io mi sono in vita ingegnato conoscere le cose, piú colla pruova che col dire di altrui; e quello che io intendo piuttosto lo compresi dalla verità, che dall'argomentare altrui. E perché uno di questi, i quali leggono tutto il dí, a me dicesse: cosí sta; io non gli credo però, se io non veggo aperta ragione.'[5] Such then is the solid gain both for Alberti and for humanism, and for our appreciation of the realities of the fifteenth century as well. The limitation is apparent, though, as well as the gain: it is a family, not a firm, which spread its branches throughout Europe and into the East as well. Its constitution reminds us of the vocabulary of the old Florentine chroniclers, who talk always of the houses, not just the house, of exiles being destroyed. Adovardo, for instance, laments that there are no less than twenty-two young men of the house of Alberti, all between the ages of sixteen and thirty-six, who remain unmarried, and so are not playing their part in the maintenance of the family.[6] That is a vital thing for them to do in an age when the lack of a tight social organisation made it safer to send a member of your family as representative of a trading house in distant parts than to send some one who might most easily decamp with any profits. In fact, this structure of the Florentine family made possible the vast development of Florentine trade and banking, which could not have ramified so securely had it not existed. But it suggests a different conception of the family than that which obtains in our

---

[1] ibid., II. ii. 124.   [2] ibid., II. ii. 210.   [3] ibid., II. iii. 373.

[4] Which itself needs a European comparison. Semprini (132) speaks of Pius II dying at Ancona blessing the ships for a crusade in which he alone believed 'in un'Europa cinica e indifferente.' Had humanism already corrupted so much?

[5] *Famigl.*, II. iii. 235.   [6] ibid., II. i. 51.

more individualistic society. Similarly, the position of the wife is typical of the time, rather than helpful for our times: Choose her young, before she has had time to leave the obedience of her father and mother, so that she will the more readily enter into the obedience of her husband. Her virtues are motherhood and housewifery, and there is an almost clinical inspection of the qualities necessary in a young woman for the successful achievement of the first, and a very careful (and authoritarian) initiation into the second. Above all, she must never be allowed to intrude into her husband's business affairs, or his relations with the outside world. She must not set foot within the study where he keeps his papers, and if she finds some paper of his about the house she must bring it to him at once without staying to read it out of curiosity.[1] It is not surprising that Alberti thinks of education as concerning boys rather than girls. That places women in a position of tutelage which few would like to see re-established. Nevertheless, Alberti (in obvious contrast to Panormita) not only praises matrimony as a necessary institution, but thinks in terms of companionship as well: 'E puossi l'amore tra moglie e marito reputare grandissimo; però che se la benivolenzia surge da alcuna voluttà, il coniugio ti porge non pochissima copia d'ogni gratissimo piacere e diletto; se la benevolenzia cresce per conversazione, con niuna persona manterrai piú perpetua familiarità che con tua moglie.'[2] That is very different from the misogyny of Petrarch, or of Alberti's youth. Moreover, so realistic is his concern for the maintenance of the marriage relationship that he gives advice which is not, I think, paralleled until the modern physiologists.[3]

The society that Alberti depicts in the *Della Famiglia* is, then, resolutely and characteristically Florentine and of his own time. It may strengthen our own belief in his goodness and in his realism, but despite its interest it remains a little alien to us. That does not prevent him at many points revealing an acquaintance with that common human nature which seems timeless. It is part of the character of Giannozzo that he should wear the best, and the best only, of Florentine stuffs, and the dialogue applies to-day as then. *Lionardo*—'Trovate voi masserizia in comperare sempre il migliore?' *Giannozzo*—'E quanto grande. . . . E durano sempre le cose buone piú che le non buone.'[4] Adovardo talks of the anxiety of children's ailments, and Lionardo interposes the remark that they are not always as serious as

[1] *Famigl.*, II. iii. 313.   [2] ibid., II. ii. 131.
[3] ibid., II. ii. 168. 'Lodano in questo (physical union) farsi ardentemente dalla donna desiderare.'
[4] ibid., II. iii. 340-1.

they seem: to-day the child lies languid and almost lifeless, and to-morrow, full of spirits, is running everywhere.[1] The same Lionardo—one of the twenty-two bachelors of the house of Alberti—laments the persistence with which his relatives draw his attention to the pleasures of matrimony, or to girls who would suit him admirably. Those who have nothing to say, those who are naturally poor at words, when they are at a loss for a topic, always begin to babble about finding him a wife, and pour out great floods of eloquence on explaining and belauding the married state. What about this girl, what about that—no-one could want a bigger dowry, better looks, a more respectable family. . . . And it isn't that Lionardo wants to be without a wife![2] But alas, the girls who suit the rest of the family don't attract Lionardo, and those he might fancy never suit the rest of the family; and so he remains with his longing for a wife and children, and almost more so with his desire to be rid of this vexation of all his friends and acquaintances who, prompted by some form of envy, dislike his freedom in remaining unmarried.[3] Or Giannozzo answers with some emphasis the query as to whether one should buy or rent a house on setting up: 'Rent it, Lord no! because in time you find you've bought the house several times, and haven't got it.'[4] How very true! Again, Lionardo enquires if he would buy a house in an out of the way district where property is cheaper, and Giannozzo nips his argument off: 'Don't say cheaper. . . . No price is small when you spend your money on something which you do not want.'[5] And, finally, there is Giannozzo's demonstration of the meaning of hus-bandry (*masserizia*): it is to use things in case of need, and to keep what is not wanted now for future need. Lionardo thinks he under-stands; it would be blameworthy miserliness to refrain from using what one has in time of need. But Giannozzo goes further: it is not only miserly, it is also actual loss. 'Have you ever observed these little widow women? They gather apples and other fruit; they keep them in a cupboard, all shut up, nor would they think of looking at them until they're going bad. So all the time they eat the rotten ones. Finally there comes the time when all are bad or blemished. Work it out: you'll find they've thrown three-quarters out of the window, and you may say that they kept them to throw away. Wasn't it better, you foolish old woman, to throw the few blemished ones away first, to take the good ones for your table, and to give some away? This isn't a keeping things, it is a throwing them away.'[6]

---

[1] ibid., II. i. 56.   [2] ibid., II. i. 53.   [3] ibid., 54.   [4] ibid., II. iii. 272.
[5] ibid., 273.   [6] ibid., II. iii. 239.

As a genre picture that is delightful, and in its kinship with the spinster aunts in Saki's story who thought things spoiled by use, and so consigned them to the dust and damp of the box-room in order to preserve them, it is not limited, like the structure of the Alberti clan, to the society of the fifteenth century. I instance these touches of comprehension of human nature both for the pleasure which I find in the observation underlying them (and once again perhaps I should observe, if human nature seems much the same as the distorting fog of medievalism clears, that there is a great difference between making one's way through streets bound in fog, and in the open sunlight), and as a specific reassurance that the humanism of Alberti is neither too much in the air, nor too uncompromisingly rooted in the fifteenth century; but not, of course, as essentials to his thought as I have outlined it in connection with his predecessors and contemporaries. It is no accident that I have been quoting here mainly the *Della Famiglia*; but I have not forgotten that Alberti wrote other works as well, one of which I think to have been more important even than the admirable dialogues on the family. On the whole, and since I intend to stop for the present at Alberti as a convenient pausing-point, I shall ignore some sides of his thought. The enlightened Voltaireanism of the *De Jure*, where he prescribes a division in justice, to leave sins against God for God to punish, so that sins only against man are the business of the laws,[1] shows him well ahead of his century. The *Teogenio* I might have quoted earlier for one opinion at least which in its form and its spirit foreshadows Montaigne. It is an idea cognate to the Epicureanism of Valla, derivative perhaps from that *suaviter* which Petrarch used for our acceptance of our bodies: 'Cosa niuna delle altre necessarie da noi richieste dalla natura si truova non piena di voluttà: il mangiare, bere, posarsi, addormirsi e simili, per quali sedati in noi gli appetiti e movimenti, stiamo non dissimili a chi sia acquietato in morte: cosí il morire possiamo persuaderci forse fie non sanza qualche voluttà. . . . E noi stolti pur pensandovi ci perturbiamo di quello che sempre ci sia maturo e necessario.'[2] That is remarkable language for any one in modern Europe before Montaigne. In the *De Iciarchia* are to be found the principal links with Machiavelli and with Castiglione, nor are Alberti's political ideas

[1] Manc., 162. 'Io penso che sia lasciata a Dio la cura delle cose divine e che solamente alle umane debba il giudice provvedere, occupandosi delle disposizioni delle leggi, memore di Dio e amantissimo del giusto.' cf. Voltaire, *Dialogue entre un Plaideur et un Avocat*. 'Peut-être que les Anglais et d'autres peuples ont pensé que l'observation des lois était de l'homme à l'homme, et que la religion était de l'homme à Dieu.'

[2] *Teog.*, III. ii. 225-6.

uninteresting or unimportant. I neglect them, then, here because they would seem preludes to the theme of Machiavelli rather than conclusions; and because I am anxious to press forward to the main contribution of Alberti.

I have said Alberti's contribution: but with him, as with the Epicureanism of Valla, it is not idle to point out that the ideas to which he gives expression are in the air of humanism. And there is a predecessor of Alberti to whom less than justice has been given: Matteo Palmieri. I have quoted the *Libro della Vita Civile* already in the one splendid phrase which is usually quoted from it.[1] Its connections with Petrarch and the Humanist Educators are plain to see, and at the other end I think the vexed question of Machiavelli's source for his remark on the *tre generazione cervelli* can receive some light from Palmieri[2] (especially since Palmieri's views on mercenary troops are unworthy neither of Machiavelli's reading, nor of Machiavelli's writing). But apart from this there is more original matter in this little treatise than might seem likely from its rather dull beginning. Palmieri precedes Castiglione in his recommendation of accomplishments: his citizen may do few things himself, but he must be able to understand and judge 'tutte le cose fanno gli altri uomini.'[3] Foremost amongst these come music, sculpture, architecture, which the citizen can practise as well as understand.[4] In this revolution by which the mechanical arts are becoming tacitly fine arts Palmieri is awake to the movements of his own time: he trounces pre-Giotto painting;[5] he praises the revolution being wrought by Brunelleschi and Ghiberti, writes of sculpture and architecture coming back to light after the 'sciocche maraviglie' of the Middle Ages.[6] It is not surprising that one so minded, in accepting from the Petrarchan tradition the humanist view of society and its progress, should strike an essential keynote of the Renascence, and strike it, I think, for the first time: 'Quinci hanno havuto principio le città, nelle quali l'uso e conversatione civile ha dimostrato infinite utilità con le quali si subministra pria alla necessità poi alla amplitudine et hornamento di nostro vivere.'[7] Those are notable words; but Palmieri caps them with the invention of one whose fortune in the Renascence was to be most great. This he uses first in considering the matter of taxation: such public money is to be employed for 'magnificentia, et utilità di commodi com-

---

[1] cf. *supra*, 140.

[2] Palmieri, *Vita Civile*, 23: 'Di quinci dice Hòesiodo,' etc. cf. *Principe* (ed. Lisio), XXII. 131, and Tommasini, *La Vita e Gli Scritti di Niccolo Machiavelli*, II. 305, who notes Hesiod, but not Palmieri's quotation from him.

[3] *Vita Civ.*, 17 v. [4] ibid., 17-18. [5] ibid., 19 v. [6] ibid. [7] ibid., 28 v.

muni.'[1] But this new quality of *magnificence* can reside in the individual, as in the community: 'Le spese del Magnifico vogliono essere in cose honorifice e piene di gloria, non private, ma publiche come in edificii, e ornamenti di templi, theatri, logge, feste pubbliche. . . .'[2] What more concise description could be found of the man who was to be endowed *par excellence* with the title of IL MAGNIFICO? This swelling theme of amplitude of life, adornment, magnificence, Palmieri develops in the most eloquent parts of his little book; and not a word fell unheeded in the life of the fifteenth century. In applying his ideas to the city Palmieri even anticipates Alberti where he has been thought most original: the first idea of town-planning belongs to Palmieri, and even if it is only a suggestion it is one of great importance. The city 'contiene gli elevati, e superbi palagi, per insigne gloria de magistrati, contiene la sublimità, e nobile magnificentia de sacrati templi, la conveniente compositione, e aptissima bellezza de privati habituri, pe quali la dignità del huomo appaia meritamente ornata . . . con questi ornamenti si convengono le piazze, i mercati, i ponti, i portici, le vie, e ogn'altra parte degnamente magnifica, e ampla.'[3] The *dignity of man* is a favourite conception of the fifteenth century, and one whose very practical application then is very often overlooked. And it is no accident that those keynotes, for Palmieri and his century, are repeated in the Proem to Alberti's treatise *Della Famiglia*: 'la magnificenza e amplitudine.' Alberti is a greater man than Palmieri; but he learnt from his predecessor.

I said before that Rossi gave a couple of lines to one of Alberti's most important works: I meant, to the *De Re Aedificatoria*. Croce remarked, in a comprehensive reference to Leon Battista and half a dozen others, that they wrote on the beautiful.[4] Mr. Blunt rightly observes that Alberti's theory of beauty derives mainly from Vitruvius, and consists of the idea of harmony of parts so that nothing can be added or subtracted without spoiling the whole.[5] That is a very useful acquisition after the increasing fidgetiness of Gothic, and it is not to be sneered at. But it is not the most important contribution made by Alberti. The anatomy of beauty is not the outstanding part of his work, and if we look to other things than aesthetic theory pure and simple we shall find him more original. The whole work has often earned for its author the title of the *Italian Vitruvius*, and in so far as Vitruvius is an honoured name, that is wholly to the good. But it must be taken to mean that he legislates for Europe as Vitruvius had

---

[1] *Vita Civ.*, 65. The background, once more, is in Cicero. cf. *De Officiis*, II (*Opera*, IV. 325).
[2] ibid., 75 v.   [3] ibid., 92 s.   [4] Croce, *Estetica*, 196.   [1] Blunt, *op. cit.*, 15.

done, not that he copies or duplicates the work of Vitruvius. He himself, it is not idle to observe, had something like contempt for Vitruvius. The latter's indigestible text, rich with unwholesome terms filched, rather than borrowed, from the Greek, gave something of a foothold for Francesco Colonna and the unfortunate work, *Hypnerotomachia Poliphili*. Alberti, who by now was clear of such stylistic aberrations (not uncommon in some parts of his prose), did not fail to note this. Vitruvius did not write intelligibly, for to the Latins what he wrote seemed Greek, while to the Greeks it seemed that he was writing Latin. 'Ma la cosa stessa nel dimostrarcisi fa testimonianza, che egli non parlò né Latino né Greco; di modo che egli è ragionevole, ch'egli non scrivesse a noi, perché egli scrisse di maniera, che noi non lo intendiamo.'[1] For a generation which has been credited with a blind veneration for the remains of antiquity that is fairly casual, and apart from this very qualified approval to Vitruvius, Alberti claimed more indebtedness to observation of extant buildings than to theorists. The gap that is thus established between Vitruvius and Alberti is extended by the varying interests of the two writers. Vitruvius (apart from the modules and the orders) bequeathed to Europe the trilogy commodity, stability, beauty.[2] He noted the progression, in the development of architecture, from uncertain to certain in grasp of symmetry.[3] He saw Nature's supply of materials for building increased by art and adorned to create the elegance of life.[4] But these are, as it were, casual observations in Vitruvius: his main purpose is to instruct the builder, and to this he sticks much closer than Alberti. In the introductory chapter of the *De Architectura* Vitruvius claims many branches of learning as necessary for the architect. It was a claim that was not without its influence in raising the status of the artist in the Renascence: he also has his erudition in antiquity and in the sciences, and is a man of learning. But, unfortunately, the claim is not that the architect should be a man of taste and learning, but that he should know jurisprudence so as to be able to handle disputes that will arise over boundary walls, and what not. He is to know astronomy in order to determine the points of the compass, the equinox, the solstice, the courses of the stars: if he didn't know all this, how could he deal with the client's clocks?[5] Similarly, he must know a lot of history: then he will be aware that

---

[1] I quote Cosimo Bartoli's able translation of the *De Re Aedificatoria* (ed. Bologna, 1782). Book and chapter indications will be the same as for the original Latin. VI. i. 131.

[2] Vitruvius, I. iii. 'Firmitas, utilitas, venustas.'

[3] ibid., II. i. 'Ex incertis ad certas symmetriarum rationes perduxerunt.'

[4] ibid. 'Et auctam per artes ornaverunt ad elegantiam vitae.' [5] ibid., I. i.

the Caryatides were used by architects to carry weights because they
were matrons captured in war, and so retained in matrons' robes with
bowed heads as a perpetual trophy.[1] This is a somewhat trifling
acquisition of learning, and a subordination of the architect to his
profession. It is not in the least surprising that the humanism of
Alberti leads him to different conclusions. He dismisses this rather
frivolous equipment of Vitruvius' architect. There is no need for
him to be a Doctor of Law, an Astronomer or a Rhetorician: what
he wants professionally is draughtsmanship and mathematics.[2] But
it is significant that in the same chapter which limits the apparatus
required for the architect as architect Alberti adds a most Petrarchan
postscript on what he expects from him as a man. Prudence and
mature counsels, obviously, but the other virtues really do not need
stating: 'Conciosia che le altre virtuti, come è la umanità, la modestia,
la bontà, non le desidero più in costui, che io mi faccia nelli altri
huomini, dediti a qual si voglia sorte d'arti. Conciosia che queste
son cose che chi non le ha, non credo io, non che altro, che sia da
reputare per huomo.'[3] That is the language which Petrarch used
about the ruler, and it is clear, I think, that there is nothing Vitruvian
about its humanism. The main difference between Vitruvius and
Alberti is that the first was concerned primarily with the technique of
building, while the second embraces in the course of his work almost
every manifestation of civil life. That makes a very considerable
difference in the texture of their two books. In the course of his,
Alberti finds room for much that coincides with European ideas
right down to the eighteenth century (it is no accident that there
are English and French, as well as Italian, editions of him then),
and much that we, in the present anarchy of our towns, may
find helpful even without reference to the canons of Vitruvian
architecture.

   This difference is visible in the introductions to the theme of
architecture in the two authors. In Vitruvius it is, as we have seen,
what contribution is required from other branches of knowledge in
order to make the architect. In Alberti it is the contribution of
architecture to the life of mankind, and in consequence mankind's
debt to the architect. Even where Alberti uses still Vitruvian terms
this divergence is sharply visible. The proem, then, to Alberti's book
advances the claim for architecture as the least restricted of the arts
to particular ends of its own. It divides the arts according to the
Ciceronian distinction that we have seen recognised in Petrarch:

[1] Vitruvius, I. i.   [2] Alberti, *De Re Aed.*, IX. x. 243-5.   [3] ibid., IX. x. 243.

some for necessity, some for usefulness, others for delight.[1] Architecture is the primal necessity, but in its development it gives above all utility, delight and greatness. The public is indebted to the architect for stability, dignity and adornment. It is he who makes it possible for us to live in our leisure calmly, cheerfully and healthily; in work usefully and with profit; and in both, without danger and with dignity. That means that the architect is among the first on his claims for honour from us. And to build is not an activity which concerns the individual alone. 'All good men approve, and are glad together, when you by building a beautiful wall or porch, and adding the ornament of doors, columns, roof, have done something for yourself, and for them as well; glad for this more than anything else, that they know that you have increased with this fruit of your riches honour and dignity for yourself, for your house, your descendants, and your city.'[2] Thus the work on architecture is attached triumphantly to the theme of social virtue of the humanist educators. A house that is built is lived in by one family, but it is seen by all the rest of the city: therefore its external appearance is as much more important than its internal arrangements as the number of inhabitants to the city (or, for that matter, of strangers visiting it as well) is greater than the number of people in the house. I draw the mathematical conclusion myself, because we are in no danger of leaping to it in our times. Indeed, we live in an age in which the opposite obtains: in which every house is on the defensive against other houses (a *view* is something which, by definition, is unspoilt by other houses), when there is no question of a visual contribution from one house to another, or of any thinking further out than the comforts that can be contrived within the house itself. We have abandoned the symmetry of Vitruvian, and of Albertian, architecture; we have abandoned also the rules which both lay down for the materials of construction. For Alberti the aim of the builder is something that will last for ever. Therefore the builders must use things that are pure, unadulterated, firm and whole and stout.[3] That is a code which holds less and less writ as the industrial revolution deepens. We build cheaply now, as we make cheaply, so that people may find employment in doing things all over again. In Alberti's time the eyes, by their nature, know and desire beauty and grace, and in this matter are fastidious and difficult to please.[4] The industrial revolution has seen the disappearance of all visual standards, partly because it has reversed those

---

[1] cf. also ibid., I. ix. 19.   [2] ibid., Proemio.   [3] ibid., IX. ix. 241-2.
[4] ibid., IX. viii. 240.

requirements in materials. One of the most brilliant of Alberti's phrases may indicate the nature of the change more sharply than I can myself. It is the opening to a chapter in Bk. iv: 'All public things, which are parts of the city, belong to all the citizens.'[1] If we think in contrast of the wastes of brick which we call modern cities we shall see that it is precisely in this that they are lacking most: there is no provision for the public things which belong to all the citizens. Or rather, if there is, it is in matters of necessity or use: drains, lamp-posts, policemen, roads. The question of delight is no longer asked. Alberti forwards Palmieri's idea of the planning of the town; and Europe could second him in what he wrote because it accepted from humanism the living trilogy which he based it on: that of necessity, commodity and delight. The architecture of the European Renascence is not merely Vitruvian: it is humanistic also. The spirit of Alberti legislates for Europe quite as much as the rules of Vitruvius. On the contrary, the dormitory-town is the natural expression of modern society, which is impelled by space-restriction, the necessity for transport and the existence of transport to escape from the place lived in in order to enjoy living at all. If one can put fifty miles between one's home and oneself by tea-time there is no need to demand delight from the immediate surroundings of the home itself, or anything more than the provision of the creature comforts. Nor in this way does one acquire responsibility for the dignity or the beauty of what one visits fifty miles away. If I go to the pictures I have no influence on what Hollywood has provided for my entertainment; if I listen to the wireless I do not dictate the music played; if I proceed to a beauty-spot I do not create beauty. It was M. Valéry who remarked that the existence of beauty-spots meant an insensitivity to beauty.[2] Under the impulse of humanism Europe set to work to dignify its surroundings; we, with the benefits of science, are impotent to deal with ours. That is an opposite conception of society to the one put forward by Alberti, and maintained in Europe until the eighteenth century. It is not possible, of course, to remedy the disease merely by mentioning it, and the passing of Town-Planning Acts to meet the opportunities of war-time destruction will not make much difference while the root causes remain. There is little suggestion of their disappearance.

That aberration from what had been the norm of European

---

[1] Alberti, *De Re Aed.*, IV. ii. 80. 'A tutti i Cittadini si appartengono tutte le cose publiche; le quali sono parti della Città.'

[2] P. Valéry, *Variété*, I. 209.

civilisation is our problem. It may help to solve it to realise the
psychology of the organisation which preceded it; but the solution
can only come by the subordination of the machine and the machine
product to the humanism which sprang from the Renascence. We
can build no Wren-like London as we are, because we lack the
aptitude, the frame of mind: what would the modern citizen of
London do with it if he had it? Alberti's conception of society in
the *Della Famiglia* was somewhat limited to its own age: but the
book on architecture mirrors the gentleman of Europe for all
the centuries until the nineteenth. It is manifest that buildings are
made for man, and the progress forward from the necessity of
protection to delights leaves him with the task of analysis. And
Alberti, after all the opinions of the ancients, sees some men as far
from men as from the brutes: 'Ma non c'è cosa alcuna, per la quale
l'huomo sia piú differente da l'huomo, che quella sola, mediante la
quale egli è molto lontano dal genere de le bestie; cioè la ragione,
e la cognitione de le buone arti; e aggiugnici se tu vuoi, la prosperità
de la fortuna.'[1] The arts have ceased to be what they were with
Petrarch, a gift of Nature to man (even if Alberti saw the principles
of the various arts in Nature): they are the contribution of the individual to society, to be accepted and appreciated only by the
development of perception in the individual. The conveniences of
the town, the pleasures of the country-house, all these are considered.
It is Alberti, not Vitruvius, who advises on how to stable your horses
and cattle; it is he who counsels against keeping hens on the
battery principle.[2] He knows the virtues of ventilation, and the
possibilities of infection by bacteria in the air. His treatise on
architecture includes a hundred themes which Vitruvius would have
found no room for. And if at times the mantle of Pliny falls on him
a little there is not much reason for complaint. He backs his plea for
fresh air and windows in every room with two little anecdotes:
there is Capitolinus' story of the golden coffer which was found and
opened. So long had it been shut that the air inside was rotten, in-
fested the bystanders and spread cruel plague out into Asia, even
as far as the Parthians. Similarly with a statue of Apollo that had
long been stopped with wax, a story told by Ammianus Marcellinus.
That is a little more enthusiastic than scientific; but it does not do
much harm, and compared with his grasp of the house as a part of
the city, and as the centre of the family life, it is of scant importance.

[1] *De Re Aed.*, IV. i. 78.
[2] ibid., V. xvi. 122. 'L'uova nate a lo scuro, e in luogo rinchiuso sono piú sciocche.'

L

Nothing must be left out of account in the consideration of a house: 'Quivi harai tu da attendere ad ottimi studii, quivi ti saranno cari i dolci figliuoli e la famiglia, quivi harai i giorni da travagliare e da quiete, quivi si consumeranno tutti i discorsi de gli anni tuoi, talmente che io non penso, che e'si possa trovar cosa alcuna in tutta la vita appresso la humana generazione (eccetto che la virtú) alla quale si debba piú attendere con ogni cura, opera, e diligentia, che a cercare di potere con la tua famiglia habitare bene, e comodamente.'[1] That is a doctrine which concerns the Florentine merchant, and the bourgeois generally, as much as it did the gentleman of Europe.

Palladio, the master of Vitruvianism, acknowledged the excellence of Leon Battista Alberti in his preface. Moreover, along with the explicit statement of his dependence on Vitruvius and other writers (though there is nothing of the enrichment of the theme of building in Palladio's book) he borrowed a phrase direct from Cosimo Bartoli's translation of Alberti, which had then been printed some twenty years: the parts of the building must be each in its due place, not less than dignity requires, nor more than use demands.[2] I am not sure that there is an exact correspondence in Vitruvius to that very important formula, though I may have overlooked it. At any rate, it can be said, I think, that Alberti established in it the canon of taste in architecture, and recommends a reticence which has other applications as well. Delight is not the negation of utility and need, and these last must come before display.[3] Alberti deplored the aberrations of Caligula and Nero and the lavish use of sumptuous materials: Agrippa did better to use terra cotta for his flooring: 'I hate sumptuosity, and I delight in those things which are the invention of the mind and are graceful and pleasurable.'[4] That is not to go back on the statements on firmness and durability in materials. Likewise, it is not good to have the walls full up with statues or pictures. Heap jewels together, and you rob them of effect. 'Therefore, I should desire stone ornaments to be placed at certain determined places on the wall, both suitable and honourable places, where statues and pictures are to be set.'[5] Europe did not always heed that lesson of

[1] *De Re Aed.*, I. vi. 14.

[2] Palladio, *L'Architectura di Andrea Palladio*, Proemio (1572). Bartoli's translation had been published in 1550; there, I. ix. 18. 'Non minore che la dignità si richiegga, né maggiore che l'uso si ricerchi.' It is significant that the parallel is in Cicero, IV. 314: 'Ornanda est enim dignitas domo, non ex domo dignitas tota quaerenda. Nec domo dominus, sed domino domus honestanda est. . . . Cavendum est etiam (praesertim si ipse aedifices) ne extra modum, sumptu, et magnificentia prodeas,' etc.

[3] *De Re Aed.*, IX. x. 244.   [4] ibid., IX., iv. 226.   [5] ibid.

discretion and good taste; but Alberti would have approved still less the way in which we heap the works of art which might leaven taste into vast mortuaries where they can only be piled up, or buried out of sight to stimulate the enquiries of a handful of researchers into the knowledge of art. We have no use for our works of art when we throw them in heaps into repositories, even if we call the repository by so grandiose a name as the British Museum. A Fitzwilliam Museum (in its best elements) in every town of size in England would be more serviceable for promoting taste than the monster of Great Russell Street.

I shall be accused of having wandered from my text, and from my subject, which is Petrarchan humanism down to Alberti. The accusation is both true and false. It is true literally, since the British Museum, or the lack of any level of taste in England now, are not parts of the fifteenth century. It is false substantially, because I myself should have no interest in the fifteenth century did not I think it had some significance for the conduct of life at the present time. On the contrary, it is because I think that humanism as it developed from Petrarch to Valla and Alberti establishes an attitude which remained valid in Europe, *mutatis mutandis*, until the French Revolution, almost, and promoted an achievement which was the effort of Europe towards the elegances of life; because I think that the effect on Europe of that movement was tremendous, and vivifying, that I take the trouble to recommend it. When the tradition broke, Europe floundered. The abnegation of the scientist has flooded society with goods which merely distract man from himself, and prevent as much as they assist individual achievement. The modern world has more wealth than the Albertis knew, even in their days of most prosperity, but it has lost the progression from necessity through commodity to delight. It has lost stability and perpetuity in its building. It has lost elegance. It has lost the possession of all public things by all citizens. It has gained movement, and its life is centrifugal in opposition to Alberti's town-planning, which was centripetal. We may never be able to recapture the humanism of Petrarch, Valla and Alberti; but it is not irrelevant to our problems.

SUMMARY LIST OF EDITIONS AND PRINCIPAL
WORKS QUOTED

Alberti, L. B., *Opere Volgari*, ed. Bonucci, 5 vols., 1843-9.
  Della Architettura (tr. Cosimo Bartoli), 1782.
Barozzi, L., and Sabbadini, R., *Studi sul Panormita e sul Valla*, 1891.
Bartoli, Adolfo, *Storia della Letteratura Italiana*, 1878-89.
Benetti-Brunelli, *Le Origini Italiane della Scuola Umanistica*, 1919.
Blunt, Anthony, *Artistic Theory in Italy*, 1450-1600, 1940.
Bruni, Leonardo, *Dialogi ad Petrum Histrum*, ed. Kirner, 1889.
Burckhardt, J., *Civilisation of the Renaissance in Italy* (tr. S. G. C. Middle-
  more), 1929.
Castiglione, B., *Il Cortegiano*, ed. Cian.
Cicero, *Opera*, 4 vols., Bâle, 1534.
Cochin, H., *Un Ami de François Pétrarque*, 1892.
Comparetti, D., *Virgilio nel Medio Evo*, 1896 (2a. ed.).
Dominici, G., *Regola del Governo di Cura Familiare*, 1860.
Gentile, G., *La Filosofia* (Storia dei Generi Lett.).
  G. *Bruno e il Pensiero del Rinascimento*, 1920.
  Studî sul Rinascimento, 1923.
Gerosa, *L'Umanesimo Agostiniano del Petrarca*, 1927.
Gilson, E., *Les Idées et Les Lettres*, 1932.
Gregorovius, F., *Storia della Città di Roma* (tr. R. Manzato). 1866-76.
Guicciardini, F., *Storia d'Italia*, 1803.
Guittone d'Arezzo, *Rime*, ed. Valeriani, 1828.
Haskins, C. H., *The Renaissance of the Twelfth Century*, 1927.
Jacopone da Todi, *Laude* (Scrittori d'Italia, Bari).
Lo Parco, F., *Petrarca e Barlaam*, 1905.
Machiavelli, N., *Opere* (Italia), 1813.
Mancini, G., *Vita di L. B. Alberti*, 1881.
  Vita di L. Valla, 1891.
Monnier, P., *Le Quattrocento*, 1901.
Nolhac, P. de, *Pétrarque et l'Humanisme*, 1907.
  Petrarch and the Ancient World, 1907.
Olgiati, F., *L'Anima dell'Umanesimo e del Rinascimento*, 1924.
Orsini, N., *Bacone e Machiavelli*, 1936.
Palladio, Andrea, *L'Architectura di Andrea Palladio*, 1642.
Palmieri, M., *Libro della Vita Civile*, s.a. et l. (c. 1530).
Passavanti, J., *Lo Specchio della Vera Penitentia*, ed. 1856.
Petrarch, F., *Opera Omnia*, Bâle, 1554 and 1581.
    I quote the *De Remediis Utriusque Fortunae* only from the

1581 edition; other references to 1554, except for following modern editions:

De Rebus Familiaribus et Variae, ed. Fracassetti, 3 vols., 1859.

De Viris Illustribus, ed. Razzolini, 1874-9

Africa, ed. Corradini, 1874.

De sui ipsius et multorum aliorum ignorantia, ed. Capella, 1906.

Rime, ed. Scherillo (Hoepli).

Piccolomini, E. S., v. Pius II.

Pius II, *Opera Omnia*, Bâle, 1551.

   Pii II Commentarii, 1584.

Rossi, V., *Il Quattrocento*, 1898.

Sabbadini, R., *Storia del Ciceroniansimo*, 1885.

Saintsbury, G., *A History of Criticism*, 1900.

Saitta, G., *Filosofia Italiana e Umanesimo*, 1928.

   L'Educazione dell'Umanesimo, 1928.

Salutati, Coluccio, *Epistolario*, ed. F. Novati, 4 vols., 1892-1911.

Sanctis, F. de, *Storia della Letteratura Italiana*, 1870.

Sapegno, N., *Frate Jacopone*, 1926.

Segrè, Carlo, *Studî Petrarcheschi*, 1903.

Semprini, *L. B. Alberti*, 1927.

Siciliano, Italo, *Medio Evo e Rinascimento*, 1936.

Symonds, J. A., *Renaissance in Italy*, 7 vols., 1875, etc.

Toffanin, G., *Storia dell'Umanesimo*.

   Che Cosa fu l'Umanesimo? 1929.

Tommasini, O., *La Vita e gli Scritti di Niccolò Machiavelli*, 1883-1911.

Tonelli, L., *F. Petrarca*, 1930.

Valla, L., *Opera Omnia*, Bâle, 1540.

Vitruvius, *De Architectura*, Giunta, Florence, 1522.

Vitry, J. de, *Exempla*, ed. Crane, 1890.

Voigt, *Pétrarque, Boccace et les Débuts de l'Humanisme* (tr. Le Monnier), 1894.

Wicksteed, P. H., *Dante and Aquinas*, 1913.

Woodward, W. H., *Vittorino da Feltre and Other Humanist Educators*, 1897.

Zingarelli, N., *Dante*, 1903.

INDEX

168

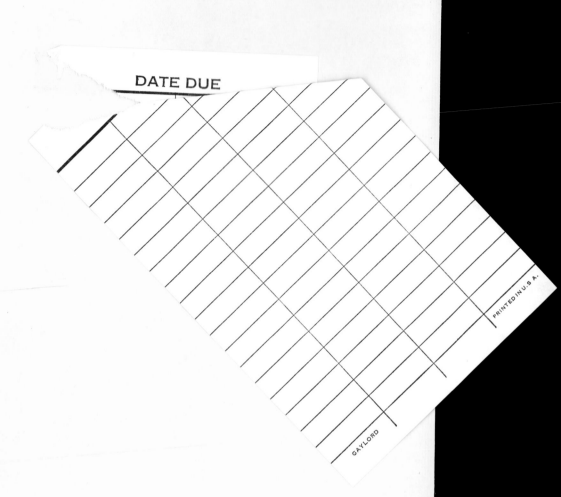

DATE DUE

GAYLORD

PRINTED IN U.S.A.